"WERBELOW is a gifted storyt colorful vocabulary, and self-dep down."
-Dave Campbell
Founding Editor in Chief of NRA's *Shooting Illustrated*

"From moose charges to mule deer migrations, being a Game Warden is so much more than enforcing the law. Warden Werbelow puts the reader in the passenger seat of his service truck (and atop his snow machine) for an inside look at what it takes to manage Wyoming's abundant wildlife."
-David Draper
Editor in Chief, Petersen's *Hunting*

"Scott "Swerb" Werbelow's dispatches from the front lines of wildlife — and more frequently, human — management remind readers that it's flesh-and-blood people on the chest side of game wardens' badges. Swerb's accounts, from the wildest Wyoming backcountry to the moose-wrangling cemeteries of small Western towns, will leave you wincing, howling with laughter, and occasionally drying your eyes. It's a treat to ride shotgun with Werbelow, whose slapstick accounts from the field have the touch of a redshirt Pat McManus.
-Andrew McKean
Former Editor In Chief, *Outdoor Life*

"Adventure at its best in wild Wyoming where a lawman deals with dangerous perps, mean moose, subzero temps, and comes out of it battered but alive. Scott Werbelow pulls out all stops with book three and has once again produced a winner. I couldn't put it down when I started reading it. I'll wager that you can't either."
-Jim Zumbo,
Former Hunting Editor, *Outdoor Life*

SON OF A POACHER III

NO TIME TO REST

SON OF A POACHER III

NO TIME TO REST

Scott C. Werbelow

ISBN: Paperback: 979-8-9904166-0-4
ISBN: Hardcover: 979-8-9904166-1-1
Library of Congress Control Number: 2024906622

10 9 8 7 6 5 4 3 2 1

To order additional copies of this book or other books, please visit my website at scottwerbelow.com

No Time to Rest

Contents

Chapter 1

UPPER GREEN RIVER

I suddenly awoke to my battery-powered alarm clock singing happily in my left ear. The time was 4:00 AM. I had slept so hard that I couldn't remember where I was or what I had been doing. The room was very dark and cold. I soon recalled that I was sleeping in the Green River Lakes patrol cabin. I jumped out of the tall bed. My bare feet hit the cold linoleum floor several feet below me. I quickly lit a propane lantern, both for heat and light. I was tired and my muscles ached from all the hiking that I had done the day before. I just wanted to sleep in and take the morning off, but I had work to do, and a lot of it. I threw my clothes on quickly and built a fire in the old antique cook stove located in the front room of the cabin. I was craving a cup of coffee and a hearty breakfast. As the coffee was brewing, I thought about the day before... the cow elk that I had seized from the Missouri hunter who called me "BOY." I thought about the river crossing that almost cost my life. I also thought about my lying on the dead cow elk to stay warm while the hunters surrounded me in the trees, all carrying loaded firearms. I thought about the dream that I had about an angel coming to take me away. I was probably lucky to still be alive. I then remembered that I had left a dead cow elk strapped to the rear rack of my ATV that was parked outside in grizzly bear country! I would need to hang this elk to keep it cool or haul it all the way back to the regional game and fish office back in Pinedale. It would be placed in our evidence freezer until it could be donated to needy people. I dreaded the thought of bouncing all the way back to town down the rutted and extremely rough road.

I needed to get back up the mountain and search for more dead elk and any evidence that could have been left in the area where the two men had killed at least nine elk the day before. All this while I was dealing with the father/son who had also wounded several elk from shooting long-range into a herd of over 300. This was not going to be a fun day. I dreaded what I might find by the end of it. I was craving eggs and bacon but didn't want to dirty any frying pans. I hated washing dishes! So, jerky and cheese sticks it would be, chased down with a frozen jelly filled doughnut. At least when the jelly is frozen, you don't drip any bright red jelly fill juice down your dirty white T-shirt. I finished getting dressed and packed a lunch for the day. I also remembered to grab my pistol from the refrigerator this time and strap it to my hip. As a game warden, it's never good to forget your pistol and have a hunter later in the day say, "Hey, where is your pistol?" That has only happened to me a few times! I finished packing my backpack and grabbed a flashlight and a roll of toilet paper. I needed to go visit the outhouse and catch up on some important reading. I headed off the front porch of the cabin in the dark and decided to turn on my flashlight to look at the cow elk that I had seized the day before and placed on the rear rack of my ATV. To my amazement the cow elk was gone. This changed my travel plans to the outhouse, knowing that a grizzly bear may be close by guarding the dead cow elk. I really needed to use the restroom, but this was how my day was starting out. I went back into the cabin and decided that I would wait until the sun came up before using the bathroom or searching for the dead elk.

Daylight soon came. It looked like it was going to be a nice day outside. I grabbed my bear spray and made sure my duty pistol was locked and loaded. I stepped out of the cabin and started yelling very loudly, "HEY BEAR, HEY BEAR!!" I wanted the bear to know that I was in the area and not surprise him/her in any way. Most grizzly bear attacks/charges are generally when someone surprises a bear, and the bear reacts by charging the threat. If you are lucky, the bear will only "Bluff" charge you, or bite you a few times as it passes by to get out of the area. When the bear continues to bite you or try and kill you, in most cases your best defense is to play dead and not move until the bear feels you are no longer a threat. Generally speaking, these incidents happen very quickly, and people often don't even have enough time to deploy their bear spray or shoot the animal with a rifle or pistol. In most cases, if grizzly bears can see you, smell you, and hear you, they will either run off or at least leave you alone.

I observed drag marks in the snow next to my ATV, indicating the direction of travel that the bear had dragged the elk. It appeared the bear was headed to the south to a nearby patch of timber. I slowly and cautiously followed the drag marks for a short distance when I noticed a large grizzly bear track in the snow. The track was the bear's front paw and it measured about 5-6 inches wide. This appeared to be a very large grizzly bear. I continued following the drag marks into the timbered area south of the patrol cabin. I yelled, "HEY BEAR, HEY BEAR!!" and fired my pistol twice into the air. This made a very loud sound "BANG", "BANG" that broke the morning silence and echoed through the trees and nearby canyons. *SHIT,* I thought to myself, *I didn't have any ear protection and now my ears are ringing.* I stopped and listened for the sounds of anything, or possibly a bear running off through the trees in front of me. I heard nothing and continued following the bloody drag marks in the snow. I was thinking to myself, *this bear probably didn't drag this whole elk carcass very far. Probably just far enough to hide it in the trees away from the patrol cabin where he could feed on it during the cover of night and be away from any human presence.* I cautiously and slowly moved forward through the thick trees. There it was, buried right in front of me! The cow elk had been nearly consumed with only the head and a hind leg sticking out of the "cache" pile. I grabbed my pistol out of my pancake holster and approached the dead elk cautiously. The elk had been almost completely covered up by dirt, pine needles, pine branches, and snow.

I grabbed the hind leg of the cow elk and gave it a heavy pull to jerk it out of the cache pile to see if there was any meat left to salvage on the carcass. To my amazement, most of the meat on the carcass was nearly all consumed. This sent a chill over my body that a bear could drag an entire elk carcass uphill through the trees for over sixty yards and consume most of the meat in one night. At this moment in time, something weird dawned on me. I noticed my hands begin to tremble as I thought to myself, *a man from Missouri poached this elk and covered it in pine boughs to hide it from the game warden. Just last night I had been lying on this elk carcass to stay warm while waiting for the Missouri hunter to return. The hunters later showed up and surrounded me with their rifles. I could have died last night because of this elk! I issued the man a citation for failure to tag his elk and seized the elk. I nearly died crossing the river during high water at night with the elk strapped to the back of my ATV. NOW, I'm sitting here in the dark timber looking over the same damn dead elk, covered in pine boughs and a grizzly bear that may eat my ass off at any moment for trying to steal it.* I decided to leave the damn elk alone and get the hell out of there while I still could. All I wanted to do was donate the meat to some family in need and now a damn grizzly bear had consumed most of it! The bear would probably return one more time and finish consuming the carcass on its next visit. I returned to the cabin and thought to myself, *I hope the Missouri hunter pleads guilty and pays his fine, as I no longer have any evidence that he ever killed an elk in the first place.*

Green River Lake

The morning sun was up now. I was enjoying the warmth of the sun. It looked like it was going to be a beautiful blue-sky day. I strapped my backpack onto the front rack of my ATV and headed up the mountain towards Union Pass where at least two men had killed nine elk the previous day. I soon arrived at the infamous river crossing at the "Bend" in the river. I had no problems getting across it during the daylight hours, but certainly remembered that I could have died there the morning before, when the ATV and I went for a ride down the river. I climbed the steep rough hill up out of the river bottom and noticed a vehicle ahead of me. It appeared that it was off the main road and several people were walking towards the vehicle wearing orange hats. I quickly grabbed my shitty department issue binoculars out of my backpack and looked the situation over. *SHIT, this was the same baby blue Ford truck that I had dealt with yesterday.* It looked like they had driven about one mile off the rough two-track road to retrieve a dead elk. Three men were dragging an elk towards the truck.

This was Mr. Adams with all his crony illegal non-resident elk hunters again. They had killed an elk and violated a road closure to get their truck as close to the elk as possible. I quickly grabbed my portable radio out of my backpack and tried to call the Forest Service Ranger for that area. I had no authority to enforce off-road travel in the National Forest. To my amazement he answered his radio and was even close by. He told me that he would head in that direction.

I knew these guys would not be happy to see me again after issuing the Missouri man a citation the previous day and confiscating his cow elk. To be honest with you, I wasn't really excited to have to visit with them again myself. Especially after they had surrounded me with their rifles pointed at the ground. I was in no hurry to contact them alone since it appeared they were going to be in the area for a while dragging the dead elk back to their truck. I patiently waited for the Forest Service Ranger to show up. Once he arrived, I explained everything to him regarding my contacts with this group of hunters the previous day. I also explained to him that the driver of the baby blue Ford was a convicted felon for child molestation. We both decided that it would be best if we set up in a location further down the road. This way we could make sure the elk was properly tagged once it left the site of kill.

The hunters drove off-road nearly one mile through the rough sagebrush and large boulders to get back to the main road where we were patiently waiting for them. They had a friendlier demeanor when two law enforcement officers approached their vehicle as it re-entered the main road. All of them were very friendly to me and wanted to shake my hand. It about killed me, but I remained professional and shook their hands. The guy from Kansas was the hunter who tagged the cow elk. Who knew who actually shot the elk? I may have witnessed that if I wasn't dealing with the dead elk behind the patrol cabin that the grizzly had stashed. The Forest Ranger would end up writing Mr. Adams a citation for driving off established roads.

As the Ranger was writing out the citation, the hunter from Missouri just sat in the cab of the truck and glared at me. This was the man who threatened me the previous morning and called me "BOY." I was tired of the man glaring at me, so I approached him while he was sitting in the passenger seat of the baby blue Ford. I tapped on the window to let him know that I wished to speak with him. He slowly rolled down the window and said, "Can I help you with something, SIR?" I replied, "You boys haven't done anything right on your hunt yet. You have worn out your welcome in Wyoming and I suggest you head back to your home state immediately. If I catch you doing something else illegal in Wyoming again, I will "Must Appear" you in front of a Wyoming judge and see how that works out for you." The man looked me in the eyes and said, "Yes, Sir, you won't have any more problems with me again. I can't speak for the rest of them." I nodded my head as the man rolled his window back up. At least he referred to me as "Sir" instead of "Boy."

I thanked the Forest Service Ranger for his assistance. He said, "No problem, by the way, I "Must Appeared" Mr. Adams so he will have to travel back later and face a federal magistrate. I will also contact ATF (Alcohol, Tobacco, and Firearms) and let them know that he is in Wyoming hunting elk with friends and was observed with firearms in his possession." I shook the Ranger's hand firmly and nodded my head, meaning good job and thanks. I then jumped onto my ATV and headed north towards Union Pass to try and find the area where I had found all the elk gut piles the previous day.

The snow had melted and much of my evidence had disappeared with the melting snow. I was so stupid the day before when I didn't even think to take pictures of all the tire and foot tracks that were visible in the fresh snow. I hadn't thought about the snow melting overnight. I took off walking down a steep timbered hill headed for the deep canyon where I found the gut piles the day before. I traveled through about one mile of heavy downed timber to finally reach a willow bottom. I was glad to finally get through all the heavy timber and find a well-used cattle trail that ran along the tall willows next to a creek. There was heavy down timber on my right and very tall willows on my left. I noticed some moose tracks in the mud on the cattle trail. Pretty soon I noticed a pile of fresh moose scat in the trail. I made note to myself that there may be a moose somewhere in front of me in the heavy willows. About that time, I heard a moose grunt. This is the sound that a bull makes when he is in rut. The sound came from just in front of me about twenty yards away.

I decided to climb the hill to my right and head up through the trees. This way I would be above the moose and hopefully be able to locate him below me and safely get around him. As I was climbing the hill and going through low-hanging pine boughs, I heard a noise in front of me. I stepped out from behind a small tree and noticed a large bull-moose standing behind a small sapling tree about ten yards away from me. I stopped quickly in mid-step and locked eyes with the large bull. He was standing behind a small pine tree staring at me through the pine boughs. I could see the whites of the bull's eyes and his hair was standing on end on top of the hump on his back. I had been in this situation before and knew the bull was getting ready to charge by his posture. I thought to myself, *Holy shit, this bull is going to charge me!*

I started looking to my left and right searching for a large tree that I could get behind if the bull charged. There were no large trees in the immediate area. I did find two medium-sized aspen trees to my left that looked like they might provide some degree of cover if the moose decided to charge. The aspen trees were about eight inches in diameter and about one foot apart from each another. The bull stepped out from behind the small sapling tree where he could now see me better. We locked eyes for what seemed like forever. In a split second the bull lowered his head and came crashing towards me very quickly. I grabbed for my people spray (OC Spray) as I did not have my bear spray on me. I quickly ran to my left to get behind the two aspen trees. I made it behind the trees and sprayed the moose in the eyes and nose with my people spray. The moose's large nose went between the two aspen trees and hit me squarely in the crotch as his large horns contacted the two aspen trees. The hit shook the trees hard enough that leaves began to fall in the air above my head. The moose backed off for just a second, raised his head high and charged me again. I was having a hard time standing and breathing because my testicles were now located where they didn't belong. The moose crashed into the two aspen trees again trying to hit me. This time I sprayed him good into one of his eyes. He raised his head high, stared at me for a moment and turned and ran away into the trees.

I was standing there with my hands trembling. I noticed I had dropped my OC spray and had my pistol in my right hand. This all happened so fast I didn't even recall dropping the spray can and going for my pistol. I thought to myself, *damn, I almost killed a moose, and he almost killed me. Between the grizzly bear ordeal this morning, running into the Missouri hunters and now being charged by a bull moose, this was turning out to be quite the day and it wasn't even noon yet.* I had to sit down and regain my composure and my breath. I had never been hit in the crotch by a moose's nose before. I finally quit shaking and headed back down the canyon to search for the elk gut piles.

I finally arrived at the bottom of the steep canyon. Most of the snow had melted so I wasn't able to find any boot prints in the snow. I searched for empty shell casings, or any other evidence that I could come up with to help me know who the shooters were that killed so many elk the previous day. I was mad at myself for not taking any pictures. I was also worried that I might encounter a grizzly bear or bears while searching over the nine gut piles in the area. I made lots of noise and yelled, "HEY BEAR, HEY BEAR", as I fired my pistol a couple of times into the side of the mountain. I just wanted the bears to know that I was in the area, so that there were no surprise encounters.

I made a large circle and didn't find any more dead elk that I didn't already know about from the previous day. The hunters had taken the entire carcasses of all the elk out of the canyon. Because of this, I was not able to recover a bullet for evidence out of any of the dead elk. I figured if they got the elk out whole, they must have used a winch on a truck and dragged them out of the canyon. I knew that there was no way that they could have dragged the elk whole up the steep mountain side. This would have taken them several days to accomplish. I decided to hike back to the top of the canyon and find the area where they drove off-road and winched the elk out of the canyon.

With the melted snow it was tough to find any fresh-looking tire tracks. I looked closely in the tall sage brush, and I could tell that someone had driven over it due to the freshly broken branches from the sage brush plants. The closer I looked I found some very faint tire tracks that had driven over to the canyon edge. I thought to myself, *this was probably the truck that they used to winch all the elk out of the canyon*. Once I got over to the edge of the canyon, I could see multiple tire tracks in the soft dirt and mud where several trucks had turned around. There was also a great deal of blood on the ground where they had loaded the elk into the beds of their trucks. I searched the area over very thoroughly for any evidence that they may have been left behind. I was just about to leave the area when a large gust of wind hit me and blew my hat off. I reached down to pick it up before it blew away and noticed a small white and blue piece of paper fly up into the air off to my right side.

I quickly lunged onto the small piece of paper and held it to the ground. I did not want to lose any possible evidence in the strong wind. I carefully opened the piece of paper and discovered it was someone's vehicle registration. This crucial piece of evidence had fallen out of someone's truck that was in the area yesterday. I read the name on the registration and recognized the name. This was a man who I knew as a known poacher in the area. I stuffed the vehicle registration in my front pants pocket and looked up to the sky. I said, "Thank you, Lord. Thanks for looking over me today!" Just as soon as I said that prayer, the wind completely quit blowing and it was dead calm. The only reason I found the vehicle registration was because the strong wind picked it up off the ground and moved it several feet while I was picking up my hat. I smiled and thought to myself, *sometimes, no matter how good of a poacher you are, someday you are going to get caught. Possibly by the grace of God.*

Even though I had a key piece of evidence, I still had a lot of work to do to prove the case. I took a DNA sample from each gut pile. I took each sample and placed them in a separate envelope and numbered each envelope with the location of the gut pile. I also took lots of pictures of everything. I would need to prove that the registered owner of the vehicle was in this area the previous day and shot an over-limit of elk. I would need to send the DNA samples to our lab quickly to get results. However, I did not want to wait for the results and have the meat from these elk disappear from someone's home or meat processing facility. I gathered up my equipment and followed the tire tracks back to the main road. On the way back I found something very interesting. There was a large patch of snow that was shaded by some large pine trees. The vehicle tracks went through that patch of snow, and someone had stopped at that location. I could see footprints in the snow. I followed the footprints and learned that someone had relieved themselves and peed in the snow. (I thought about collecting a sample of the pee for DNA testing as well.) I also noticed something unique about the footprints. Whoever made the tracks in the snow was wearing cowboy boots.

I asked myself, *who in their right mind would be elk hunting during the fall months at 11,000 feet elevation wearing COWBOY BOOTS? There was snow on the ground the day that all the elk were killed. There would be no way that someone could walk down into the steep canyon and get back out wearing cowboy boots. The terrain is too damned steep! If the driver of the truck was the registered owner, he probably didn't shoot any elk. He probably showed up to put his license on an elk that was already shot.*

I was also able to get some good pictures of tire impressions left in the snow. If it wasn't for this shaded area that he drove through and stopped to pee, I would have no other evidence. I couldn't wait to get back to civilization and interview my suspect. This was going to be a huge case and I was going to solve it! I could picture myself standing in front of all the game wardens at the annual Game Wardens Association meeting giving them a power point presentation on the huge case that I had solved. I headed back down off the mountain, packed up my stuff at the cabin and headed for Cora. I knew the man who I was looking for lived just north of Cora. I also knew that he drove a baby blue early seventies Ford pick-up. *What is it with baby blue Fords and poaching?* I thought to myself. As soon as I had radio service, I called dispatch and had them run this man's name and date of birth to see if he had any outstanding warrants or any prior Game and Fish violations. He had no warrants and a few minor violations. I also let dispatch know that I would be at the subject's address in reference to a follow-up poaching case. I already had his address, as I had his vehicle registration in my front pocket.

As I pulled into the suspect's driveway, I noticed a baby blue Ford pick-up parked out back behind the house. I decided to knock on the front door to see if anyone was home. After several minutes waiting for someone to open the door and listening to the neighbor's dog bark at me, the door slowly opened. A very frail man dressed in only his white boxer shorts and T-shirt answered the front door. He was wearing black socks and a black cowboy hat. He was also wearing black square-framed reading glasses with very thick lenses. The man looked to be in his mid-seventies. He looked a little nervous as he opened the door and said with a frail voice, "May I help you with something?" After looking this man over quickly, I knew in my heart that he did not hike down a steep canyon to recover a dead elk. He simply wasn't in good enough physical condition to do so. I introduced myself and told him that I would like to ask him a few questions if he had a minute. The frail man invited me into his house and offered me a cup of coffee. The inside of the house smelled horrible and was an absolute mess. I don't know how many cats were running around the house, but more than I could count. He offered me his recliner to sit in as that was the only available place to sit in the entire house. I chose to stand and told him to have a seat in his recliner and get comfortable. He nervously sat down and started to shake a bit.

I asked the man if he had recently been elk hunting. He replied, "Yes." I asked the man if he had recently killed an elk. He replied, "Yes." Then I asked him where he had killed the elk? He described the area that I had been doing my investigation in. I asked the man to explain to me where he had killed the elk. He told me that he had killed it down in a steep canyon. I asked the man if there was anyone with him. He replied, "No." I asked the man to show me what boots he was wearing when he killed the elk. He pointed over to the front door and said, "Those cowboy boots right over there." I asked the man where he had shot from. He replied, "From the top of the ridge where I parked my truck." I asked the man if there were any other dead elk in the area or anybody else hunting in that area. He replied, "The only dead elk that I saw was the one that I shot. I did not see anyone else in the area." I told the man that I had done my investigation and did not observe any cowboy boot tracks in the canyon. I also told him that there was no way that he could have hiked down to his elk by himself wearing slick cowboy boots in the snow. I then told him that my investigation showed that the elk was hauled out of the canyon whole, and that there was no way that he could have done that by himself. He replied, "No, I never even walked down to the elk because I was wearing cowboy boots. A couple of guys showed up with a winch on the front of their truck and asked me if I would like them to drag my elk out. I told them, Hell Yeah, I'm seventy-six years old." I asked the man if he knew the names of the men who helped him. He replied, "No, I never did get their names. I wished I would have, so I could do something to pay them back someday."

This man had sat there in his recliner, looked me straight in the face and lied, and lied, and then lied some more to me. I got frustrated and walked out back to check the dead cow elk in the back of his truck. His license was neatly displayed and filled out correctly, hanging from the rear leg of the cow elk. I knew from listening to my portable scanner the previous day that two men had killed nine elk in this area. This old man was probably called on his CB radio and told to come up and tag his elk. I doubt the man ever even got out of his damn truck. Whoever shot the elk winched it up the hill and loaded it into his truck. I knew pretty much what had happened but couldn't prove a damn thing. This man had been around the block a few times and knew to keep everyone else out of it. Even though I had found the man's vehicle registration, I guess the game warden lost this time. I was more interested in finding the two men who killed nine elk. I had DNA samples but would need the other elk carcasses to sample and compare to my samples. I would keep an eye on this guy in the future.

Party hunting in Wyoming is illegal. If I can find out who he hunts with, that will be good information in the future. I shook the old man's hand and thanked him for being totally dishonest with me and headed out the door. I thought to myself, *sometimes when you think you have a huge case, it can turn out to be nothing very quickly.* I was beginning to learn how frustrating it can become to be a game warden at times. Sometimes you know exactly what happened and who did what, but you cannot prove it.

I loved doing law enforcement work during the fall months, but this was also a very busy time for my real job which was Feed Ground Manager. I couldn't devote too much time to being a game warden or

I would fall behind in my other duties managing all the elk feed grounds. This included purchasing hay, hiring elk feeders, hauling draft horses into feed grounds, and maintaining all the hay sheds, stack yards, hay sleds, hay wagons, and anything else that broke along the way. The minute that I felt caught up on maintenance, the hay shed roof blew off on North Piney and Finnegan feed grounds one day in October. The road washed out going into Franz feed ground and required a new culvert. It was just one thing after another. The hay was still being hauled into all the feed grounds to stock them for the winter months. Heavy snowstorms would be coming soon, so it was a priority to get all the hay hauled before roads became impassible. All draft horses would need to be trimmed, roached, wormed, and hauled into feed grounds as well. It seemed that I rarely got a day off and I rarely had time to do much law enforcement work. My title was still Feed Ground Manager/Game Warden. I had been doing law enforcement work for over two years now and the Department still hadn't sent me through the 13-week law enforcement academy in Douglas, Wyoming. I was starting to worry that if they didn't send me to the academy soon, I may be a Feed Ground Manager for the rest of my career which was alright, but just not the direction I wanted to go with the Department. Permanent jobs were very tough to come by and you better appreciate what you had. If you ever showed signs of being negative, poor attitude, etc. you were gone or never going anywhere with the agency. I would cross my fingers, continue to work hard, and hope for the best.

The Pinedale Regional Wildlife Supervisor, Bernie Holz, called me into his office one day to visit about how things were going for me. I was honest with him and told him that I felt overwhelmed most days. I told him that I couldn't keep up with all the maintenance. I asked him if there was any chance that we could hire a contract Feed Ground Maintenance position to help me during the spring and summer months. He replied, "If you can come up with a funding source for this position, I will run it by Wildlife Administration." I thought for a few moments and said, "What if we create like a stamp or something that sportsmen would need to purchase to hunt elk that are fed on state-operated feed grounds. We could charge like $10.00 per stamp. We could maybe call it a "Feed Ground Stamp." Bernie looked up towards the ceiling as if in deep thought as he smoked his Cuban cigar. He became quiet for a few minutes as he stared into my eyes. This made me very uncomfortable. He finally replied, "I suppose that idea may have some merit. Let me run it up the ladder." I replied, "Thank you, I appreciate that." It wasn't long after that discussion the idea got traction and we soon had a Feed Ground Management Stamp. If sportsmen hunted elk in any of the hunt areas with feed grounds in western Wyoming, they would need to purchase this stamp for ten dollars. The Department generated about $150,000 after the first year of selling the stamp. The total operating costs of the feed ground program at that time were about 1.2 million. So, the stamp didn't do much to pay for the program but certainly generated some additional income.

After several months, it was agreed upon by Wildlife Administration that we could hire a 9-month contract position to assist with maintenance in the feed ground program. I was very excited to have this position. I contacted Pinedale Office Manager, Des Brunette, and asked her to quickly help me get the position advertised statewide. She did so the same day and we soon started receiving applications for the position. A man by the name of Gary Hornberger called me from Nebraska to ask questions about the position. I really liked the man after talking to him on the phone. He seemed like he had a great deal of work experience that would be compatible to the position. He also seemed like he had a strong work ethic and was eager to come to Wyoming. After interviewing several other candidates, it was decided to hire Gary Hornberger as the new Feed Ground Maintenance Assistant. Gary would start his position January 1, 1998. This was the best decision that we could have ever made. We really needed this position. I was extremely happy and felt relieved to have someone finally assisting me with all the maintenance projects.

Chapter 2

STAND BACK MADAM - I'M A TRAINED PROFESSIONAL

It was January 1998. I was lucky in the fact that all my elk feeders had returned from last year. I only had to hire one elk feeder and that was to replace my wife Lana at Soda Lake feed ground. I ended up hiring Mike "One Beer" Stevie to feed at Soda Lake. Mike was the brother to outfitter Todd "Roundy" Stevie. He was a top hand at guiding, shoeing horses, and just about anything that he put his mind to. I was looking forward to working with Mike and my new Feed Ground Assistant Gary Hornberger. By now the hay was all hauled for the year and the draft horses had also been hauled into all the feed grounds. We were feeding elk on all 22 feed grounds by the end of January. It was always a relief to finally have all the draft horses hauled and all the feeder's feeding elk. This winter proved to be another good one again. Heavy snows started falling early. We also had a number of elk displaced onto private property that we would have to move to nearby feed grounds almost daily. Gary proved to be an excellent snow machine operator and an excellent hand at anything that needed to be done. Tim Baxley was again hired to feed two feed grounds-Finnegan and North Piney. Hopefully he wouldn't get in over his head this winter with broken down snow machines and lame draft horses. Lucky's leg had healed completely and would again be used to feed at

North Piney with his mate Rooster.

My wife Lana was still working for Kathy Miller up Horse Creek feeding cows in the mornings. She also helped Kathy put up her hay this past summer. Lana was really wanting to find a house with some property for our four horses. I started looking at the market and everything was very expensive. I told Lana that we might be living in Kathy Miller's hired hand house for a long time to come. Big Piney game warden Brad Hovinga and I had become close friends. We worked hard together, and we played hard together. Brad would find an excuse to come to my house nearly every Monday and Thursday night to watch NFL football games. Brad's favorite team was the Minnesota Vikings, mine was the Denver Broncos.

Things were shaping up at the office. My boss Bernie Holz had asked me if I would like an office on the main floor next to the main desk. I was excited about this because I was tired of hitting my head on the ceiling back in the corner of my small cubicle upstairs. Once I moved down to the front office, I could hear every conversation that went on at the front desk. I learned a great deal from listening to Office Manager Des Brunette as she answered hunter and sportsman questions all day long. By the end of the fall, I don't think there was a question that I couldn't answer just from overhearing all the different conversations.

One day Bernie and I were the only two in the office over the lunch hour. Des had locked the front office door and went to lunch. I heard a loud bang on the front door. BANG, BANG, BANG!! Even though the sign said "CLOSED" on the front door, someone wanted to talk to someone pretty badly. I jumped up and opened the door. It was a rancher from the Bondurant area. I asked him if I could help him with something. He replied in a loud voice, "I NEED

SOMEONE TO PAY ME FOR ALL THE DAMN HAY THAT I HAVE FED TO YOUR DAMN ELK!" I kindly told the man that we didn't ask him to feed the elk or encourage him to feed the elk. He had chosen to feed the elk over the years until the population was well over one hundred head. He screamed back, “WITH CURRENT HAY PRICES I CAN’T AFFORD TO FEED THEM ANYMORE. YOU EITHER CUT ME A CHECK FOR MY HAY OR REPLACE THE HAY THAT I HAVE ALREADY FED THEM. THEY ARE YOUR PROBLEM, NOT MINE!!” The man was wearing a scotch cap with the ear flaps down, Carhartt coveralls, and muck boots with his pants tucked in them. He was yelling very loudly at me. Bernie overheard the conversation and came walking out of his office. Bernie knew the man and the situation well. Bernie asked the man if he allowed any access in the fall for hunters to try and harvest some of the elk. He also asked the man if he continued to lock his gates so that no one could access public property in the area. The man yelled, “I DON’T WANT ANY F---ING HUNTERS ON MY PROPERTY, AND YES, THE GATE IS LOCKED AND IT’S GOING TO STAY LOCKED!” Bernie pulled the cigar out of his mouth and said,” Well, it looks like you are doing absolutely nothing to try and solve your own problem, so why don’t you just get the F---k out of here and quit bothering us with your problems.” The man’s jaw dropped to the floor. He was speechless and so was I. The man turned around and blasted out the front door, slamming it as he went out. I looked at Bernie speechless, Bernie said, “Well Shit, it's not that hard to figure out!” and calmly walked back into his office. I don’t think that man ever returned. One thing about Bernie, he was a small man, but he didn’t take any crap from anyone.

North Pinedale game warden Duke Early was the next guy to come through the office door. It was always a pleasure to visit with Duke. He had a great personality and was always upbeat about something. Duke stepped into my office and asked me if I would be available to move elk early in the morning north of Cora. It sounded like a bunch of Black Butte feed ground elk had left the feed ground and were on private property. Duke told me that he had a crew lined up and that we would meet at the Wrangler Café at 7:00 A.M. for breakfast to make a game plan. We always met at the Wrangler café for a "Game Plan." This was a good time for the locals to visit (bullshit) with their local game and fish employees and a good time for us to have a nice hearty breakfast.

The next morning, we all met at the Wrangler Café. It was -30 degrees. The "A-Team" would be Big Piney game warden Brad Hovinga, wildlife biologist Dean Clause, south Pinedale game warden Dennis Almquist, and north Pinedale game warden Duke Early better known as the ICE man (Incident Commander Early.) We had a nice breakfast and Duke organized a game plan to move the elk. It sounded like there were about 150 elk that needed to be moved about 4-5 miles to the Black Butte feed ground. Duke led the pack of game and fish trucks pulling single-wide snow machine trailers and we headed north towards Cora. I was excited to get to ride my brand-new 600 Powder Special snow machine. Duke asked me to lead the pack to find the elk, and that he would go up on a high hill to the west where he could see the elk and direct us to them with our portable radios. I dressed very warmly and started my new snow machine. It pulled over very stiff and didn't want to start. I grabbed my portable radio and stuck it in a pouch that was mounted to my handlebars. I then clicked the mic to the top of my windshield so that I could talk without removing the portable from the carry bag.

I let my snow machine warm up for a few minutes and headed north. I could see about 150 elk on a high ridge about one mile away. Everyone was following me as we left the parking area. I came upon a large snow drift in the two-track road that I was traveling on. I decided to "Mash" the throttle and catch some air as I jumped over the drift. I gave it the onion and caught some air alright! The throttle stuck wide-open as I hit the large snow drift, and it launched me off the snow machine. As I was lying face down in the snow, I looked up to see my snow machine going wide-open towards the large herd of elk. The snow machine must have been doing nearly 90 MPH with no rider on it. I stood up and was standing in the road watching my runaway snow machine when wildlife biologist Dean Clause pulled up next to me on his snow machine. I could hear Duke talking over Dean's portable radio. He was yelling, "I don't know who is in the lead, but they are going too damn fast, and they are going to "bugger" that herd of elk all over the damn countryside!" Dean looked at me and gave me this weird look and said, "Where is your snow machine, Swerb?"

I pointed to the north and said, "Can you see that rooster tail of snow way out there on the flat by that lone telephone pole? That is my snow machine." Dean laughed and said, "Damn, looks like your runaway machine is going to bugger that herd of elk." My machine was now far enough away that I was looking at it through my shitty department binoculars. It looked like it was headed for a lone telephone pole and still traveling at a high rate of speed. At this point in time, all the other guys had pulled up to watch the event. Just before the snow machine was going to hit the telephone pole, it hit a large piece of sage brush that was about five feet tall and went into the most spectacular endo that I had ever seen. The machine went end over end at least four times and finally came to a rest on its hood upside down. I jumped on the back of Dean's sled, and he gave me a ride over to my snow machine.

When we arrived, there was steam rolling out of the hood and the engine was silent. I could hear Duke on my portable radio still yelling, "GF-84, GF-84, is that you in the lead, you need to back off those elk right now!" I went to answer Duke on my radio and noticed my mic was missing. Dean laughed and said, "Swerb, your mic is lying over there in the snow," as he pointed to the south. I couldn't talk to Duke even if I wanted to. The mic had been torn completely off my portable radio. I looked up on the hill above us, the elk were gone. My runaway snow machine had the large herd of elk headed somewhere.

We flipped my machine over, and I noticed sage brush sticking out of my hood vents. The hood and windshield were busted up and the skis bent. I noticed the kill switch was in the off position. When the snow machine was doing its final acrobatic moves apparently the ground hit the kill switch and shut the machine off.

I didn't dare try and start it with fear that it would take off wide-open again. Dean towed me back to my truck and the others went looking for the herd of elk. I took the machine straight to our repairman south of Pinedale who was named Ken. I dropped the machine off and told him what had happened. Ken ran his fingers through his hair and shook his head and said, "I sure haven't seen that before. I'll call you when it's done." Ken was never happy to see game and fish employees come in after an elk drive. He told me that he had never fixed so much broken shit in his entire life. I later spoke with Duke. He told me that the elk nearly made it back to the feed ground on their own after seeing the runaway snow machine coming towards them.

The next morning, I received a phone call at 6:30 AM from a rancher who lived next to the Green River north of Daniel. The rancher told me that he had a sick cow moose in his haystack that needed to be put down. He told me the location of the haystack and said he would be out feeding cows somewhere but wanted me to know about it. I headed that direction and soon arrived at the rancher's house. I banged on the door, and no one answered. I decided to go look for the sick moose in the location he had told me. After about one hour of looking, I was pretty sure that I had found the haystack he was talking about, except I didn't observe a sick moose in the haystack. I did however notice a cow moose lying in the willows behind the haystack a short distance away. I didn't want to shoot this moose until I was able to get a closer look at her, to make sure she was indeed the sick one that I was searching for. I thought about just walking up to her and shooting her in the head with my 9mm Beretta pistol. I decided I better grab my pump shotgun instead.

I made sure that it was fully loaded with seven rounds of slugs, this included one in the chamber. The moose was about 200 yards from my truck and the snow was deep and crusty. I took off walking towards her post holing through the knee-deep snow. She could see me coming the entire time as I walked right towards her. I ended up approximately thirty yards from her. She looked right at me and never attempted to get up or show any signs of aggression. I noticed her left ear was hanging down alongside her face and her body looked very emaciated. I was breathing hard from hiking through the deep snow. I stopped to get my breath and look her over carefully.

I had finally determined that this was indeed the sick cow moose that I was looking for. I decided I would put her down with my 12-gauge shotgun from where I was standing. We had a lot of moose dying at this time of unknown causes. Our lab folks wanted us to send in the head of any dead moose so they could run tests to see what was making these moose sick and die. If we were to send in a moose head, they didn't want us to shoot the moose in the head and destroy any tissues that they needed for sampling. I decided to wait for the moose to stand up, and I would shoot her behind the front shoulder. It seemed like I had stood there for eternity and the moose was not going to stand up. I was not afraid of the moose, and she had still not displayed any signs of aggression towards me. However, I still felt that I was close enough to this moose and didn't want to get any closer. I finally decided that I would just shoot her behind the shoulder as she was lying down.

I raised up my shotgun to aim. The moose saw the movement of my shotgun raising up and immediately jumped up and charged me at full speed. My first thought was, *oh Shit, she is coming fast. I need to make the first shot count.* I found the front sight on my shotgun and quickly put it in the center of her chest and pulled the trigger. I expected her to drop in front of me immediately after the first shot.

That didn't happen and she kept coming fast. I had been through some earlier law enforcement training and was taught that when you get in a life and death situation, your brain slows down and you will get tunnel vision. This is absolutely true. This was the weirdest thing that I had ever experienced. My brain slowed down, and everything was happening in slow motion. I quickly jacked another round in the chamber and aimed at the chest cavity of the charging moose. I could see steam leaving her body on her right side. This was where the slug had exited her rib cage. Every time she took a breath, I could see steam exit her side in the cold morning air. I fired again and again. Now I was running backwards cycling another round into my chamber. I could now see three separate streams of steam exiting her right side every time she took a breath. I knew I had hit her all three times, and she was still coming right towards me very fast. I continued running backwards and shooting at her chest area. My back was now leaning against some heavy willows, and I could no longer run backwards. I started to "rack" my final slug and realized I didn't have any more time before she was going to hit me. I held the shotgun up along my side to protect my face. Her nose hit me in the side of my face and knocked me down hard. I hit the ground face first and felt pinned to the ground. The moose had died on top of me. I was able to struggle and get out from underneath the heavy moose and stand upright. My hands were trembling, and the moose was dead.

I couldn't have told you how many times I shot. Everything happened in very slow motion. The whole event probably only took less than five seconds to unfold. Because there was snow on the ground, I was able to go back and recount everything that had just happened. I went back to the location where she first stood up. I noticed blood in the snow indicating that I had hit her the first shot. I then found a string of red shell casings lying on top of the snow spaced evenly apart. Each shell casing was about two feet apart, as I was running backwards while shooting. I found six empty shell casings on the ground with one final slug left in my shotgun. As I stood there still shaking, I thought, *thank God I grabbed my shotgun and fully loaded it before I left my truck.* After further investigation, I determined that I had hit the cow moose in the chest all six times and not one of them slowed her down. I had shot many animals with a slug before in my life and had not seen anything like this. Most animals drop in their tracks when they are hit with the velocity of a large lead ball.

I also determined that the moose was completely full of ticks. Some of the ticks were as large as a super ball. I would probably have nightmares about a tick-infested moose dying on top of me and I wouldn't be able to get out from underneath her. I happily cut her head off and threw it in the back of my patrol truck. I also thought about donating her meat to the needy and quickly decided that the coyotes could have this one. The rancher had pulled up in his tractor just as I was cutting the head off the moose. He said he was feeding cows and heard six shots and thought either I was a poor shot or needed help. I replied, "Probably both." I told him the story and he just laughed almost uncontrollably. He said, "Shit, I was going to just put her down myself, but I'm glad I called you."

I sent the moose head to our lab and did not tell any of them about the moose charging me. I received an email from the lab about two weeks later that read. *Dear Scott, thank you for submitting the cow moose for sampling. Our lab tests determined that the moose had Elaeophora. This is a worm that gets in their carotid artery and reduces the flow of blood to their brain. This moose was probably nearly blind and very cantankerous.* Boy, did she get that one right. If someone would have captured this on video, it would have made an excellent training video for wardens across the country. The video would have shown that thirty yards from a sick moose with seven slugs may have been too close and doesn't always work.

I returned home that evening covered in moose blood and hair. I told my wife Lana the story about the cow moose dying on top of me.

She just laughed and said, "You better check yourself for ticks before crawling into bed." Shit, I hadn't even thought of that. I quickly jumped into the shower.

I soon found myself headed to our research lab in Sybille, Wyoming for some capture/immobilization training for a few days. This training was to teach how to load drugs, what drugs to use on certain animals, and proper dosages. We got to walk around the facility and dart different big game animals such as deer, bighorn sheep, elk, and antelope. We, as students, would have to determine which drug to use based on the animal that we were going to put down. We would then have to calculate the proper dosage, load the drug into a dart and load the dart gun. Once all of that was done, we would try and shoot the animal preferably in the hind quarter or other large muscle mass area. When the animal was down, we would keep it sternal, take its temperature and either draw blood, or place a radio transmitter collar on the animal. Each animal had a different scenario of what we were to perform as students once the animal was down. We would also keep track of how long the animal was down and how long it took the animal to recover after the antidote was administered.

My job was to dart the nine-year-old full curl ram named Chester. Chester was extremely aggressive and hated all men wearing red shirts. I think Chester had been darted so many times that he became very cranky and unhappy with life in general. If Chester ever had a clean shot at you, he would take you in a second. I jumped in the large fenced-off area that held Chester. Luckily, he was lying down facing away from me. Except, I would need to low crawl for about thirty yards to get close enough for the dart to fly accurately and penetrate his heavy coat. Just as I was pulling the slack out of the trigger, Chester spotted me in the tall grass behind him. He jumped up out of his bed and came charging towards me with his head down at about 30 MPH. I was instructed to place the dart in his hind quarter. This is not possible when the ram is charging you with his head down and coming very quick. I could hear other students laughing in the background. I even heard a loud voice yell, "RUN, SWERB, RUN!"

I carefully and calmly placed the crosshairs of my rifle scope on the chest cavity of the charging ram. It was going to be a very difficult shot as the ram had his head lowered as he charged. I started having flashbacks of the cow moose that had charged me earlier. Everything went into slow motion again as I thought, *nice easy trigger pull, focus on crosshairs,* BAM, I pulled the trigger. I had firmly placed the loaded dart right into the very tip of the ram's nose. I quickly placed both of my arms around my head for protection. The ram lowered his head with large horns and smacked me a good one rolling my entire body over as he went over the top of me. Thankfully the ram kept running away from me and later succumbed to the drug that was injected into his nostrils. Some of the other students were giving me a hard time and laughing at me. Saying things like, "Nice shot, Swerb, you were supposed to shoot him in the ass not the nose!" I slowly got up, brushed the dirt off my clothes and replied, "That's the work of a trained professional right there, Sir. The nose is the softest tissue on the ram and that is exactly where I was aiming."

I returned to Pinedale and soon became the region's "trained professional" at darting animals as I had just received all this fancy training at our research facility. Soon after, our lab was looking for some moose to do some research on. The lab requested ten moose and suggested that if we were having any problem moose in residential areas, that we should target those moose and remove them from towns and human conflict. We were currently having conflict with 7-10 moose that an elderly couple had been feeding alfalfa hay to in Pinedale next to the middle school. The couple really felt that they were doing the moose a favor by feeding them. They had named all the moose personally and were very attached to all of them. From my experience, once moose are fed and lose fear of humans, they can become very dangerous. They expect a food reward and when they don't get one, they can become aggressive. I had already had several calls on these particular moose chasing young children into the school building while kids were playing during recess. I had even used my patrol truck to haze an angry cow moose out of the playground one day to get it safely away from the playing children. I literally used the front quarter panel of my patrol truck to push the running moose away from the playground and over the chain-link fence that surrounded the playground. Thankfully she cleared the tall fence when she jumped and was not injured.

I met with our local wildlife biologists and south Pinedale game warden Dennis Almquist. We all agreed that these moose would be great candidates to remove from town due to human safety concerns. Our lab personnel had recommended that we use Telazol for the drug of choice and gave us recommended dosages for the adult and calf moose. The biologists loaded up several darts and handed me the loaded darts and the Palmer dart gun. I guess I was designated as the "shooter" on this project due to my recent training. We all jumped into our game and fish trucks and headed to the address of the elderly couple who had been feeding these moose for several years. Once we arrived on scene with four game and fish trucks parked across the street from the elderly couple's house, I noticed that all the moose were busy eating hay out of a feeder in the elderly couple's yard. The elderly couple noticed all the green trucks parked across the street from their house and came out to see what was going on.

The elderly lady, who looked to be in her late 70's, was wearing a pink bath robe and had her hair rolled up in curlers. She was wearing house slippers and had a cane in one hand. The elderly husband also had a cane in his hand and was fully clothed. The temperature was very cold, and the snow was about a foot deep in their yard. I approached the elderly couple as they stood on the edge of their property with their arms crossed and the moose herd standing behind them happily eating hay. The elderly lady squinted her eyes at me and said with her arms crossed, "Can I help you with something?" I informed the lady that we would like to dart the moose in her yard and move them out of town due to human safety concerns with the school just down the street. She yelled at me, "OVER MY DEAD BODY! THOSE MOOSE BELONG TO US AND YOU AREN'T STEPPING A FOOT ON THIS PROPERTY OR WE WILL CALL THE SHERIFF AND HAVE YOU TRESPASSED!" I really tried to "smooth" talk the elderly couple but was not getting anywhere. They were adamant that we were not allowed on their property.

The neighbor lady across the street came running out of her house towards us. She was also in her bathrobe and had a Camel cigarette hanging out of her mouth. She joined our conversation and yelled at the elderly couple. "YOU GET THESE DAMN MOOSE OUT OF YOUR YARD. THEY ARE A HUMAN SAFETY CONCERN TO ALL OF US. WE ALL WANT THEM THE HELL OUT OF HERE!" The elderly lady in the pink bathrobe grabbed her cane and pushed the lady backwards off the curb and back into the street. She replied, "I'M ALLERGIC TO CIGARETTE SMOKE, YOU GET OFF MY PROERTY RIGHT NOW OR I WILL HAVE YOU TRESPASSED!" I ended up jumping between the two old ladies and a cane and tried to calm them down. I thought to myself, *what have you gotten yourself into now, Swerb?* Dennis could see that things were going south, so he came over and tried to calm the ladies down. By now, there were other people coming out of their houses to see what all the commotion was all about. I whispered to Dennis, "Let's get out of here and come back later before the situation escalates even more."

We all left the area. I stayed several blocks away where I could keep an eye on the moose. After several hours the moose walked across the street onto the property of the lady who smoked un-filtered Camels and was now an ally to the department. I quickly drove up and parked my truck along the street in front of her house. She came out the front door and yelled, "GO AHEAD, GET EVERY ONE OF THESE FLOWER-EATING SONSABITCHES OUT OF MY YARD!" I radioed to Dennis to bring in the "A" team and be prepared to dart some moose.

Dennis rolled up and handed me the Palmer dart gun. He looked at me with a very serious look and said, "Here ya go, Swerb, try not to F—k this up. We have a lot of spectators watching." I was very nervous, I had only darted one animal prior to this and shot charging Chester in the damn nose. I grabbed the dart gun and headed into a tall patch of willows to try and get a shot at one of the cow moose. As I was sneaking through the willows trying to get within shooting range of a cow moose, I heard a voice behind me. "What kind of drug are you administering and what is your dosage?" I turned around to see the little old lady still wearing the pink bathrobe and slippers following me through the thick patch of willows. I very calmly replied in a whisper, "Madam, I'm a "trained professional" and you need to stand back."

I looked up and noticed a cow moose walking away from me in the willows about twenty yards away. I took careful aim and placed my dart perfectly into her left hind quarter. She felt the impact of the dart and quickly ran forward into the thick willows. I slowly and quietly walked through the willows until I could locate her. There she was lying down right in front of me. I looked at my watch and decided to give her a full ten minutes to let the drug fully absorb her system before approaching her. After ten minutes I walked very quietly up to her as she was lying down facing away from me. The crusted snow made it difficult to be quiet. As I approached her, she heard me coming and jumped up and ran off into the thick willows. I thought, *damn she didn't get enough drug. Once an animal gets up and starts running, their adrenalin kicks in and they can be very difficult to put down after that.*

Game and Fish personnel darting a cow moose

I walked back to our trucks and told Dennis what had happened. He had been patiently keeping the little old lady at bay. I didn't dare let the lady know that I needed another dart as I told her that I was a "trained professional." The biologists kindly loaded me up another dart and snuck it to me as Dennis was still trying to calm the lady down. I snuck back into the willows and located the cow moose again. She was lying down facing away from me. I made a perfect shot on her right hip, and she jumped up and headed up the hill towards another neighbor's house. I followed the cow moose up the hill and watched her from a distance. The cow finally lay down in the neighbor's backyard. We were starting to gain an audience now. After waiting several minutes, which seemed like forever the cow would not go down. I went back down and met with Dennis and told him I needed a third dart. Dennis replied, "Swerbe, you need to get this cow put down right now, we are attracting an audience!"

I had my dart gun loaded and was now belly crawling in front of the picture window of the house where the moose was lying down in the backyard. An old lady in the house looked out her picture window and saw me with my rifle. She started yelling at me and flipped me off. She grabbed her cordless phone and called someone as she was flipping me off. Within minutes two sheriff's deputies showed up and wanted to know why I was poaching a moose in the lady's backyard. They soon realized that I was a game warden and not some crazed person crawling around in people's backyards poaching moose. I apologized to the lady and explained what I was trying to do. She apologized for the call to the sheriff's office and allowed me to enter her backyard to dart the moose again. I shot a third dart into the rump of the moose and waited for the moose to go down completely. The moose would not go down. Dennis approached me and said, "Swerbe, we need to get this cow moose down right now even if we have to tackle her."

Dennis grabbed a couple biologists, and they made a "Game Plan." The moose was now lying down facing away from them as they slowly approached her from behind. Dennis grabbed her head and pulled it to the ground. He then put his knee on her neck and pulled her front leg up close to her body (like how cowboys would hold a calf down while branding them.) The other two men jumped into the middle of it and were trying to place hobbles on the moose's hind and front legs. The moose quickly lunged up and game and fish personnel went flying everywhere. Except Dennis, he held on tight. The next thing I knew Dennis was straddled over the moose's back. The cow moose was headed right towards me with Dennis yelling, "GRAB HER SWERB GRAB HER!!" Dennis's eyes were the size of silver dollars, and he was hanging on very tight. The moose was headed right towards me. This is when I realized just how big moose really are. The moose's head stood about one foot higher than mine. She had to be at least seven feet tall. I did the quick math and quickly decided that there was no way that I was going to try and stop the moose. I stepped back and let the moose run on by me. The moose was now headed straight towards a wooden yard fence that stood about six feet high. She had three brightly colored darts sticking out of her butt, and Dennis straddled across her back with two fists full of moose hair. The moose lunged to jump the tall wood fence and Dennis shot off the back side of the moose like a cowboy being bucked off a rank bucking bull. The moose did not clear the tall fence but knocked it over as she busted through it. Boards flew everywhere as she knocked down about ten feet of the nicely constructed fence.

The moose then ran through a small group of little old ladies who were standing nearby. I would have never believed that they could move that fast! Never underestimate the speed of little old ladies when a cow moose is coming right towards them. They screamed, one of them even dropped her cigarette as she quickly took off running. The cow moose had three darts sticking out of her rump and was dazed from the drug, which made her run like she was drunk. The moose crashed through a second fence. I thought, *oh dear God the moose has entered the town cemetery.* I walked over and gave Dennis a hand's up. He was moving very slowly, and his face was squished up as if he were feeling a great deal of pain. Dennis looked over the knocked down wooden fence and said, "Dammit, Swerb, she is in the cemetery." We stood there in shock as we watched the moose run away from us. She would stagger to her left and then stagger to her right. About that time, she ran into a large headstone that stood about six feet high and knocked it over. I continued watching her run through the cemetery knocking over large headstones that got in her way. Finally, the moose went down. I was very relieved except we now had about 10-15 spectators. I was no longer feeling like a "trained professional."

I walked through the cemetery and stood up several headstones. Some of them were very heavy and Dennis had to help me prop them back up. Each one that I set back up, I whispered "*Rest in peace, sorry to bother you*." I finally reached the moose; she was down on her belly with her head still up. She was feeling the effects of the drug and didn't seem too concerned about our presence. Several of us got into position and grabbed her all at the same time. Dennis again put his knee on her neck and raised up her front leg close to her body. The others put their bodies over the top of the moose to try and hold her down while they put hobbles on the moose's legs. Again, the moose made a lunge as she got up and flipped Dennis over her head. Dennis landed on his belly facedown. The moose then used Dennis's back and shoulders for traction as she suddenly took off again. The moose ran several more steps, hit another large tombstone and fell to the ground. We all tackled her and finally got the hobbles and blindfold on her.

We needed to get the moose loaded into a horse trailer some distance away. We couldn't drive the truck and trailer into the cemetery, so we needed to figure out a way to get the large bodied moose back to our trucks. One of the spectators told me that he had a large car hood in his backyard and that we were welcome to use as a sled. I thanked the man, unloaded my snow machine, and hooked a rope to the man's car hood in his backyard. The snow was deep, drifted and crusted in the cemetery. We finally got the moose loaded onto the car hood. I tried to get the rope tight and take off slowly, but I kept getting stuck. Finally, I got some slack in the rope and gave it the onion. I hit the end of the rope so hard that the sled took off and the moose stayed there. I circled back around, and we loaded the moose again. This time we also loaded two other biologists to sit in the sled with the moose and hold her down in the car hood sled. I gave it the onion again and hit the end of the rope. It was a little "Western", but we were up and moving towards the truck with the horse trailer. I held the throttle wide open on the snow machine to keep from getting stuck. If I slowed down at all, I would be stuck in the deep snow. I had to make a sharp turn to get through a small gate to get out of the cemetery. As I made the turn the old car hood full of people and a moose swung out to my right and collided with a large tombstone. The biologists had an undisturbed flight into a snowdrift, but the moose stayed in the sled. I kept on the throttle to keep from getting stuck and blew by all the spectators with the moose hanging halfway out of the sled blindfolded. I bet the moose would have enjoyed seeing where she was headed. I finally made it to the horse trailer with the moose flailing around trying to get up off the car hood. With a great deal of grunting, we were all able to get the moose into the horse trailer. Once the moose was in the trailer and the door was closed, I went through the small side door and removed the hobbles and her blindfold. The cow moose immediately jumped up and started trying to jump out of the trailer. She was making noises that I had never heard a moose make before as her head kept hitting the top of the horse trailer.

We didn't want to travel all the way to Laramie with only one moose in the trailer, so we darted a cow moose and her two calves. We had a similar experience with the other three moose not wanting to go down in a timely manner. Just before nightfall, we had a horse trailer with four moose headed for Laramie. The biologist who was driving the truck arrived in Laramie at approximately 11:00 PM. He exited the truck and walked underneath the front of the gooseneck trailer and hit the top of his head on a sharp piece of angle iron. This split his head wide open requiring a trip to the emergency room in the middle of the night for stiches. He was not able to return to Pinedale until the next day. As for Dennis, when the cow moose stepped on his back and shoulder, he sustained an injury to his shoulder that later required shoulder surgery. We soon learned that Telazol was not the drug of choice for moose. Carfentanil turned out to be a much better drug for putting moose down quickly.

Dennis Almquist qualifying with his department issue shot gun

Chapter 3

WYOMING LAW ENFORCEMENT ACADEMY

It was April of 1998. My wife Lana and I were still living in the little white house up Horse Creek across from Kathy Miller's ranch house. The Green River which was located about 200 yards behind the house was raging with high water due to high spring run-off with snow melting in the upper elevations. Later that spring the water would end up coming out of its banks and flood around our house. This caused a very muddy driveway and yard. The mosquitoes became absolutely horrendous that spring and summer.

I received a phone call from regional wildlife supervisor Bernie Holz that I had been accepted to attend the Wyoming Law Enforcement Academy (WLEA) starting in early May. I was really excited to hear this news as this meant that I would be receiving the proper training that I needed to become an official permanent Wyoming game warden. It also meant that the department would be more vested in me, and it would really help me to get a warden district someday if I ever wanted to give up the Feed Ground Manager/Game Warden position. The downfall to attending the WLEA would be that I would need to be gone for thirteen weeks and only home on weekends. I would again be away from my family, and how would I get all the hay purchased for the feed grounds and all the maintenance jobs completed? I would need to rely heavily on Gary Hornberger our new

Feed Ground Maintenance guy. I would also only have about one month to get into good shape so that I could pass the rigorous physical training that the WLEA required each officer to pass on the first day of training. This involved running a mile and a half in twelve minutes and doing a set number of push-ups and sit-ups in one minute.

At first, I was not concerned about passing the physical fitness test because I was pretty active. I had run a six-minute mile while playing college football. What I didn't realize was that was over ten years ago, and I had gained some weight. I jumped in my truck and drove a mile and a half down the Horse Creek Road from our house to mark how far I would need to run for training. I would need to complete this in twelve minutes. I thought to myself *this should be a breeze.* I went home and threw on some old holey, faded sweatpants and hit the highway running with my stopwatch in hand. I never was much of a runner, and I soon realized that there is not much oxygen in the air at over 7000 feet elevation. I hadn't even made it a mile when I tripped on my tongue and fell face first in the gravel. I stood there along the highway with both arms held above my head trying to catch my breath. I looked at my watch and it read nine minutes. Heck, I still had another half mile to go, and I couldn't catch my breath. This was a humbling experience for me. Ol'Swerb would end up running up and down that damn road for several weeks before I could make my mark in twelve minutes. I also spent hours in the evenings doing as many push-ups and sit-ups as I possibly could.

The day would soon come when I was packed up and headed for Douglas, Wyoming to attend the WLEA. I was in great shape and my morale was high as I had just got a brand-new Ford one-ton patrol truck. This truck was badass. It had a lift kit, heavy duty front bumper with a warn winch, and a cassette player. All the other wardens were jealous that I was able to bid a one-ton truck. As the Feed Ground manager, I needed more truck to pull a long gooseneck trailer loaded with a tractor. I also needed the extra power to pull a horse trailer loaded down with heavy draft horses.

Brand new game and fish truck

I was so excited about my new truck, I grabbed my bag phone and called my brother Wade A.K.A. (Dumbass) who was now living in Riverton, Wyoming. I asked him if he would meet me at the Walmart parking lot in Riverton and check out my brand-new patrol truck. Wade was excited and told me to call him when I was at Walmart. It was a beautiful spring day as I flew over South Pass headed for Lander. The V-10 truck had lots of power and an awesome stereo system. I played my one cassette tape Match Box 20 over and over. As I was driving through Riverton my bag phone rang. It was a Pinedale rancher wanting to discuss hay prices. I sat in the Walmart parking lot talking with him for several minutes with my foot on the brake. I hung up with the man and headed into Walmart to purchase a pair of tennis shoes to run in for the physical fitness test at the Academy. I didn't own a pair of tennis shoes in Pinedale, and you couldn't even find a pair to buy over there.

I had tried to call my brother to let him know that I was in town, but no answer. As I was paying for my white tennis shoes with Velcro straps, I heard a loud voice come over the Walmart speaker inside of the store. The voice said, "Could the owner of the Game and Fish truck in the parking lot please come to customer service?" I thought to myself, *my brother has done it now, he is trying to page me over the Walmart intercom system.* I headed to Customer Service and did not see my brother standing around anywhere. Instead, there was an older Native American standing there with beaded ponytails about two feet long wearing a cowboy hat. He looked at me and said, "Hey man, is that your game and fish truck out there in the parking lot?" I replied, "I think so." He replied with a smile, "Man, your truck rolled all the way across the parking lot and T-boned a brand-new white Cadillac, man! I ran along side of it trying to open the door, but it was locked, and I could not get it stopped before it hit the car."

I thought to myself, *boy my brother is really messing with me on this one.* I kept waiting for my brother to appear, but he never did. I nervously walked out into the parking lot to find my brand-new Ford truck stuck right in the side of a brand-new Cadillac. I had evidently left the manual transmission in neutral while talking to the rancher and had forgot to put it in gear before heading into the store. As I approached the accident scene a little closer, I noticed my Warn winch was planted deeply into the passenger side door of the white Cadillac. I was extremely embarrassed as I stood there looking around the Walmart parking lot. Every car in the parking lot was an old beat-up ridge-runner except the car that I had hit. I had literally hit the only nice car in the entire parking lot.

Spectators were starting to gather around the scene, and I was very embarrassed. I jumped in the truck, started it up and backed it away from the Cadillac. About that time a Riverton police officer arrived at the scene and questioned me. I told him what had happened; the officer chewed my ass for leaving the scene of an accident. I told him that

I had only left the scene for about thirty feet because it was embarrassing to me. I jumped in my truck and ran the license plate number of the car through our dispatch to find out who the registered owner was. I wrote the name down on a McDonald's napkin and sat in my truck for nearly thirty minutes waiting for the owners to arrive. They never arrived so I went into Walmart and had Customer Service call the man's name over the store speaker system. I waited for about ten minutes, and nobody showed up.

I walked back out into the parking lot and noticed an elderly man and women getting into the white Cadillac from a distance. They got into the car, started it, and drove off. I chased them in my red shirt through the parking lot yelling, "HEY, HEY." They never heard me or saw me as they pulled out on the main highway and headed for Shoshoni. I thought to myself, *I can't believe the old lady never saw the huge gaping hole that my winch left in the passenger side door as she entered the car.* I jumped into my patrol truck and chased them down the road. Once behind them I turned on my red and blue lights and my sirens and followed them for nearly a mile before the old man finally pulled the car over. This was really embarrassing. Now I had to pull over the car that I smashed to tell them what I had done! As I approached the car on foot, the old man jumped out of the car and started coming towards me. He yelled, "WHAT THE HELL DID I DO WRONG? I HAVEN'T HUNTED IN YEARS!" I said, "Sir, you didn't do anything wrong, but I need to show you the damage that I did to your car while it was parked at Walmart."

The old man walked around the other side of the car and observed the damage. He ran his fingers through his hair and said, "How in the Cornbread Hell did you do that?" I explained what had happened. The man and I exchanged insurance information. The man was not impressed to say the least. He asked me if I had received my driver's license from Sears. I felt horrible about what had happened and still needed to call the regional wildlife supervisor Bernie Holz in Pinedale and inform him of the incident.

I called Bernie and explained to him what had happened. He just giggled and said, "Good thing that didn't happen while you were parked in front of a strip joint somewhere." I was glad that he could find some humor in the situation because I did not. I headed onto Douglas and decided to stop at the Game and Fish regional office in Casper and say "hi" to my old boss Terry Cleveland. I met Terry at the front door of the office as he was leaving the building. He shook my hand and stated, "I heard that you got in a fender bender in Riverton this morning." I could not believe that he had already heard about the news, and he wasn't even my supervisor anymore. I responded, "Yea, I guess it could have been worse, at least I wasn't parked in front of a strip joint." Terry laughed and stated, "Yea, that would require a few more phone calls and some additional paperwork for sure." Mr. Cleveland wished me the best of luck at the Academy, and we said our goodbyes.

I was nervous about going to the Academy. I thought to myself, *what if I do not pass the physical fitness test on day one and they send me home. What if I cannot pass the classes and fail, and the Game and Fish Department fires me?* I had heard that the instructors were hard on some officers and ran the place like a military boot camp. I arrived at the Wyoming Law Enforcement Academy (WLEA) parking lot. The front door had a punch code. I am glad that I remembered the code because I had left it on a sheet of paper at home. I entered the building and looked at the room assignment sheet hanging on the wall. My roommate would be a deputy sheriff named Ned Fogerty from Jackson Hole Wyoming. Our room number was 111. I about fainted when I saw what our room number was. This is the same number of the hospital room that both my dad and grandpa had died in years ago. This was also the same room number that I had to meet the psychologist Dr. Whyme in, prior to going through the psychological exam to get hired by the Department. This really freaked me out. Did this mean that my dad and grandpa would again be with me every step of the way or was this a bad omen?

I used a key that was provided to me to open my room door 111. My roommate had not yet showed up. I flipped on the light switch and the room was very neat and clean and smelled of fresh cleaning detergent. The room was like a college dorm room. There was a single wide bed on each side of the room with a desk beside each bed. The beds had no bedding on them just stained mattresses. Apparently, I would need to pick my bedding up at the commercial laundry room on the other side of the building and make my own bed. This would be a challenge for me as I was used to just sleeping in a sleeping bag on top of a mattress. Hell, I did not even know how to properly make a bed military style. There was also a small bathroom in the corner of the room and two large closets with a small mirror and sink between the closets.

I was not too excited about learning how to make my bed that night, so I just crawled under the sheet and blanket and fell asleep on top of the stained mattress. About 10:00 PM I was awakened by the sound of a key turning the lock on the front door. The door swung open, and the lights were turned on. The lights were so bright that I was having a difficult time focusing my eyes on the person walking through the door. The man was slender and tall with a dark mustache. As soon as the man observed me sleeping in bed he said, "Oh, I'm sorry man, I didn't realize that you were already here and sleeping, my apology." He then walked over to me while I was lying in bed and reached out to shake my hand. He said, "Nice to meet you, my name is Ned Fogerty. I shook his hand and introduced myself as well. I was not impressed. I thought to myself, *who in their right mind shows up to the academy at 10:00 PM the night before when we have physical fitness training at 0700 hours?* The man was very kind and apologized several times for waking me up. He shut the light off and slept on top of his mattress with his clothes still on, because he did not have any sheets or blanket yet. I think he would have made his bed if it were not for me trying to go to sleep. Breakfast was at 0600 hours and our physical fitness test would begin at 0700 hours. I decided that I would skip breakfast because I did not want to puke it all out after the mile and half run. I set my alarm for 0530 hours and did not sleep very well that night.

We met in the gymnasium at 0700 hours. Several of the instructors were there and introduced themselves to the class of approximately 25 officers from all over the state of Wyoming. They then issued each of us a pair of blue sweatpants that had white lettering down the legs that read WLEA. We were also issued two blue t-shirts that also had the white lettering WLEA across the back of the t-shirts. The Custody and Control instructor advised all of us to go back to our rooms and change into our sweatpants and t-shirts and return to the gymnasium in ten minutes for our physical fitness test. I had purchased a pair of white tennis shoes at Walmart. The shoes did not have laces, only two Velcro straps on each shoe. Once we were all back in the gymnasium, I noticed that I was the only officer in the room with Velcro straps on my shoes. One officer from Rock Springs walked by me and said, “Nice shoes, man!” as he laughed. This was starting to give me a complex for some reason. The instructors explained the whole physical fitness test to all of us and partnered us up with another officer. My partner was a city police officer from Gillette who did not appear to me to be in very good shape He was over-weight and looked to be about 40 years old. We all lined up and took off running around orange traffic cones in the large gymnasium. I worked my way to the front of all the runners and slid in behind a cute gal who was leading the pack. This gal was very cute and built like a brick shithouse. My view of her behind was pretty good and it certainly motivated me to keep up with her every step of the way.

I do not know how many laps we ran, but I felt good and was able to keep up with the cute gal in the lead. I could not pass her, but I kept up and started lapping other officers who were falling behind. The heavy-set man, my partner, had tripped and fell. It looked like some of the instructors may have been performing CPR on him back in the corner of the gymnasium. I finished in second place behind the cute gal. I later found out that she had set the new Academy record for the women's division in the mile and half run. I do not remember what my time was, but I had passed with flying colors and was excited about that. At the end of the run, I walked up to the Rock Springs police officer who was bent over puking in a garbage can and said, "Hey buddy, I think you should get some shoes like mine, maybe you could have kept up a little better." He did not look at me or say anything, he kept puking in the garbage can and gave me the bird.

Next it was off to do sit-ups and push-ups. I did fine in both events and did quite a few more than I needed to do for the Academy standards. My partner, the heavy-set man from Gillette didn't fare so well. He only needed to do 17 sit-ups for his age and weight. I held his feet flat to the floor and counted each sit-up. He made it to 12 and could not do anymore. He would later tell the instructors that he did 17 sit-ups but that I had miscounted them. I told the instructors that I had not miscounted them and that he was not even close to getting them done. This man was sent home that day for failing the physical fitness test. The Academy has now installed a camera in the gymnasium to keep everyone honest. The lady officer who beat me in the running also set a new Academy record for the most push-ups and sit-ups by any other woman in the history of the Academy. I would later nickname her GI-Jane.

The academy ran a tight schedule and kept us officers busy Monday through Friday from 0700 hours to 1800 hours nearly every day. Officers were required to wear their department uniform, have a clean shave, and make their beds daily. All the instructors dressed for class each day wearing a nice shirt, slacks, and a tie. My department uniform consisted of blue jeans, cowboy boots and a red shirt. The instructors and other officers did not appreciate that I could get away with wearing blue jeans and a red shirt. All the food served at the academy was cafeteria-style food. Most meals were just ok, enough said about that. Some instructors were very arrogant, as if they all wanted to become the Director someday. Other instructors were great to deal with and be around. The current Director had been there for well over thirty years.

Sitting in the classroom all day almost killed me. There were days that I could not stay awake and days that I could not focus and pay attention. I remember staring at the clock, and it seemed like a couple of hours had gone by and the hands on the clock only moved about five minutes. We spent a great deal of time together and our class became really close with one another. My roommate Ned was a great guy. We became very good friends and it appeared that he and I were the top shooters in the class. He was the firearms trainer for the sheriff's department in Jackson Hole. I would need to step it up if I wanted to win the top shooting award for the class. The hallways in the academy were filled with pictures of other classes and all the top award winners. It appeared to me that many game wardens over the years had won many of the top awards. The awards included top academic student, top firearms proficiency, top physical fitness, and all-around top officer of each class. I did not want to let my department down. Hopefully I would receive some of these top awards. However, GI Jane was going to be very difficult to beat for the physical fitness award and my roommate Ned was going to be very difficult to beat for the top shooter award. I had no expectation of winning the top academic officer award, no matter how hard that I tried. I was never good at school, and it generally takes me an hour and a half to watch 60 Minutes.

I did not realize how tough these thirteen weeks were going to be on me. I soon realized that it was May and I needed to purchase about 6-9 thousand tons of hay in small bales to stock all the elk feed grounds for the coming winter. The academy had a pay phone down at the end of the hall on the second floor. I found myself sitting in a chair talking to hay producers on the pay phone nearly every night of the week for several hours while other officers were down at the local tavern having drinks and telling stories. I spent a great deal of time arguing with hay producers over the price per ton of hay. The department bought so much hay that we kind of set the price for the entire market in Western Wyoming. If we paid too low it made everyone's hay worth less and if we paid too high, everyone was stuck paying at least what the Department paid per ton of hay when they needed to purchase hay themselves. We also had to contract with the hay producers before their hay was even fully grown and before the market was established due to our lengthy contract process that took well over a month to process.

I would drive home to Pinedale every Friday evening to see my family for the weekend. The drive was over five hours one way. I would get home after 10:00 PM on Friday night and needed to leave each Sunday around noon to travel back. About week number three I learned that one of my classmates named Jade, who was also a deputy from Jackson Hole, Wyoming had his own airplane and flew back and forth to Jackson each weekend. I asked Jade if he would mind flying me to Jackson on Friday evenings and I would have my wife Lana pick me up at the Jackson airport. He agreed to do this, I offered to pay for his fuel. He just smiled and said, "Don't worry about it buddy, you can't afford it anyways." He was probably right. The next week I rode down to Douglas with my roommate Ned and left my patrol truck home so that I could fly home with the other deputy. I was excited about this and was feeling a little bit cocky. *How many other officers got to fly home* I thought to myself. Heck, I could be in Jackson by 6:00 PM, take my wife to dinner and be home at a decent hour.

I could not wait for Friday afternoon to finally come. I was excited about flying to

Jackson with Jade and Ned. We headed out to the Douglas International Airport to find a small Cessna plane secured to the ground with ropes and cables. The wind was blowing about 30 miles per hour with some dark looking clouds to the south. Jade told Ned and I to get into the plane with all our gear while he unhooked all the ropes and cables. I was a little nervous to say the least, especially after I crawled into the little, tiny seat behind the pilot. I was really scrunched in there with not much room to even die if we were to crash. Jade jumped into the plane and started flipping switches with his cool Aviator glasses on. I asked Jade if he thought it was safe to fly. Jade responded, "We have a great head wind so we should be able to take off quickly. Those black clouds to the south do not look good, but maybe we can fly around the storm." He then told us to make sure our seatbelts were fastened tightly, as we may have some turbulence once we fly over the Gros Ventre Mountain range.

Everything went smooth until we reached the Gros Ventre Mountain range. We tried to fly around the storm, but we were unable to avoid it. Suddenly, the plane started bouncing up and down very hard. I hit my head on the roof of the plane a couple of times. Jade stayed calm and said, "Hang on, things are going to get a little western for a moment. We need to fly into the center of the cloud (known as the eye of the storm)." I looked over the pilot's seat and could see a huge black cloud moving in a circular motion. It looked scary as hell to me with hail and bolts of lightning reaching out across the sky below the cloud. Jade said, "Hold on tight we are going to fly into the center of the storm." That little plane must have jumped straight up 20-30 feet and dropped back down just as hard. Up and down, side to side we went through the black clouds. I could now hear the loud sounds of heavy rain hitting the plane and could see bolts of lightning flashing off each wing tip. I closed my eyes and interlaced my fingers and said a quick prayer to the man upstairs. I prayed, "Lord, please get me through this storm safely to Jackson Hole and I promise I will never put you or me in this situation again." I would have rather ridden a moped or a camel back to Pinedale to avoid this situation again.

The ability to fly home quickly was not all it was cracked up to be. We finally entered the "eye of the storm" and the plane smoothed out. It was a weird feeling. It became very quiet and smooth, almost an eerie feeling. Jade shifted from side to side and stayed in the center of the storm when he could. Jade yelled, "HANG ON, we are leaving the eye of the storm and it's going to get rough!" I looked over Jade's shoulder and he was white knuckled as he held tightly onto the controls of the plane. We bounced back through the black clouds and lightning and could start to see blue sky in the distance. *THANK GOD!* I thought to myself. We literally flew right through a horrible thunderstorm at high elevations over mountainous terrain. I was proud of Jade and had a new level of respect for that man. We made it to Jackson Hole safely and my wife Lana was at the airport to pick me up. She told me that she was really worried about me having to fly through that horrible storm. She asked me how it went. I replied, "Oh, not bad honey, just a little rough." I did not tell her that I was in the fetal position shaking and crying like a little schoolgirl in the principal's office most of the trip. We had a nice dinner and returned home at a decent hour. To say the least, this would be my last trip flying to and from the academy.

I would return to the academy with only nine weeks left. We had a surprise room inspection on Monday afternoon. I was ordered to remake my bed and shave before returning to class in ten minutes. I did not do well with this sort of military boot camp attitude that a few instructors had. I just grinned and bared it and said, "YES, SIR!" I thought to myself, *only nine more weeks!!* We were now doing firearms training, custody and control training and EVO (Emergency Vehicle Operation.) I absolutely loved EVO training. I have never had more fun driving a car in my entire life. I learned that if your tires don't leave the asphalt, you can't roll a car. Trust me, I tried. I would get up at a high rate of speed in the asphalt parking lot and whip the steering wheel hard to the left and go into a spin. The smoke would roll off the tires as they made a loud squealing noise. I almost ended up in the North Platte River, but I could not get the car to roll.

For our final exam we had to drive the car through an obstacle course as fast as we could drive without going outside the orange traffic cones. An officer that I knew from Greybull, Wyoming had set the record, and it was my goal to beat his time. I had an instructor who rode with me. We both wore bubble helmets without the full-face mask. We looked silly wearing those stupid helmets, but it was a requirement. Every sharp corner that we came to, I swerved the car so hard that my instructor would hit his head on the passenger window. I kept hearing this "DONK" sound and finally figured out that was his bubble helmet bouncing off the windshield. After a bit the instructor mashed on his brake on the passenger side of the car and made the car come to an abrupt stop. I almost hit my teeth on the steering wheel. As soon as we came to a complete stop, he looked over at me with a bloody nose and yelled at me. "GODDAMIT WERBELOW, YOU ARE NEVER GOING TO BEAT THE RECORD IF YOUR TIRES ARE SQUEALING!! YOU NEED TO SLOW YOUR ASS DOWN; YOU ARE LOSING TIME WHEN THE CAR IS SLIDING ON THE PAVEMENT." I looked over at the instructor trying not to laugh at his bloody nose and bubble shaped helmet and responded, "Thank you sir, for that bit of valuable information, now HANG ON!" as I gave it the onion. I never could get the car to quit sliding sideways and it was not much fun unless the tires were squealing. Nonetheless, I did not set the new academy obstacle course record.

The daily physical fitness training was rigorous to say the least. The entire class would go on a group run through the town of Douglas with temperatures over 100 degrees. We would run single file with an instructor in the lead and another instructor at the rear following all the officers. We played a game called "Drop Rock" where a rock was passed down the line of officers as they ran. If you accidentally dropped the rock, you would have to drop down and do twenty push-ups as all the other officers kept running. Then you would have to sprint to catch up with the officers and pass the rock off to someone else before one of the instructors yelled "DROP ROCK" again. The lead instructor would yell "DROP ROCK" without turning around to see which officer had the rock. An officer in front of me just happened to have the rock in his hands four times in a row when he was instructed to "DROP ROCK." This meant he had to drop and do twenty push-ups every time he had the rock. The poor guy had done eighty push-ups and had to keep sprinting to keep up and pass the rock off to another officer. He was almost caught up and "DROP ROCK" was yelled before he could pass it off. The officer stopped running and threw the rock as far as he could. He then flipped off the instructor who was leading the pack. What the officer failed to realize was there was another instructor behind him who saw all of this happen. This instructor yelled, "EVERYONE STOP RUNNING." He ordered the officer to go and find the rock and return it to him. Surprisingly to me, he found the rock and returned. The instructor then ordered the officer to leave the group and return to the academy. I was pretty sure this officer would be sent home and fail the academy.

I felt sorry for this officer, so I stopped by his room when we returned to the barracks. His door was open. I found him lying face down on his bed weeping. I asked him if he was doing alright. He responded, "I shouldn't have reacted the way I did, but look at my damn feet." He sat up on his bed as he cried and pulled his bloody socks off. I looked at his feet and thought, *Oh my God!!* Both of his feet had huge bleeding blisters on his heels and the underside of both feet. This man had been running for miles in a great deal of pain. I helped him wash up his feet and put bandages on them. I got a glimpse of two instructors coming down the hall. I shook the man's hand and told him to be strong and honest as I exited the room. The instructors never made eye contact with me as they walked right by me in the narrow hallway and entered the officer's room. Both were looking straight ahead with a very determined look as they entered the officer's room and slammed the door shut. I said a short prayer for the officer and went back to my room to get dressed for dinner.

Over the weeks our class became very close. My nickname became "Big Red" because of my size and the fact that I wore a red shirt, I guess. We had spent the entire day on the shooting range. We had to qualify with our shotguns, rifles, and pistols. Each course was a timed event and each officer needed to score at least an 80% to qualify. This can be a very stressful time because if you fail to qualify, you cannot carry the firearm that you failed to qualify with. If you cannot carry a firearm, you cannot be a game warden or other officer of the law. To qualify you need to be very accurate and very quick. In some instances, I would need to get three shots off in four seconds. This included time drawing from my holster and getting on target. At the end of the hot day, we were all tired and sore from shooting so many 12-gauge shotgun slugs. The instructors decided to have a competition among themselves. They were trying to shoot a clay pigeon with their .40 caliber Glock pistols. The pigeon was round and about five inches in diameter. It hung from a piece of wire about 50 yards away. They shot and shot and shot and none of them could hit it. I overheard one of the officers tell the firearms instructor, "Let Big Red try it."

The firearms instructor looked at me and said, "You want to try it, Big Red, go ahead." Pretty quick the entire class of twenty some officers started chanting. "GO BIG RED, GO BIG RED, GO BIG RED!" I stepped up to the line and drew my 9mm Beretta pistol from my holster.

I took careful aim and slowly squeezed back on the trigger. When the pistol fired it surprised me. What surprised me even more was that I actually hit the small clay pigeon at approximately 50 yards and completely disintegrated it. The class went wild and gave me a standing ovation. The instructors seemed embarrassed. They just stood there with dumb looks on their faces. I held the barrel of the pistol up to my lips, blew off the smoke that was slowly coming out the end of it, and quickly holstered my firearm. I looked at the class and said, “Let’s go get a bite to eat shall we.” All the officers jumped up and slapped me on the back and gave me high fives as we headed to the cafeteria for lunch. I do not know what happened that day. I could have shot at that damn clay pigeon a thousand times and never hit it. I dang sure did not want to try it twice in a row.

The following morning, we were back in the gymnasium running laps around the gym for physical fitness. The instructors were shooting baskets as the officers ran around the orange cones in each corner of the gymnasium. One of the instructors yelled out, “Who would like to try and make a full court basket? If you make it, we instructors will do fifty push-ups.” The class started chanting “GO BIG RED, GO BIG RED”. One of the instructors passed the basketball to me quickly, nearly hitting me in the face. I stopped running and squared up with the basket at the other end of the gymnasium. I dribbled the ball a few times and let it fly. That ball flew all the way across the gymnasium completely undisturbed and made a “SWOOSH” sound as it went through the hoop. HOLY COW, nothing but net!! The instructors could not believe it, I could not believe it, and the fellow officers could not believe it. The officers stopped running and applauded me as the instructors got down and did fifty push-ups. The officers counted every one of them out loud...1,2,3,4, etc. I had never played a game of basketball in my life. Hell, I was a wrestler and football player. Where did that shot come from? I wonder if my grandpa Lyle was watching over me that day with a smile on his face. I certainly did not try that one again either.

It seemed like after that moment some of the instructors and my fellow classmates treated me a little differently. I was treated like a leader, someone they wanted to be friends with. Hell, I could never make that shot again if I tried. I have no idea where that shot came from or the pistol shot for that matter. The class voted and I was elected to be "Class Speaker" for our class at graduation. This seemed like quite an honor to me. I would have to start focusing on what my speech was going to be about. I would also have to meet with the director of the academy and get my speech approved prior to presenting it. I was happy to see that the officer who flipped off the instructor during "Drop Rock" was allowed to stay and finish the academy. This cadet's attitude had changed dramatically. They must have given him a stern attitude adjustment.

We had made it to the final week of the academy. I was so excited to get out of there and go back to Pinedale and become an official game warden with professional training under my belt. I had taken my last exam and passed with flying colors. I certainly was not going to win any academic awards, but I passed in the top of my class. It came down to a final shoot-out between my roommate Ned and me for the firearms proficiency award. We both shot 100% in our qualifications with all firearms. We would now have to compete against one another in a second qualification round. My roommate again shot 100% with all department issue firearms. I was nervous and stepped up to the firing line. I would need to be perfect. I shot a 100% with my pistol and rifle. I grabbed my shotgun and shot a 100% with slugs. Now, the final round. I would need to shoot ten rounds of buck shot through my 12-gauge shotgun. On my tenth round, I threw one pellet out of the bull's eye circle. I was so disappointed, 99% would be my score. My roommate Ned would win the firearms proficiency award. It was well-deserved and I was very happy for him, but disappointed in myself that I could not control all my buckshot pellets and keep them in the center of the target.

Since it was the last week of the academy, many of us officers decided to go down to a local bar named "Shoots" and have a few drinks. You could walk from the academy and not have to worry about driving home after a few drinks. I had become good friends with a Rock Springs police officer named Tad. Tad was a big man and a great guy to hang out with. Tad invited me to walk down to the river with him and have a whiskey before we went to the local bar. Well, that one whiskey ended up the two of us killing a bottle of Makers Mark straight from the bottle. I am not sure how we stumbled to the bar, but we made it. Once we arrived at the bar, everyone was having a Big and Rich time. Including a young officer who had never consumed alcohol before. I asked the bartender what his most potent drink was. He smiled and said, "It is called Liquid Cocaine." I said, "Make one up for that young man at the end of the bar. He's never had a good drink before." I am not sure what was in that drink, but smoke rolled out of the glass and pretty quick it caught on fire as the bartender was mixing it. The bartender blew the flames out as he handed it to the young officer. The bartender said, "Here, try this, it's from Big Red." The young officer grabbed the drink and swigged down about half of it. He looked at me and held his drink in the air towards me to give me a toast. We made eye contact and he started to smile and thank me for the drink. About that time his head hit the bar and he was out like a light. Tad looked at me, smiled and said, "Lightweight." I do not know to this day what was in that drink, but I never ordered another one. The young officer ended up visiting the throne, and we later got him safely tucked into bed.

Once we were back at the academy one of the girls in our class invited Tad and I to come watch TV with her in the day room. Tad and I had the munchies, so we raided the vending machine for a bunch of junk food. We sat down on a sofa while the gal turned on the TV. Once the TV came on it showed a naked girl dancing on a brass pole. This channel must have been HBO or something. Tad smiled and asked the girl if she could dance for us on the pool table. The girl smiled and said, "Sure." Next thing I knew this girl was dancing naked on the pool table in the day room of the academy and Tad had a dollar bill hanging out of his mouth. He had a Snickers in one hand and a bag of Cheetos in the other. It was now that Swerb, aka "Big Red", decided it was time to make a mile and get the hell out of there. I was hoping there were no cameras in the room. We only had one day left and I dang sure did not want to get fired and sent home. I do not know what happened after I left, and I don't think I want to know.

I had been preparing my graduation speech each night as I lay in bed thinking. I had the most beautiful message to give to all the officers at graduation already made up in my head. I rehearsed the speech over and over in my head each night. It was quite an honor for me to be selected as the class speaker. I was going to write my entire speech out on a piece of paper. I thought *no, that will look silly if I am up in front of the class reading my speech. I know it inside and out and don't need any notes.* The final day came and now it was time for graduation. I could not wait to get out of that building and be done with it all. My entire family showed up to watch me graduate. They were all so proud of me. They could not wait to hear my inspirational speech to everyone in the gymnasium. Finally, my name was called to come present the class with my well-thought-out inspirational speech. I was nervous and stood behind the podium and adjusted the mic. I looked up and observed about 250 people watching me. You could have heard a pin drop it was so quiet. I heard one man cough in the back row. As I looked at everyone staring at me, I completely drew a blank. I had no idea what to say or how to start my speech. My speech completely left me and was not coming back, ever! I have never had this happen to me before. *Damn,* I thought to myself, I should have written down some notes.

I welcomed and thanked everyone for coming to the graduation. I told everyone how close our class had become over the past thirteen weeks. I told some funny stories that had happened to some of the officers while attending the academy. After that I drew another blank and could not recall what message I was going to flatter everyone with. I stood up there the next fifteen minutes and told every clean joke that I could remember. Once I told all the clean ones I ended my speech with a dirty Johnny joke. The class stood up an applauded and started chanting. "GO BIG RED, GO BIG RED, GO BIG RED!!" I really screwed that one up and wish I could have done it over again. As for the infamous Velcro tennis shoes, I donated them to the academy. I think they are still in a glass display case somewhere in that building today.

Chapter 4

A New Home and a Package of Moose Burger

I was happy to return to Pinedale and sleep in my own bed again. I was behind with all my maintenance work on the feed grounds. Much of the hay had been purchased but still needed to be tested for protein and moisture requirements. The small bales would also need to be weighed so that I could determine the average weight per bale. This would determine total tonnage and what we owed all the producer's based on price per ton of hay. I was missing my family from being gone over the past thirteen weeks. My wife Lana reminded me that I should start looking for a house and some property that we could purchase and have a place for our horses. The housing market continued to rise and there just were not any affordable houses on the market that came with any horse type property.

One day while working, I noticed a small log cabin for sale next to the highway north of Boulder. It was a very small cabin but fairly new construction and kind of cute. The property also had a nice shop and came with ten acres. No corrals, no barn, and no irrigated property to grow grass on to feed our horses. I decided to call a realtor and see what they were asking for the small cabin. I about ran off the road when the realtor replied, "They are asking $350,000. There was no way with my income that I could ever afford something in that price range. The realtor asked me several questions on what type of property that I was looking for. I explained to her that it needed to be out of town and suitable for several horses. She told me that she would keep her eye out and let me know if something became available. She asked me what my price range was, and I told her about $150,000. I don't think she meant for me to hear her laugh in the background, but I certainly heard her laugh. I didn't expect to ever hear back from her again.

About three weeks later the lady realtor called me back and told me that she had a two-story log home that just got listed on the market. She said it had ten irrigated acres, and a cute little horse barn. It was located right off the main highway about ten miles outside of Pinedale next to the Pinedale airport. She also told me that it was listed for $250,000. This was out of my price range, but I decided to go check out the property. The exterior of the logs needed refinished, all the carpet inside needed replaced, and there was no yard fence. I could do all the improvements myself with the carpentry skills that I had learned over the years. The master bedroom and living room had a huge moss rock fireplace that I absolutely fell in love with. There was even a really cool bar in the living room and tall ceilings to hang some of my wildlife mounts. It had a one-car attached garage and two bedrooms upstairs that my children Wes and Wendy could call their own. I fell in love with the place, and it would be perfect for our horses. I was excited to show it to my wife Lana, but I knew we could not afford it.

Several days later I drove Lana out to check out the place. I didn't want to bother the realtor with getting a key and doing a showing, so we were just going to look through the windows and show Lana the property and the horse barn. I wanted to make sure that it passed her approval first before I got too serious about trying to get a thirty year home loan. As I approached the front door, I noticed an arrest warrant addressed to the owner of the property taped to the front door. I did not read the warrant, but it certainly gained my attention. After showing Lana around the property, she fell in love with it. We could both envision what we were going to do to improve the house and the property once we became owners. I knew in my heart to not get too excited because we had no savings, and we were living month to month on our pay checks. There was no way that we would ever qualify for a loan for $250,000.

The next morning, I called the realtor and told her that we really liked the property. I also told her that there was an arrest warrant on the front door for the owner of the property. She told me that she was not aware of the arrest warrant but had just found out that the owner of the property was going through a foreclosure on the property. Apparently, he had skipped town and was on the run. This really spiked my interest. If this man was going through foreclosure and had an arrest warrant, he was probably ready to make a deal before he lost his house. I would need to investigate this further and figure out who this man was and what his bottom dollar was. For some reason I didn't trust realtors. I put them in the same category as attorneys, maybe even a bit lower. It's all about making money! I didn't waste my time asking the realtor what the man's bottom dollar was. I decided to find him myself.

After a short investigation interviewing the man's neighbors and figuring out who his friends were, I learned that he had moved to Farson, Wyoming and was living in a camp trailer behind the gas station. I also learned that he broke horses for a living. I didn't tell any of the neighbors why I was looking for him. They probably just assumed that he had poached something because I was a game warden. I would end up driving to Farson and finding the owner of the house. There was only one camp trailer parked behind the gas station. The Chevy pick-up truck that was parked next to the camp trailer had Sublette County plates. The truck was a black flatbed with three different colored quarter panels and a large steel vice mounted to the rear corner of the flatbed. It definitely looked like a horse trainer/cowboy's truck to me. It was dark out. I noticed a propane lantern shining through the window on the side of the small camp trailer. I decided to knock on the trailer door. The tall slender man who opened the door was wearing a dirty black cowboy hat and had a large black handlebar mustache. Three blue healer dogs also met me at the door and were all eager to tear my windpipe out if given the command by their owner.

The tall man had a .44 magnum revolver "Hog Leg" hanging off his right hip. He placed his right hand on it and said, "Can I help you with something?" I reached out and shook the man's hand as I introduced myself over the sound of the barking blue healers. I asked him if his name was Juan Stone and if he had a house for sale near the airport. He replied, "Yes, it is and yes, I do." The man invited me into his trailer and offered me a seat at his kitchen table. His eyes were blood shot, and his speech was slurred when he talked. There was a strong smell of whiskey on his breath. He opened the small cupboard above the small sink on the counter. He pulled out a bottle of Old Crow and offered me a drink. He did not offer me a glass or ice, so I just took a pull off the bottle. It was warm and tasted like shit and I almost blew it back through my nose. I didn't want to show any weakness, so I swallowed hard and said, "AH, that's my favorite, thank you for the pull." He grabbed the bottle and tipped it back for several seconds, swallowed and said, "AHHH, that's good shit." As he slammed the bottle down on the table. I told him that I had looked at his house and that I really liked it. I didn't say anything about the arrest warrant on the front door. Hell, he may not have even known anything about it. I asked him lots of questions about the house and property. I told him that the reason I was here to visit with him was because I wanted to make an offer to the realtor, but that I could not afford his asking price of $250,000 dollars. He took another pull off the bottle and offered me another. I accepted the offer. The second shot didn't taste any better! He told me the whole story about the house. When he purchased it, whom he purchased it from and everything he had done to improve it. He then told me that he had recently divorced and that he was struggling financially. He then said, "I just want to pay the damn bank off and walk away from this whole damn deal. She's going to get half of it anyways." I asked him what his bottom dollar was on the house. He replied, "I owe the damn bank $134,000." I told the man that I would submit an offer on Monday and that he could take it or leave it. I thanked the man for the drink, shook his hand and told him that I would be in touch.

Monday morning, I called the realtor and told her that I would like to make an offer on the property for $134,000. She gasped and said, "Ok, but I think you are a long way off from getting this house bought for that amount. I replied, "Just submit the offer, please." She said she would and that she would let me know what the owner's response was. Several days later she called and said, "Oh my God, congratulations, you just purchased this house for $134,000 dollars." I was overwhelmed. Now I would need to meet with the bank and try and get my first ever big loan from a bank. This process took me three months to close. I had to pay off all my debt, sell vehicles that I owed money on, pay off all credit cards, etc. My wife Lana and I showed up for the closing of the house. The realtor told us, "Sorry, I have some bad news. You guys will need to come up with another $5,000, as that is what is needed to pay the bank off to release the title." I was heartbroken. I did not have another $5,000 dollars. I told the realtor that we were done with the deal and could not come up with the additional money. The realtor had spent three months on this deal trying to get it closed. She ended up knocking $5,000 off her commission to get the deal to go through. I'm guessing she didn't make much if anything on the deal. Now I was starting to like realtors a little more. We ended up purchasing our first home. Our payments would be $1284.00 a month. Hell, I was only making $1600.00 per month. We would be eating lots of pork and beans to pay for this house over the next thirty years.

I ended up borrowing my neighbor's sandblaster and sandblasted the entire outside of the log home. I re-stained the entire house and applied about 10 five-gallon buckets of log jam into all the cracks between the logs. I applied the log jam with a sausage maker gun that I purchased with my Cabela's bonus points. This was a very tedious process using a kitchen spoon and a water spray bottle. This project took me almost a month to complete. The outside of the house now looked awesome and new. We replaced all the carpet in the house and re-stained all the wooden interior walls. We also built new fence, planted trees, and dug new ditches to irrigate our nine-acre pasture. I built a large elk horn chandelier with an old wagon wheel to hang in the front living room by the rock fireplace. I had a friend build some beautiful log bar stools for the bar as well as a beautiful king-size log bed made from some old aspen wood with lots of character.

My friend, Big Piney game warden Brad Hovinga, came over to look at the new house for the first time and watch Monday night football. He said, "Man, you need to get you some new fancy bar stools." My eight-year-old son Wesley responded, "My mom says if we buy new bar stools, Brad will never go home." My wife Lana was in the kitchen doing dishes and overheard what Wesley had said. I heard her say, "Wes, get your butt in here!!" Brad just laughed and said, "True story!" We were living the "American Dream" in debt up to our ass and really enjoying our first home.

It was now October 1, 1998. I was scheduled to work the opening day of hunting season for the moose openers in the Pinedale area. I started out on the New Fork River just east of my house at daylight. I pulled my patrol truck down along the New Fork River on a state section right at first light. I pulled up to a canal and waited for it to get light out. About thirty minutes after sunrise, I noticed a man and a young boy running in a panic on the other side of the canal from me. They ran right in front of my pick-up and never even looked my direction. They both looked scared to death and were pale in the face. I watched them run about another 100 yards and cross the canal on a culvert to my right. Then they ran right in front of my patrol truck again. I rolled my window down and yelled, "Is everything all right?" They both stopped and looked at me. The father walked up to my truck breathing hard and stated, "Man, I really screwed up." I responded, "What's going on?" The man stated, "I shot what I thought was a cow moose right at daylight. I walked up to her and realized that I had shot her calf and not the cow. I started to dress out the calf and the mama moose charged me. I have been trying to dress out the calf for the last hour and mama won't let me touch the calf, she just keeps charging me." I checked the man's license and told him that I would help him dress out the calf moose, as we couldn't just leave it unattended. He replied, "I hope you are tougher than me, because she will kill you if you're not careful." I thought to myself, *well, here we go again Swerb, just another day as a Wyoming game warden.* I said, "You lead, and I will follow you to the location of the dead calf moose."

We had to cross the New Fork River before arriving at the location of the dead calf moose. Now, I was soaking wet and cold from my waist down. When we arrived, the mother was nowhere in sight. I told the father and son to dress out the calf and I would stand guard and keep the mama moose away. Just as soon as they started to dress out the calf, the mother moose came charging out of the thick willows headed right towards me with her ears pinned down and coming quick. I thought, *oh shit, she is coming fast and very upset.* I broke off a dead nearby aspen tree and armed myself with the tree. She charged. I hit her hard right across the end of her nose with the dead tree as she approached. This stopped her but she didn't run away. She stood on her hind feet and began pawing her front legs towards me. I kept hitting her with the dead tree until I had broken it into tiny little pieces. Once my defense mechanism was broken and gone, I started throwing rocks and small pieces of wood at the mama moose. It seemed like I had been holding off this angry moose for quite some time. I turned around and looked at the father and son. They had a small yellow pocketknife that they were trying to dress out the calf with.

Hell, they hadn't even gotten started opening up the calf moose. I threw another log at the mama moose and yelled at the father, "You hold off the mama moose and I will gut out the calf.

I grabbed his small yellow pocketknife and gutted out that calf moose in a New York minute. The man looked at me and said, "Holy Shit, I can see this is not your first rodeo." I said, "No, it's not! Now keep her away from me while I drag it back to the truck." My adrenaline was pumping.

I grabbed a hold of the calf and hauled ass dragging it back to the pick-up. I finally arrived at the canal across from my truck breathing very hard and hands trembling. The man and son were able to fend off the mama moose. They soon came running back to my location. They were so relieved that the calf moose was back to my truck, and no one was hurt, and so was I. I helped them drag the calf across the deep water in the canal and load it into their truck. I was cold, soaking wet and completely exhausted. I thought to myself, *Man, I didn't even have the license or kill the moose and ended up doing all the hard work. I'm soaking wet, cold, and exhausted. I sure hope they appreciated all that I had done for them this morning.* Sometimes as a game warden you end up "Conserving Wildlife and REALLY Serving People." The man shook my hand and thanked me for all my help. I returned home and changed into some dry clothes and boots. It was still early morning hours, so I decided to head for New Fork Lake and try and find some more moose hunters to check in that area.

I drove through the campgrounds around New Fork Lake. I did not find any more moose hunters in this area. I decided that I would head up to Green River Lakes and see what was going on up there. As I approached the main highway and came to a stop, I could see a huge plume of dust coming up from behind a large patch of willows across the main highway in front of me. This was private property. I had never observed any hunters on this property before. I decided to wait and watch to see where all the dust was coming from. Pretty quick I observed a white pickup hauling ass down a two-track road towards a closed barbed wire gate. The driver mashed on the brakes and came to a sliding stop at the closed gate. I could barely see the man exit his truck to open the gate with all the dust billowing through the air. The man seemed in a hurry. He threw the gate open, ran back to his truck and sped off without closing the gate behind him.

In Wyoming it is pretty common practice to leave all gates as you find them. If they are closed, you should close them. If they are open, leave them open. As I watched the man speed off towards me, I noticed a cow moose running down the two-track road behind him. The moose stopped at the open gate and turned around. She ran back down the road out of my sight and into a thick patch of willows. It appeared to me that the moose was chasing the man down the road, and that's why he was in such a hurry to get out of the area. I crossed the main highway and headed over to the road that would take me to the person driving the white truck.

I observed a plume of dust coming towards me, so I found a place and pulled off the rough road to wait. I rolled down my window and held my hand out the window to indicate that I wanted to speak to the man. He sped right on by me as if he never even saw me. Finally, I saw his brake lights come on in my rearview mirror. He came to a stop and backed his truck up even with mine so that we could visit. The man was breathing hard and pale white in the face. He rolled down his window and yelled, "I have a goddamn cow moose trying to kill me, and I don't have time to stop and bullshit with the game warden right now." I told the man to calm down, that I had observed the cow moose go back down the hill and into the willows and that it was no longer a threat to him. I asked him what had happened. He told me that he had shot what he thought was a cow moose but had accidently shot the cow's calf. When he started to dress out the calf, the cow charged him from the heavy willows and chased him to his vehicle. Once in the vehicle he claimed the cow moose attacked his truck standing on her hind legs and kicking the side window and hood of his truck with her front legs. He started his truck and sped off to get away from her. This was about the time that I had observed the man open the gate and leave it open. I told the man that I would help him retrieve the calf moose as we couldn't just leave it to go to waste. The man said, "Sorry, but I'm not going back there ever again, and I hope you have good insurance on your vehicle because she will destroy it." I told the man to wait at the gate and that I would go down and get the calf. He parked at the gate and closed it this time.

I drove down the road a short distance and noticed the dead calf lying next to the heavy willows. As I approached the calf, the mother moose charged my truck and nearly hit me as I sped by the dead calf. She went back and stood next to her calf to guard it from danger. I thought to myself, *Swerb, how in the hell are you going to deal with this one?* I parked my patrol truck a short distance away from the moose. I exited the vehicle and dug my lariat rope out of my toolbox in the back of the truck. I tied one end of the lariat around my rear receiver hitch ball and placed the loop end in the cab of my truck through my open driver's side window. I grabbed my 12-gauge shot gun and loaded it full of rubber bullets. I had not tried rubber bullets on a moose before and did not know how effective they would be. Hell, they might just really piss her off after being shot in the rump. I drove my patrol truck slowly towards her. Once I was about thirty yards away, I held the shotgun out of my driver's side window and smacked her in the butt with a rubber bullet. She charged towards me and then turned quickly to run back to her calf.

While she was running away from me, I sent another rubber bullet into her rump, and she ran past the calf and into the thick willows.

I hauled ass towards the calf with the other end of the lariat in my left hand. I drove up next to the calf, quickly opened my door and put the loop end of the lariat around the calf's neck. I looked up and the cow moose was coming towards me and my patrol truck. I romped on the gas, gave it the onion, and headed back up the road towards the closed gate. The calf moose hit the end of the rope and flew about five feet in the air as I sped off. I looked in my rearview mirror and could see the calf moose skipping along behind me with the cow moose running a short distance behind the calf. I was headed up the road towards the man in the white truck. I yelled, "OPEN THE DAMN GATE AND GET OUT OF THE WAY!" The man quickly opened the gate, jumped into his truck, and sped off down the rough two-track road towards the main highway. I made it through the gate and the cow moose stopped and headed back down towards the willows. I thought, *Thank God!!* I walked back and closed the gate just in case. Not that a moose can't jump a fence, but it might deter her from coming back down the road after me.

I caught up with the man in the white truck a short distance down the road. By the look on his face, he couldn't believe what he had just witnessed. I jumped out of the truck and said, "Well, that got a little western, but here is your calf moose." The man thanked me and couldn't believe that I was successful in retrieving the calf. The man said, "Well, I better get the guts out of this calf and get her cooled out." I told the man that would be a good idea. The man grabbed his razor-sharp skinning knife and began cutting up the stomach of the calf. I noticed the man's hands were trembling as he was making his cut. The man was now shaking uncontrollably. Just as I was about to ask "Sir, are you alright?" the man cut his hand with the knife and was bleeding badly. The man stepped back away from the calf and placed his fluorescent orange stocking cap over the cut on his hand. He looked at me still pale in the face and said, "I'm sorry man, I'm just too shaken up over this whole ordeal to safely use my knife. Would you mind gutting this calf for me? I would greatly appreciate it."

The man looked like he was in his seventies. I grabbed the man's knife and said, "Not a problem, tend to your wound and get the bleeding to stop." The man sat in the cab of his truck while I finished gutting his calf. Once I was finished the man said, "I'm sorry. I'm feeling a little lightheaded right now. Could you please load this calf in the back of my truck for me? I would really appreciate it." I said, "Not a problem sir, you just sit tight and relax." What I was really thinking to myself was, *Swerb, how do you get yourself in this type of situation twice in one day?* I literally recovered, drug, gutted, and loaded this man's moose for him. The only thing he did was make a poor decision by shooting the calf in the first place. I understand how mistakes can happen, but this was the second and same mistake in one day made by two separate hunters. The man had finally got the bleeding to stop. I took my water jug and poured cold water over his wound to help him clean it out. I dug into my toolbox and found my first aid kit and applied some dressings and bandages over the cut for him. He thanked me for my generosity and drove on down the road.

Heck, I was so busy with all of this, I forgot to check for his moose license and ask him if he had permission to hunt on private property. I would need to follow up on this with the ranch manager of the property. I would also look his name up in the department license database to make sure he had the proper license. My guess is that he certainly never filled out his license before he left the site of kill as he was too busy running from the mama moose. He probably hadn't filled out his license at all. Sometimes I felt like I was a horrible game warden.

The elderly man showed up at the regional office in Pinedale about one month later. He asked for me and told our office manager Des Brunette that he had a gift that he would like to present to me. Des took the man to my office. The man had the biggest smile on his face that I had ever seen before. He reached into a brown paper bag and said, “I have a special gift for you for all your help awhile back.” The man pulled out a small white package and handed me a one-pound package of ground moose burger. This would barely make a meal, but the man was so excited to give it to me! I shook the man’s hand and gave him a game warden hug and thanked him for his generosity. Heck, the charging cow moose could have killed me, but at least I got one pound of moose burger out of the deal.

Hunting seasons were starting to get into full swing. I was excited to get out and check some hunters. Since most of my feed ground maintenance projects were nearly completed. We still had several feed grounds that needed hay hauled into them. There would be more work later on getting draft horses hauled into all the feed grounds, but as for the time being I had some free time to spend checking hunters in the field.

I was just outside of Pinedale when my mobile radio blared “GF-84 this is GF-24, you copy?” I grabbed my mic and replied, “GF-24 this is GF-84, go ahead.” This was north Pinedale game warden Duke Early. Duke rarely called me on the radio. I knew if he was trying to get a hold of me it was probably something important or he was stranded somewhere. Duke replied, “Do you have cell phone signal? If so, please call me right away.” I responded, “10-4, I will call you in about ten minutes or so when I have better cell service.” I turned around and headed for a tall hill where I knew I could get decent cell service. Once on the phone with Duke he relayed to me that he had received a report of a woman with long black hair driving a white van had been reported for shooting a doe deer during a buck-only season and leaving it lay south of Soda Lake. Duke said he was headed that direction, but he was a long way away and didn’t want the lady to get out of the area without being identified. I told Duke that I was in the area and would head that direction. Duke relayed, “I don’t have a lot of information and I haven’t even seen the dead deer yet. But if you see a white van with a woman driving who has long black hair, please stop her and hold her until I can get to the area. I agreed to do so and headed towards Soda Lake on the Soda Lake Road.

Approximately 3-4 miles later I observed a white Dodge van headed towards me at a high rate of speed. The van looked like it was an early 70's model as is roared past me. It was difficult to tell, but it appeared to me that the driver of the van had long black hair and looked more like a man than a woman. The van was going so fast, that it left a rooster tail of dust lingering in the air for about two miles. There was so much dust coming from behind this van, that it made it difficult for me to pursue and get this driver stopped. I turned around, gave it the onion, and flipped the switches to run my sirens and my tiny little red and blue lights that were mounted to my front push bar. The siren wailed as I disappeared into the heavy dust cloud behind the van. After several miles of heavy pursuit, the van quickly pulled off to the right side of the road. So quickly, that I almost ran into the rear of the van. I came sliding to a stop on the gravel road right behind the van.

I was going to call in the plate number so that our radio dispatch SALECS would know who I was dealing with, except there was no license plate on the vehicle. I jumped out of my patrol truck and headed alongside the old beat-up van towards the driver's side window. While walking alongside, I noticed a large yellow and orange fire flame that had been painted on the side many years ago. The flame ran the van's entire length. I also noticed that the tread on the tires was completely bald. The van had no side windows making it very difficult to see the driver. I slowly put my hand on my pistol. I was thankful that it was still in my holster and not lying on top of a toilet somewhere in a dingy restaurant. (This has only happened to me once before.)

As I slowly approached the driver's side. I could hear a voice yelling from inside, "DON'T TELL HIM ANYTHING, JUST KEEP YOUR DAMN MOUTH SHUT!!" I reached up and tapped on the driver's side window behind the driver with my knuckles. The window slowly rolled down and I saw a light film of smoke exit the vehicle. It smelled strongly of marijuana. I had never tried marijuana before, but I dang sure knew what it smelled like. As I slowly crept up to look through the driver's side window, I ordered the driver to place his/her hands on the steering wheel where I could see them. I observed what looked like a male's hands with dark-colored skin. The man had long dirty fingernails with a ring on almost every finger. One ring was a large skull, and crossbones, another was a black widow spider. I stepped forward a bit and could now see the man's face. He was a Native American with long black hair all the way down his back. The passenger was an older man probably in his sixties. He had a long grungy beard and was wearing a dirty rawhide coat and rawhide pants. He looked like a mountain man. His gray chest hair protruded out of his leather top. The buttons on the coat were made of elk ivories. The man was loud and wouldn't shut up. I couldn't understand what he was saying over the sound of the stereo and the van's motor running with no muffler or exhaust pipe.

As I peered through the window looking for weapons, I observed a small alligator head mounted to the top of the gear shift knob on the manual transmission. The little beady eyes of the alligator were staring right at me. The whole situation was starting to give me the heebie-jeebies. I asked the man to please shut off his loud music and turn the van off. The man reached up and pressed a large button on the stereo and ejected an eight-track tape. I hadn't seen one of those in a while. It kind of made me giggle. The man shut the van off and I asked him for his keys. He reluctantly handed me the keys without saying a word or making eye contact. Meanwhile, the mountain man wouldn't shut up. I could tell he had been drinking heavily. I asked the driver for his driver's license, and he replied, "Sorry, I don't have one." I thought, *great, no driver's license, marijuana, and a drunk mountain man. Swerb, what have you got yourself into again?"*

From my previous experience dealing with Native Americans, I had learned that it's always a good idea to take their keys before you end up in another high-speed chase. They like to run, especially if they are near the reservation boundary. Once they cross the line, we have no authority to enter the reservation unless we have a Federal Agent assisting us. I asked the man for his name, and he replied, "Dakota." I asked the other man for his name, and he replied, "They call me Trader." After hearing this, I could recall seeing this man during Rendezvous Days in Pinedale throwing tomahawks into the side of an old building on Main Street. He was quite skilled with a tomahawk. I asked the driver Dakota if he had been hunting. He replied, "I don't think so." I asked, "What do you mean, you don't think so? Either you have been hunting or you haven't." He told me he couldn't remember. I asked him to please step out of the van and open the back. He nervously agreed.

I ordered Trader to stay seated and not get out. Dakota walked around to the back of the van and opened the two swinging doors towards us. I observed a scoped rifle and a florescent orange hat lying in the bed of the van. I asked Dakota if that was his rifle and orange hat. He replied, "Yes, it is". I grabbed the rifle and looked at it carefully. The rifle was a .243. I told Dakota that another officer had recovered a .243 bullet out of a dead doe deer just up the road. (I lied.) I asked him if the bullet might match his gun. Dakota replied, "I don't think it will." I finally got Dakota to admit that he had been hunting, but he couldn't remember where. He finally said, "Maybe that direction somewhere," as he pointed to the west. He was adamant that he hadn't killed or even shot at a deer all day.

I could overhear Duke trying to call me on the radio. I told Dakota to stay put and walked back to my truck to answer the radio. Duke informed me that he had found a dead doe deer that was shot and left. He also told me he had some good footprints in the mud of whoever was in the area. I informed Duke that I had the suspect stopped and with me. I also told him that it was a man and not a woman as reported earlier. Duke asked me if I could bring the man to his location several miles up the road for questioning. I informed Duke that we would be there shortly. I then informed Dakota that I would like him to drive ahead of me until he came across a green game and fish truck parked along the roadside. I did not want to give Dakota a chance to follow me. I always wanted him in my eyesight.

We finally arrived at Duke's location. Duke stepped out of his patrol truck and introduced himself to Dakota. Trader stayed seated in the van. Duke light-heartedly joked with Dakota about several things and asked him if he could follow him through the sagebrush for a short distance. Dakota agreed and set off following Duke with me following behind. Duke came to a mud hole with a foot track in it. Duke looked at Dakota and said, "Could I get you to place your foot in the mud next to that track?" Dakota looked very nervous but agreed. Once done, Duke carefully looked at both tracks and ran his fingers through his hair as if he was in deep thought. He then looked up into the sky and back down towards the ground and said, "Dakota, does that track look like it matches the other track?" Dakota dropped his head and stated, "Yes, sir, it does." Duke stated that whoever left that track in the mud was responsible for killing the doe deer and leaving it.

Dakota finally admitted to the whole story. His license was only valid for a buck deer. Dakota explained that as he was getting ready to shoot a buck deer, the small herd of deer gathered up and started to run. He was not going to shoot but Trader was yelling at him. "HURRY UP AND SHOOT, HURRY UP AND SHOOT BEFORE THEY GET AWAY!"

Dakota got excited and made a bad shot killing the doe deer. Once the doe went down Trader yelled, "NOW YOU HAVE REALLY F---ED UP, LETS GET THE HELL OUT OF HERE BEFORE THE GAME WARDEN SEES US!" Another hunter had been up on a hill above them and observed what had happened. All that hunter saw from a long way away was a dead doe deer and a long-haired woman headed for a white van. This is when he reported the incident to the game and fish department.

Once Dakota had admitted to his mistake, he began to cry and apologized for leaving the deer to waste and for lying to us. He said he would have never left the area and lied to us, but Trader was yelling at him and made him nervous and crazy. After listening to Dakota's story. I began to feel sorry for the man. Judging by the vehicle he was driving and the company he was hanging out with, it became clear to me that he had no money and probably very few friends. Not to mention he had no driver's license, vehicle registration, and was smoking pot. I could have called the Sheriff's department and had a deputy come up and arrest him. Not to mention, Duke and I could have arrested him as well for shooting the wrong sex of deer and allowing it to waste in the field.

I requested Dakota to sit down on a rock and told him that I would like to visit with Duke alone to discuss how we were going to handle the situation. Dakota put his hands over his face and started weeping again. After visiting with Duke, we both decided to write the man one citation for taking wrong sex of deer. We would let him keep the deer and tag it with his license. At the end of the day if he didn't take care of his $250.00 fine, he would be arrested and go to jail. I walked back and told Dakota how we were going to handle the situation. He jumped up off the rock and gave me a huge hug. Tears were streaming down his face as he said, "Thank you so much, officer, you have no idea what I'm dealing with right now in my personal life. I will take care of that deer and see to it that every part of the deer is utilized for something." He then shook both of our hands and thanked us for being fair and professional with him.

I left the area feeling like I had done the man a favor even though he had violated the law and lied to me. Sometimes making the right decision as a game warden can be very difficult. Hopefully we made an impression on this man to have a better respect for wardens and the law even when times are tough. I have always felt as a game warden, if you can issue someone a citation and they shake your hand and thank you afterwards, you have probably done something right and may have earned their respect to do things right in the future. Dakota and Trader left the area to retrieve the dead deer. I looked at Duke with a smile and said, “I don’t know Duke, do you think that track in the mud matches that track?” Duke started laughing out loud and replied, “I have never tried that one before, but it damn sure worked.”

Chapter 5

Perfect Christmas Tree and a Poached Deer

We were really enjoying our new home. We were absolutely broke, but it was really nice to finally have a home that we could call our own. We were so broke that I decided, with the kids getting bigger, that we should buy a brand-new Ford pick-up right off the lot in Jackson Hole Wyoming. Heck, if you are already over $100,000 dollars in debt, what's another $50,000 spread over six years? It was a beautiful and very black four-door ¾ ton 4x4 turbo diesel pick-up. We all know some of the best deals on trucks are from a dealership in Jackson Hole, Wyoming. Heck, I think my payments were only like $600/month for the rest of my life. Man, we were going to be able to pull a horse trailer now and look cool doing it! We would probably need to purchase a brand-new $70,000 dollar 20' aluminum horse trailer, as well, to haul all our $600 horses around the countryside. We drove the brand-new truck home from Jackson. Lana was pretty happy that she would finally have some real horsepower when towing a trailer full of horses. This was the cleanest this black truck was ever going to be. I swear that I could wash that truck three times a day and it would be dirty before I ever got it home and parked back in the garage. The new car smell was worth every penny that we paid for it. The smell only lasted for about five days until our three-legged registered cow dog puked in the backseat. Oh well, I guess it's an official ranch truck now. This was the first and last brand-new truck that I have ever purchased. I guess we all have to do it at least once, just to say we did.

It was getting near Christmas time. One Saturday morning I heard the wail of sirens going down the highway next to our house. I grabbed my binoculars and looked out the front window to see what was going on. What I observed was south Pinedale game warden Dennis Almquist responding to a poaching call of some sort. He was traveling at a high rate of speed with his front red and blue lights flashing. What really gained my attention was the Christmas tree that was tethered in the back of his patrol truck. The tree would fly high in the air above the cab of the truck and come back down. I stood there and watched in my binoculars as the tree flew all over the back of his truck as he sped by my house. I looked at Lana and said, "Looks like Dennis has found the perfect Christmas tree." She responded, "We should take the new truck and kids for a drive and cut a Christmas tree today." I was always excited to search for the perfect Christmas tree. As a matter of fact, several game wardens in the Pinedale region had a friendly competition each year to see who could find the perfect tree. We all had a full year to scout for the perfect tree and we all had covered hundreds of mountainous miles each year patrolling for hunters giving us plenty of opportunity to scout out the perfect tree. Some wardens would buy a forest service permit and do it legally. Others would not purchase the permit and claim that they were going to "Poach a tree." One warden claimed that he would poach one in the night and carry it over his head not leaving any drag marks or evidence in the snow. You wouldn't dare show your tree until everyone had cut one down. This way no one could see your tree and then go out and find a more perfect one. First place was generally a bottle of not so expensive whiskey of the winner's choice. In order to receive the bottle of whiskey the winner would have to volunteer to host a party at their house the week following the judging. The bottle of whiskey never survived the night, as all your friends made sure it was gone before they went home. During the party, everyone would stand up and tell their story of everything that they went through to finally find the perfect tree.

My story goes something like this: We all loaded up into the brand-new black Ford pick-up that Saturday morning before Christmas. I told my wife Lana that I had the perfect spot for a perfect tree. I had found this spot in the Upper Green River area while riding my snow machine the previous year checking pine marten trappers. It was in a very remote area, well off the beaten path. I wasn't sure that I could even remember how to get there anymore, because I hadn't traveled on any roads with my snow machine when I found it. I could remember a very rough two-track road that should get us close to the area. All I remembered was a valley full of young pine trees. The pine trees were spread out and most of them looked young and perfect. I think this was a regrowth area of trees that had been through a forest fire years ago. After miles of driving, I found the rough two-track road. I told Lana that we were close, and the road would be a bit rough for a while. The snow was about one foot deep as we approached a very steep hill. The hill went straight up and was on a side hill. I stopped at the bottom of the hill and looked up. Lana said, "I don't think this is a good idea honey, especially with our new truck and all."

I said, "Oh, honey, don't worry about it. We have brand new tires and a very powerful turbo diesel engine. If I can take it slow and avoid spinning, I think I can keep it on the road and over the top of the hill." Lana said, "HONEY, I don't think we should...." And away I went. I said, "Hold on, punkin', nobody ever said it was going to be easy to find the perfect Christmas tree." I was nearly to the top of the hill and started sliding to my left. The road was extremely rough, and the snow was getting deeper. I had a large aspen tree coming up quickly on my left. I knew if I stopped, I would slide into the tree and be stuck. I gave the ol' turbo diesel the onion and lunged forward. It was a real Tank Slapper for a minute! Just as I was about to clear the tree, the truck slid hard to left. I heard Lana scream, and I also heard the sound of brand-new metal wrapping around the large aspen tree. I didn't quite clear the tree. Now it was embedded into the left rear quarter panel of our new truck. Not only did I have a large dent in my new truck, but I was also stuck. If I moved at all, it would continue to tear up the beautiful black quarter panel. The truck came to a quick stop. Both kids were bawling in the backseat. I looked over at Lana and she said, "Smooth move, dumbass!!"

Now, nobody likes to be called a dumbass in front of your young crying children. The truck was on a steep side-hill leaning against a large aspen tree. The snow was so deep that I couldn't open my driver's side door. I asked Lana if she could please help me get out on her side, so that I could figure out what we were going to do. I hadn't even been able to see the extent of the damages yet, nor did I really want to. Once out of the truck I noticed an orange plastic marker nailed to the aspen tree. It read C/D. *Oh shit,* I thought to myself. *I'm on the Continental Divide snow machine trail that goes over Union Pass. This is not an open road for vehicle travel.* I had not noticed any closed road signs. I guess now I was officially in violation while poaching a Christmas tree. Lana said, "Look at this sign, what does C/D stand for?" I replied, "I think it stands for "Casual Dent". Lana looked at the damage to the truck and said, "Casual Dent, my ass, this is going to cost thousands to repair." I said, "Oh honey, that's why our full coverage insurance is so damn expensive. Aren't you glad we have it now?" Lana replied, "There is probably a clause in the policy in fine print that doesn't allow payment for being a dumbass!" I said, "Honey, would you please knock off the dumbass talk in front of our already upset children. Besides we are supposed to be having a fun family day together. Now fetch me that Husqvarna chainsaw in the back of the truck so I can get rid of this damn tree."

I gave the saw a few pulls and it actually started. Generally speaking, a saw will never start when you need it the most. I told my wife not to take any pictures of me cutting down the large aspen tree that held the small orange Continental Divide trail placard. She just laughed and said, "Oh, I'm getting pictures, nobody will believe this story at the Christmas party without proof." I cut down the large tree and it even fell in the right direction, which was not on top of our new truck. I placed the saw back in its case and told Lana to get back in the truck, calm the children down, and just shut up for a few minutes. I jumped in the truck through the passenger door and fired up the diesel engine. Now that the tree was not holding me back anymore, I was able to give it the onion and paw my way to the top of the hill. Lana breathed deep and said, "Thank God, now let's turn around and get the hell out of here!" I said, "Oh honey, we are almost to the perfect tree patch, I think it is right over the next ridge." The road didn't look good, but I could tell that there was an old road underneath all the snow. I told Lana that we would turn around in just a bit.

We headed on down the rough road and came to a nasty creek crossing. The water was still flowing over the top of the ice and all I could see were large boulders sticking up out of the snow. Lana said, "STOP, don't do it!" I said, "Oh, honey, it's not that bad." As I gave it the onion, Lana's head hit the ceiling, my head hit the driver's side window, both kids flew around in the back of the truck like a couple rag dolls and we were stuck!! Now both kids were bawling again. Lana was calling me a huge sack of dumbass, and she was probably right for the first time in her life. The kids were driving me nuts with their crying and carrying on. I told them both to get in the back of the truck because we needed added weight in the bed of the truck for better traction. This way, they felt like they were doing something useful to get us out of a bad situation. It was getting dark. I kept digging and stacking ice-covered rocks for better traction. Finally, the truck lunged forward, and we made it over the creek crossing. The only problem was, we were going to have to go back across it again to get home. I could tell Lana had lost her enthusiasm to find the perfect tree, so I turned around and approached the creek crossing. Lana said, "What are you going to do now?" I replied, "There is only one way home, honey, put on your big girl panties or get out of the truck." Lana chose to exit the truck with my entire family. I backed up, gave it the onion, and sailed across the nasty crossing. It wasn't pretty and I'm sure I caught some air, but I made it, nonetheless.

The beautiful new black truck was now muddy, dented, and had no Christmas tree in the back. We finally made it back to the main road just before dark. Lana hadn't said a word to me since the creek crossing. I reached over to turn up the radio since nobody else wanted to visit on our family day. Lana yelled, "LOOK, OVER THERE, THAT LOOKS LIKE A NICE TREE!" I hit the brakes, grabbed my binoculars and focused in on the tree. I said, "Are you shitting me right now honey that is the ugliest tree that I have seen all year. That, my dear, is definitely a Charlie Brown tree." Both kids jumped out of the truck and yelled, "COME ON, DAD LET'S CUT IT DOWN!" I told them that they couldn't use the chainsaw to cut it down, as that was not part of the Christmas tradition. I handed them a small red tree saw and they ran as fast as they could all the way out to the ugly tree. I had to remind myself that this was a family day and winning the perfect tree competition was not the most important thing in the world, (but it kind of was). The tree looked bigger than the inside of our house, and man was it ugly. Lana said, "We will just put it in a corner to hide the two bad sides." We loaded the large heavy tree and headed home in the dark with a dent in the new truck singing Christmas songs. I would end up cutting about five feet off the tree and using a come-along to winch the tree through the front doors of our house. I had to borrow the neighbor's extension ladder to put the star on top of the tree. Not only was the tree big, but it was also ugly.

Sometimes it's not how pretty the tree is, but the memories that are built spending time together as a family. I will always cherish those memories.

I can't remember who won the perfect tree competition that year. But I do remember the story that Dennis Almquist told during the annual Christmas party. He apparently had found the perfect Christmas tree up near the Prospect Mountains somewhere. He didn't have a tree cutting permit and didn't want to poach the tree, so he left it alone. He bought a tree permit a few days later and headed back to the area to retrieve his perfect tree. When he arrived, he noticed that someone else had already cut down and taken his perfect tree. He spent several more weeks looking for another perfect tree. He finally found it while working and cut it down and placed it in the back of his patrol truck. Shortly after he hauled it home, he received a Stop Poaching Report south of Pinedale. He and his wife Mary Ann jumped in the truck and responded to the call. The tree was tied in the back of his truck and eventually blew out along the highway somewhere. When Dennis arrived at his poaching call, he discovered that his perfect tree was missing. He went back searching for his perfect tree and never found it. Someone had stolen his perfect tree. I know this was a true story because I saw him go by my house that morning with the tree trying to escape his truck. Nonetheless, Dennis was forced to cut down a third tree and it did not cut the mustard to win the annual perfect tree competition. He and I had a drink together to discuss our downfalls in procuring the perfect Christmas tree. Oh well, there would always be next year.

It was January 1999. I received a call late one night from regional wildlife supervisor Bernie Holz. Bernie informed me that the sheriff's department had just contacted him to advise that a man had been arrested on South Pass earlier in the evening. The man was pulled over for no taillights. Once stopped, the highway patrolman discovered that the man had been drinking heavily. He also had a warrant for his arrest and was on probation for a multitude of previous violations. He was driving with no valid driver's license or vehicle insurance. The patrolman searched his truck and found fresh deer hair and blood in the bed of his old Chevy truck. The patrolman questioned the man about the fresh deer hair and blood. The man denied knowing anything about it. The man had a girlfriend with him who appeared to be sober. When questioned by the patrolman, the lady admitted to poaching a deer on a ranch they had worked on located on the lower Green River. Apparently, her boyfriend had recently been fired and they were leaving the area headed for Riverton. She claimed that she knew a game warden by the name of Scott Werbelow who lived in the Pinedale area. She stated that he bought hay for the feed ground program from her previous boss and that she knew him pretty well. The patrolman asked her where the deer was located. She claimed that it was hanging in the old red barn on the ranch where they recently used to live. The patrolman asked her why she had shot the deer out of season. She responded, "Because we are hungry." The patrolman identified her, got her contact information, and allowed her to drive the old Chevy on to the town of Riverton. The patrolman then contacted supervisor Holz and relayed the information to him. Bernie knew that I had worked with these people before and decided to call me late at night. Bernie suggested that I hurry up and get out to the ranch and confiscate the deer before it ended up magically missing in the night.

At the time, I had just quit chewing for several months. I was proud of myself for quitting the nasty habit. After I hung up the phone with Bernie, I suddenly felt this strong urge for a fresh chew. I didn't know what my authority was to enter private property in the middle of the night and seize a poached deer out of the owner's barn. I didn't know if the owner of the ranch was even home or where exactly the red barn was located. This would probably involve me driving onto the private ranch property in the middle of the night and having to use my spotlight to locate the barn. The owner of the ranch had recently purchased the ranch and moved to Wyoming from California. I had purchased a great deal of hay from him earlier that year and had several disagreements with him over the quality of his hay. I had also met his hired hand and his girlfriend but didn't know them well at all.

I jumped out of bed and tried to get dressed in the dark. I didn't want to turn the bright light on and really wake up my wife Lana. I started to put my second leg into my pants and tripped. After three jumps across the bedroom floor trying to maintain my balance with one leg in my pants, I fell headfirst into the oak dresser. It pert' near killed me. I lay on the floor with a pop knot on my head big enough for a calf to suckle on. Thank God my head missed the rock fireplace. Lana stood up in bed with her eyes squinched and said, "What in the hell are you doing, it's 11:30 PM?" I replied, "Not much honey, just trying to get dressed in the dark and not wake you. Someone poached a deer down on the lower Green River and I need to go retrieve it before it disappears." Lana responded, "Well, be careful and put another log on the fire when you get back home." "Yes, dear." I grabbed my pistol from off the top of the refrigerator and headed out the door. It was very cold outside. My patrol truck barely turned over. Luckily, it started. I looked at my gas gauge, *Shit, I'm nearly out of gas*, I grabbed my large metal flashlight and clicked the on button. No light, shit, I needed new batteries. I raced into the town of Pinedale that was about ten miles away hoping a gas station was still open. I needed gas, flashlight batteries, and I really needed a chew. Luckily a gas station was open. I was able to get everything I needed including a brand-new can of Copenhagen. I took a three-finger dip and shoved it in my lower lip. This feeling had to be like being addicted to cocaine or something. That was the best chew I had ever had in my life.

As I was speeding down the east Green River Road, I heard Bernie trying to call me on my mobile radio. "Gf-84, GF-7" I grabbed the mic, "Go ahead, Bernie" I responded. He asked me my location and estimated time of arrival at the ranch house. I told him that I was about ten miles out. He responded, "10-4, I will see you there." I was excited that Bernie was going to join me on this mission in the middle of the night. We arrived at the ranch headquarters and drove through the front yard of the owner's house. It didn't appear to me that anyone was home. At least there were no lights on, and no vehicles parked in front of the house. I thought that I could remember where the red barn was located but I wasn't sure. I kept driving down a narrow road in the deep snow searching for the red barn in my headlights. I came around a corner and the red barn appeared in my headlights. Bernie and I grabbed our flashlights and tried to open the small walk-through door next to the two large sliding doors. The door was locked. It took both of our strengths to slide open the large sliding door that was buried deep in snow. The inside of the barn was huge, dark, and cold. I could see my breath with the light of my brand-new flashlight batteries. In the far rear corner of the barn, I could barely see something hanging wrapped in a blue plastic tarp. As we approached the blue tarp, a large great horned owl flew out of the rafters from above and nearly took my hat off as it went by. HOO…HOO as it flew the length of the barn and landed in some rafters at the opposite end of the barn. If you never had the opportunity to see the glow of green owl eyes in your flashlight five feet from your head in an old, abandoned barn, you truly haven't lived. This scared the shit out me, but I showed no fear in front of my boss. The large chew that I had taken was starting to give me the spins. I hadn't felt this way since the first chew that my stepfather Martin gave me out in the hayfield years ago.

We approached the object that was hanging in the air, wrapped in the blue tarp. Bernie held up his flashlight and I snapped a few shitty pictures of it with my shitty department camera. Because this is what you do in an official investigation before you touch or move anything. To my amazement this was a huge mule deer buck hanging from the rafters. The rack had several non-typical points and approached thirty inches wide. If you were ever going to poach a deer, this would be the one. The lady told the highway patrolman that she poached the deer because they were hungry. I thought, *and a rat's ass!!* She poached this deer because it was a huge buck. I was already suspicious as to why the lady had poached the deer and not her boyfriend. The deer was hanging with its head high up in the air with a rope around its neck tied off to the rafters of the barn. Bernie grabbed a near-by ladder and climbed it nearly to the top step. He pulled out a small knife that he had hidden in the small of his back and cut the rope with his flashlight mounted securely between his teeth. The large deer was completely frozen and dropped like a ton of bricks. The deer landed on its frozen hind legs and fell right towards me in slow motion, like something you would see in a horror movie. The tongue was hanging out of the deer's mouth, and the green eyes of the deer illuminated in my flashlight. As it slowly fell towards me to the ground, it made a large thud noise as it hit the dirt floor. Bernie giggled and said, "Sorry, I didn't realize that you were standing under the deer when I cut the rope. I should have warned you." We left the blue tarp wrapped around the deer and drug the carcass the length of the barn to the front door. Again, the large great horned owl flew directly over my head, HOO, HOO and back to the other end of the barn. I said, "Sorry to bother you buddy, now get some rest."

It was all the two of us could do to load the deer into the back of my patrol truck. The body of the deer was absolutely huge. I was really glad that Bernie was there to assist me. This would have been very tough for me to do alone at night. I thanked Bernie for his assistance and asked him if he would meet me at the office in Pinedale to hang the deer in the heated shop and thaw out overnight, so that I could do a complete necropsy in the morning. Bernie agreed and we left the ranch. As I headed back down the east Green River Road, I had so many unanswered questions going through my head. Who really shot this deer? Did the owner of the ranch know that the deer had been poached? Where was the deer poached? Where is my can of Copenhagen? Was I ok to enter the red barn on private property without a search warrant and the owner of the ranch not knowing anything about it? I had a confession from the lady. I had probable cause that a violation had occurred. I had the evidence in the back of my patrol truck. But still, did the patrolman read the lady her rights when she told him everything. What if the lady changes her mind and denies everything that she told the patrolman? Did the patrolman get a written statement from the lady? I would need to interview the girlfriend soon and make sure that all of our ducks were in a row.

I returned home shortly after 2:00 AM. I was surprised that Bernie hadn't questioned me about the huge knot on my forehead. Maybe he couldn't see it in the night? I snuck through the house as quiet as a mouse wearing slippers. I didn't want to wake Lana again. I stoked the fire and grabbed a large pine log out of the wood bin to throw in the wood stove. My toe caught the corner of the rock fireplace, and I tripped throwing the pine log halfway across the living room. The log made a loud thud as it hit the floor, rolled across the carpet, and smacked into the wall. I heard Lana yell, "HONEY, IS THAT YOU?" I replied, "Yes dear, just putting another log on the fire, pumpkin, love you!!" I sat in the kitchen with an ice pack in one hand and a stiff whiskey in the other. What a day! What would I learn in the morning about the poached deer?

I awoke early, eager to learn more about the poached deer. I grabbed a cup of coffee, skipped breakfast, and headed for the Pinedale regional office. I had left the deer on the cement floor in front of the overhead heater. The deer was still wrapped in the blue tarp and partially thawed out. I removed the blue tarp for the first time and found something interesting. The cape on the large buck had not been cut all the way up to the throat area. Indicating to me that someone had plans of getting this deer mounted in the future and didn't want to ruin the cape. The deer was also shot perfect right behind the front shoulders. I doubted that the lady actually shot the deer, gutted it, preserved the cape, and hung it in the barn by herself. But why would she take the fall for this poached deer? I grabbed my shitty metal detector to try to retrieve a bullet from the carcass. I don't think this metal detector had ever found a bullet. I was beginning to doubt it again, when suddenly, I heard the sweet sound BEEP, BEEP, BEEP. I thought to myself, *awesome, I'm going to actually find my first bullet with a metal detector.* I looked and looked for a bullet or even a fragment of a bullet, and nothing! I finally hung the deer in the air off the cement floor and tried the metal detector again. This time, nothing, no more beeps indicating that it had found something made of metal. I ran the metal detector over the cement floor below and again I heard BEEP, BEEP. This had me puzzled for a few minutes when it finally dawned on me that the cement floor contained rebar. Rebar is a metal rod that helps strengthen cement and keeps it from cracking. I felt so stupid. I would never make this rookie mistake again. A bullet was never recovered out of the buck deer. I dragged the entire deer out to the shop and hung it from the rafters. Back then we had no walk-in evidence freezers to store confiscated wildlife. We simply hung them in a storage shed and locked the doors to preserve the evidence.

I tried to call the suspect's girlfriend with the number that the patrolman had provided. No answer. It went straight to her boyfriend's voicemail. I knew that he was in jail and probably already used his one phone call. I left a message indicating who I was and that I needed to visit with his girlfriend regarding the poached deer. I then tried to call the owner of the ranch and no answer. I decided to go back out to the ranch, knowing that someone would be around, as several hundred cows needed fed daily. I arrived back at the ranch and found the owner out feeding his cows. He was surprised to see me. The last time we had talked it ended badly. I had cancelled his hay contract for roughly 2000 tons of hay due to poor hay quality. He simply got in over his head, didn't know what he was doing and contracted for three times the amount of hay that he could actually produce. The bales had too much moisture in them and would probably catch a hayshed on fire from spontaneous combustion from all the moisture trapped in the bales. The bales were also too long to even haul legally on a semi. It was a mess to say the least. When I told him his contract was cancelled, he started crying and told me how important the contract was to him. He probably needed to make his yearly interest payment on the ranch from the sale of hay to the department.

This was all water under the bridge. I shook his hand and asked him if he still had a man and his girlfriend working for him. He shook his head and looked at the ground. He said, "Nope, they don't work for me anymore, I fired him the other day." I said, "Are you aware they poached a large buck mule deer and hung it in your barn?" His eyes got large, and he said, "WHAT, THEY DID WHAT?" I told him that I had retrieved a poached deer out of his barn late last night. He couldn't believe what I was telling him. He wanted to know more details. I told him, that so did I. He told me that he had been away for several days and had just returned to the ranch to feed his cows. He had no one to feed now that he had fired the man. I visited with him for a few more minutes and told him that I would keep him updated once I learned more. I jumped in my truck and headed out the driveway.

On my way out of the ranch yard, I ran into an old Chevy truck with a woman driving it. We met on a sharp corner, and she almost ran me off the road. I stopped and she said, "Oh my God, are you Scott?" I replied, "Yes, Madam." She said, "I think my boyfriend knows you and I have talked to you before out in the hayfield last year sometime." I vaguely remembered talking to the woman. I asked her for her name, and she told me. It was the same name that the patrolman had relayed to Bernie. This was the women who had admitted to shooting the deer. I told her that the reason that I was out at the ranch was to visit with her about shooting the deer. She said, "Can you please come to my camper trailer where we can talk in private?" I agreed to follow her to her camp trailer.

I jumped out of my patrol truck and shook her hand. She had a firm handshake like a man, and she was a big ol' gal to say the least. She had long, red hair tucked up in her scotch cap and was wearing muck boots. I looked at the size of her hands and it was quite possible that she had shot, gutted, and hung the large buck deer in the barn without assistance. She invited me into the trailer house. Once in, there was no place to sit. The trailer was cluttered. She apologized for the mess and told me that her boyfriend had been fired and she was just coming back to get their camper trailer and head back to Riverton. She made a small place for me to sit down. Once seated she looked at me and tears started to well up in her eyes. She said, "Please excuse me, I'm very upset right now." She reached into the inside coat pocket of her Carhartt coat and pulled out a bottle of peach brandy. She took off the cap and took a pull off the bottle. She offered me the bottle. I declined. This was very tough for me to decline because I loved Peach Brandy. This was the same brandy that my dad had drunk himself to death with. I decided it wouldn't be very professional of me to drink with her, even though I wanted to.

She took another pull off the bottle and said with a crackle in her voice, "I know why you are here. I poached that deer and I want to take full responsibility for it." I told her that I appreciated that and that I would like to hear the whole story from start to finish. She told me that yesterday morning the deer was standing out in the field next to the river while she was feeding. She had never seen a buck deer that big before, so she went back to her trailer and grabbed her 30.06, returned and shot the deer. She told me that she only took one shot and hit the buck behind the front shoulders dropping it like a cow patty hitting a flat rock. I had never heard that saying before. She took another swig off the bottle and started crying some more. I interrupted and said, "You told the patrolman that you shot this deer because you were hungry. Why did you kill such a big buck deer if you're hungry?" Her eyes lit up and she moved her face close to mine and whispered, "Because that is the biggest damn buck deer that I have ever seen in my entire f---ing life! I have always wanted to kill a big buck deer!" She then went on to say that once she was done feeding, she took the old Chevy truck out and gutted and loaded the deer. She then returned to the barn and hung it from the rafters. She said, "There is a big ol' f---ing barn owl living in that barn, so I covered it with a blue tarp so the son of a bitch wouldn't eat the meat." I told her that I had personally met the owl last night. I asked her many more questions. She was adamant that she poached the deer alone and her boyfriend knew nothing about it until he was stopped on South Pass and the patrolman found the blood and deer hair in the back of the truck. She said, "My boyfriend is in a lot of trouble right now and he will be lucky to ever get out of jail again."

I reached over and grabbed her bottle of peach brandy and took a pull. I slammed the bottle on the table and looked her directly in the eyes and said, "You and I know that your boyfriend killed this deer, and you tell me you had nothing to do with it! You are only protecting your boyfriend because he is already on probation and in a bunch of trouble. You need to knock your shit off and tell me the truth." She grabbed the bottle and took another drink. She stood up, standing over the top of me. I felt compelled to stand up as well. She gave me a hug and whispered in my ear as she was crying, "Sometimes things are better left unsaid do you understand?" I tried everything in my power to get her to tell the truth. She said, "Just write me the damn ticket and get on down the road." This was one of the hardest things that I had ever done, but I did it. She paid the heavy fine and lost her hunting privileges for three years. I know in my heart that she never killed that deer. She protected her boyfriend from getting into more trouble. It never ceased to amaze me that a woman could love a man that much, even while he was going to be sitting in jail for a long time. I kind of admired her for that. She was a tough ol' ranch gal who stood by her man through tough times.

At the end of the day, it probably didn't matter who actually pulled the trigger. Bottom line, they got caught and weren't allowed to keep the trophy deer. They didn't have any money and had to pay a hefty fine, on top of all their other problems they were dealing with. I jumped back in my truck and headed down the road. I noticed the can of Copenhagen on the console in my truck. I grabbed the full can and took another three-finger dip. I have never quit chewing again since that moment.

Chapter 6

BLIND HORSES, BIG FISH, AND A GREAT SCOTCH

It was another busy time for me, but all the elk feed grounds were up and running. All the hay had been hauled, elk feeders hired, and draft horses hauled into each feed ground. I always felt relieved once all the feeders were feeding. Now, I would just have to react to problems, broken equipment, lame draft horses or whatever hand Mother Nature decided to deal me. I would hire Tim Baxley back to feed North Piney and Finnegan feed grounds. I would also hire Kathy back to feed at Fall Creek feed ground. The only new feeder was Mike (One Beer) Stevie to feed Soda Lake feed ground. It was always nice to not have to train a bunch of new elk feeders. I was hoping that Tim Baxley would not have so many problems this year due to broken down snow machines and deep snow.

A local rancher up Horse Creek called me one day and said that he had four draft horses that he was going to sell if I was interested. He told me that he would sell all of them to me for canner price. I asked him what he had for horses that he wanted to sell. He told me that he had a colt, two really old mares and one three-year old beautifully marked Clydesdale. He said that the three-year old had been started and was easy to handle. I figured that the one three-year old was probably worth canner prices alone. I would also be getting a colt and maybe two mares that could be used as a spare if needed. The rancher told me that if I wanted to drive up to the ranch, he would catch and weigh all the horses on his free-floating scale. I agreed to come up and look at the horses. When I arrived at the ranch, I was joined by no less than eight barking cow dogs that wanted to eat my leg off. The owner of the ranch was running around beating dogs with his cowboy hat and yelling, “BLUE, GINGER, HANK...NO!! BAD DOG! LEAVE HIM ALONE!”

I shook the man’s hand firmly and introduced myself. He pointed over to his right and said, “Well there they are standing on the scale.” I looked over and he had all four draft horses tied to a Powder River panel, all standing on a free-floating scale. He had built a makeshift corral with panels around the large scale. The scale was moving back and forth, which made all the panels shake and rattle around the horses. I thought to myself, *any horse that can stand on a moving floor with rattling panels and barking dogs in the background is probably a pretty good horse.* All the horses looked fat and sassy. The colt already had long winter hair and the three-year old Clydesdale was absolutely beautiful. The horse resembled one of the Budweiser Clydesdales. I don’t think I had ever seen a prettier draft horse. The rancher reached up and patted the three-year old on the neck. He said, “This is ol’ Clyde. I think he is going to make someone a great horse someday. I just don’t need any more damn horses around here with hay prices at $80.00/ton.” Clyde kind of pulled back on his lead rope and spread all four legs out wide as the scale was moving back and forth. His eyes were the size of silver dollars. I could tell that he was a little nervous. But who wouldn’t be under the circumstances? The rancher asked me to step off the scale and keep an eye on the horses while he went into a nearby little red shed to read the total weight of the horses.

He stepped out of the little building and yelled, “LOOKS LIKE RIGHT AT 6000 LBS. HOW ABOUT 3,000 FOR ALL OF THEM?” I walked over and shook the man’s hand and said, “That sounds fine, I think we can do that.” I remembered still having some cash in the coffee can back at the front office, but I didn't remember how much was still in it. I would need to call my Office Manager, Des Brunette and have her count the money. The rancher told me that the two older mares were very well broke and probably still had a few good years in them. "They will both make you a good spare, if you need one," he replied. I backed up the horse trailer and loaded all the horses including the colt without any problems at all. I was really pleased with the deal and was excited to give the three-year old Clydesdale to one of my feeders who I knew would finish breaking him and enjoy doing it. On the way back to the office, I decided to give the horse to Kathy up at Fall Creek. She would love to break him and would do a great job. I would have to call her and see if she was interested in the challenge. I took all the horses out to Soda Lake and dumped them off on the department's 5,000-acre wildlife habitat management area. I decided to bring Clyde to the office and put him in the corral so that he was accessible, and I could get him hauled into Fall Creek feed ground if Kathy was interested.

I called Kathy and she was delighted to take on the challenge of a new horse, especially a good-looking horse at that. I had already hauled her team of horses up earlier (Clyde and Lucky.) Lucky was the horse that had the spike stuck in his foot the previous year up at North Piney feed ground. We had to walk nine miles out to rescue him. My wife and I had doctored Lucky for most of the summer to get him sound again. Lucky had lost sight in one eye over the summer. I did not realize this until fall round-up. Lucky and about thirty other draft horses were running behind my patrol truck chasing me back to the holding pen at Soda Lake. I had grain in the back of my truck and the horses knew it. I was traveling at a high rate of speed on a two-track road to stay ahead of the running draft horses. Lucky was the biggest grain pig of the bunch and was running right beside my truck looking towards the back of my truck and not watching where he was running. I was watching him in my driver's side mirror and heard a god-awful noise. WHAPP! Lucky ran smack into a boulder about the size of a Volkswagen. Two thousand pounds of draft horse launched about ten feet into the air as he did a complete front flip. He landed on his rear end and slid about twenty yards in the snow. The reason he didn't see the large rock was because he was looking towards my truck while running and was blind in his left eye. This caused him to not be able to see the large rock. Once harnessed with another horse, Lucky did fine pulling a sleigh or wagon. Kathy already had a horse named Clyde. She may have to re-name the new Clydesdale.

I left the new horse in the corral at the office and fed him for several days. He was easy to catch and seemed really calm and gentle. I finally got some time and hauled him up to Fall Creek feed ground. I could only drive about halfway in with the truck and horse trailer, due to deep snow conditions. I would end up leading the new horse Clyde for several miles to get him settled in the horse corral at the feed ground. Once there, Kathy was delighted to see the horse. She seemed really excited about breaking him. I helped Kathy feed about 800 elk and headed back down the trail. As I was walking away, I turned around and yelled to Kathy, "GOOD LUCK WITH HIM. LET ME KNOW HOW HE DOES OVER THE NEXT FEW WEEKS!" Kathy replied, "Will do, I think he will be just fine."

Over the next several weeks I had received several calls from Kathy. She told me that the new horse was difficult to catch in the round corral each morning. She said that he runs in circles in the corral and will never face her or look at her ever. She also told me that he runs in circles always looking outside of the corral. I could tell that Kathy was getting discouraged. It didn't sound like she had even caught him to get a harness on him yet. I thought that was kind of weird because I hadn't had any problems catching him earlier. The word **can't** was not in Kathy's vocabulary. She prided herself in working hard and doing a great job at everything she did. I offered to come up and help her and she replied, "Naw, I can get it, I'll keep you posted."

Kathy would call me at least once a week and give me an update. It sounded like she finally got the horse caught and harnessed. She said that she had even hooked him up with Lucky a few times and fed the elk. She also said that he was really skittish and nervous all the time. I knew if anybody could get this horse broke, she could do it. I told her to be careful and call me if she needed help. She just laughed and said, "Give me a few more weeks, and I will have him broke. Oh, by the way, I named him Spook."

Tim Baxley and his gray cat, Cow Cat, finally got settled at North Piney and Finnegan. He had decided to live in the Hantavirus hotels again. Both were camp trailers that the department provided him to stay in. I'm sure he probably had to clean the filthy rat nests out of each one of them to make them livable again. Maybe this is why he brought his Cow Cat to live with him. Except, I'm not so sure that those rats might be big enough to eat the cat. I was excited to have Tim back and was glad that he started the feeding season with an almost new snow machine. Tim hadn't changed a bit. He still called me "Boss Man" and was always in good spirits and thankful for each day. I had never seen anyone with such a great attitude. In Tim's mind there was nothing that he couldn't accomplish. And if things went to shit, he would just laugh and say, "You don't know, what you don't know, well now I know, I won't try that again."

I would also spend a few days getting Mike Stevie (aka One Beer) set up to feed at Soda Lake feed ground. There was a shortage of small hay bales that year. This forced me to have to buy large one-ton square bales for this feed ground. This would be a gamble, since we would have to load the large bales with a tractor. The plan was to load the hay sled with the tractor and still use the team of draft horses to feed the elk. The tractor had a diesel motor and would be difficult to start when the temperature dipped down to -30 degrees or even colder. If the tractor didn't start, the large bales would not be loaded, and the elk would not get fed. If the 1000-1500 head elk didn't get fed, they may end up right in the town of Pinedale or on some rancher's cattle feedlines on private property somewhere. Mike was one of the lucky feeders as he had a water well to water the draft horses daily. He did not have to haul any water or shovel any snow and melt it for the horse's drinking water. A pair of draft horses could easily drink 30 gallons of water a day. All he had to do was fire up the little Briggs and Stratton motor each morning and pump the water into a large holding tank. If the motor started, the water flowed. If the motor didn't start, there would be no water for the horses. I always hated when I had to rely on something mechanical starting in the wintertime to have a successful day.

One Beer got pretty creative with the orange diesel tractor. He built a small garage out of one-ton square bales to park the tractor in. The tractor was strategically parked each day to face in the direction of the morning sun. He also draped a black canvas tarp over the hood and engine compartment of the tractor each day. This would help protect the motor from the extremely cold wind chill. The black tarp would also radiate some heat onto the engine after sitting in the morning sun for several hours. I purchased him a generator and a heavy duty jump box to boost the tractor's batteries each morning before starting. I would lose sleep at night worrying about that tractor not starting each day. It was my idea to purchase the large bales and use the tractor to load with. If things went to shit, it was my fault.

My bag phone started ringing, it was Kathy. I hadn't heard from her in over a week. I was really excited to hear how Spook was coming along. I picked up the phone and heard a loud voice. "Hello Scott, this is Kathy." I replied, "Hey, Kathy how is everything going up there at Fall Creek?" Kathy started laughing and replied, "I finally figured out what is wrong with this new horse Spook!" My heart sank for a second and I replied, "Yes, what is wrong with him?" She replied still laughing, the damn horse is completely blind, he can't see a damn thing, no wonder he is so spooky all the time." I about died when I heard this news, I thought to myself, *Swerb, did you buy a damn blind horse?* I told Kathy that I was sure that the horse could see when I took care of him and caught him at the office three days in a row. He stepped in the horse trailer just fine. He went in and out of the horse trailer several times without missing a beat. Kathy giggled some more and said, "Well, I don't know about any of that, but he just acts lost all the time and was stumbling a lot. He is plumb gentle and helps Lucky pull, but he can't see a damn thing. I can take my finger and poke him in each eye, and he don't even know it's coming towards him." I couldn't help but laugh, and I was at a loss for words. I replied to Kathy, "Bet you never thought you could break a blind draft horse, did ya?" I told her that I was sure it wasn't blind when I bought it, but hell, maybe it was? Maybe that's why the rancher was selling such a nice looking three-year old draft horse for canner prices? If that rancher knew that horse was blind and he just sold it to the dumbass game warden, I'll bet he is drinking beer with his buddies and they are all laughing their asses off at me, all the way to the bank. Hell, I even paid him in cash. He didn't have to wait the customary 45 days to get paid by a state agency. I paid him with a coffee can full of cash! I was glad that the girls who worked for the fiscal division in Cheyenne didn't know anything about this horse, and they weren't ever going to know anything about the other three horses either. My dad always told me, "Son, sometimes things are better left unsaid." I now understood the meaning of that phrase. The gal who took the rap for poaching the large buck deer also used that phrase while I was interviewing her.

I asked Kathy if she thought she could finish out the year with a blind horse named Spook and one-eyed horse named Lucky. She laughed and said, "Oh Hell yeah, as long as he is harnessed up with Lucky, he just puts his head down and pulls. Hell, nothing scares them because neither one of them can see!" I felt pretty stupid and wondered how the blind horse would do during the summer months in a 5000-acre pasture with 30-40 other draft horses. I guess time would tell. We just needed to get through the winter months and get the elk fed daily.

The winter progressed. We were moving elk to feed grounds with our snow machines almost daily. I loved to ride a snow machine, but this was getting old. The days were cold, and we moved elk through some absolute rock piles with our snow machines. I felt sorry for my machine, bouncing it through the boulders all day long, denting the belly pan and tearing up the skis. Heck, one game warden broke a ski completely off his snow machine one day. He had to limp it all the way home leaning to one side to keep the broken ski off the ground.

I had received several calls from a complaining rancher who lived below Finnegan feed ground. He complained that he thought the elk feeder had been double feeding the elk and they were getting hungry and coming down to eat with his cows. This rancher was very critical of the department and not liked by many. This rancher had fed the elk at Finnegan feed ground years ago and knew elk behavior pretty well. I would need to visit with Tim and make sure he wasn't double feeding the elk causing them to leave the feed ground and get into trouble on private property. Double feeding is a situation when an elk feeder can't feed the next day for whatever reason. So, they feed the elk twice the amount in one day, hoping it will hold them over the next day when they are unable to feed. I had requested my elk feeders to never double feed without contacting me first. That way I could feed for them or find someone else to cover for the day. I had also requested all my feeders to have a back-up feeder that they could depend on in case they needed a day off. I visited with Tim, and he apologized for double feeding. He told me that he needed to get his truck to a mechanic and have them put a new engine in the truck. I completely understood his situation but emphasized to him that because the elk had brucellosis, we could not risk them coming down on private property and co-mingling with cattle. If the rancher's cows contracted brucellosis because of our elk and a feeder not doing his job properly, this would create a very serious and expensive situation for the rancher. I told Tim to please notify me if he ever needed to double feed again. I stopped in and visited with the rancher as well. He told me that approximately 150 elk had been down with his cows several times over the last few weeks. As I left his house, the rancher stated, "If my cows get brucellosis because of your DAMN elk, there will be hell to pay. Feed your damn elk!" I apologized to the rancher and told him we would do a better job in the future.

Tim Baxley's infamous Ford truck

It was a beautiful blue-sky day. I hadn't been in to feed with One Beer at Soda Lake yet. I decided to snow machine into the feed ground and see how things were going. The tractor had been starting pretty well. There were only a few mornings that the tractor wouldn't start. One Beer designed a heater that he could plug into the generator and put under the engine block of the tractor to warm it up on the really cold days. This seemed to work pretty well. One Beer was a tall slender man. He was a very good roper and had spent a great deal of time on a horse. He shod horses for a living and guided hunters in the Upper Green River for his brother Todd "Roundy" Stevie. He was a heck of a hunting guide and knew his way around the mountains very well. He was a jack of all trades. I always enjoyed visiting with One Beer because he was always happy and had a great attitude about life. While feeding, he always wore sunglasses and an old grungy scotch cap with the ear flaps down. His short goatee would be covered in frost with his red handkerchief nestled around his neck. He wore the scotch cap high on his head, most the time his ear flaps wouldn't even cover his ears. When he talked, his voice was loud, and he always had a lot of energy. I always told him that he reminded me of a fart in a hot skillet bouncing around.

One Beer had some really nice bulls on the feed ground. We fed a couple lines of hay and stopped the team of draft horses in the middle of the herd. There must have been nearly 1000 elk on feed that day with a couple hundred branch antlered bulls. It was really enjoyable to just stop and enjoy the moment looking at all the large bulls. Most of his elk were very tame and some of them would even eat hay off the feed sled as we were stopped. I looked behind me and observed a spike elk eating hay off the back of the hay sled. I said to One Beer, "Boy, that's a tame one." One Beer giggled and said, "Yea, that's ol' Norm, I named him after your BFH biologist. Norm was the Brucellosis, Feed Ground, Habitat biologist that got crossways with the previous feeder that I had ended up firing the year before. The feeder told Norm to get the F—ck off his feed ground and to never come back.

One Beer looked at me and giggled as he said, "Hey, Swerb, you care if I take ol' Norm for a ride?" I looked at him and replied, "You think you can ride that spike elk?" One Beer replied, "I have always wanted to try and ride an elk." I replied, "Hell, I have always wanted to watch someone try and ride an elk, so getter done!" One Beer eased his way over to the edge of the sled next to the spike elk. He slowly scratched the elk on top of its head. The spike seemed alright with everything and just kept eating hay off the back of the sled. Pretty quick, One Beer grabbed the spike by one of its horns and threw a leg over the back of the elk. I thought to myself, *oh my God!! This can't be good. We don't even have a first aid kit with us.* The spike elk lunged sideways and reared its front legs into the air. One Beer was on board for an eight second ride. I thought to myself, *this is going to be good, you don't get to witness this every day.* I expected the elk to buck but he didn't buck much. He just ran thirty miles an hour through a herd of 1000 elk. I never seen so many elk blow up and run ten different directions all at once. One Beer held on tight. He even started acting like he was spurring the bull and held his right arm above his head. The elk ran about fifty yards and came to a dead stop in the middle of the feed ground. I sure wished I had had a camera with me that day. One Beer sat on him and spurred him a few times with his muck boots. The elk wouldn't move. One Beer swung a leg off and landed on both feet, just like you see the professional bull riders do. One Beer grabbed the brim of his dirty scotch cap and flung it high into the air while raising both hands over his head. I think I could hear the crowd cheering in the background as well. That was the first and last time that I had ever witnessed someone ride an elk. He probably didn't buck much because he didn't have a cinch strap around his flank area. He also probably didn't have the hot blood lines of being a rank bucking bull, hell, he was only a spike. I was pretty proud of One Beer and gave him a high five as he jumped back up on the sled. I told him that if the elk leave the feed ground and end up on private property, I may have to fire him until the dust settles. The elk never ended up leaving the area and I don't believe the spike ever came back to eat off the back of the hay sled again.

I returned home and had a nasty voice message on my answering machine. Apparently, the Finnegan elk had left the feed ground and went back down to the angry rancher's property to eat with his cows. The message on my machine said, "I'm headed out the door to get on my snow machine and run all your goddamn elk out of my cows. If they don't cooperate, I'm going to start shooting." I thought to myself, *oh dear God, hopefully Tim didn't double feed again.* It was late in the afternoon. I called Big Piney game warden Brad Hovinga and told him about the situation. Brad said, "Oh, that's not good, hopefully Tim didn't double feed again." I told Brad that I would be hooking up my snow machine trailer and get headed his direction. I also asked Brad if he would mind going with me. If Tim double fed those elk again, I was going to fire him, and we would need to feed the elk ourselves. Brad agreed to go with me. I told him that I would be at his house in about an hour.

I drove fast all the way to Big Piney. I was really hoping that Tim hadn't screwed up again. I really liked this guy and certainly didn't want to have to fire him. I was also hoping that the rancher didn't shoot any of the elk or Tim. If his cattle ended up with brucellosis, this would be a bad deal for everyone involved. I met up with Brad. He told me that he had called the rancher, and no elk were killed. The rancher was very upset but had successfully moved the elk back to the feed ground himself. Brad was upset because this was one of his landowners that he had been trying to build a positive relationship with for several years. I was upset because I told Tim to never double feed again without letting me know.

I stopped at Brad's house to meet up with him. He told me that he got a major ass-chewing from the rancher and that this better not be Tim's fault. We took separate trucks and headed south of Big Piney. It was starting to snow and was very cold out. After meeting at the Forest boundary, we snow machined up the big nasty hill to get into Finnegan feed ground. When we arrived at the feed ground, there were approximately 450 elk standing on the feed ground with no feed. Tim was nowhere to be found. Maybe he was at North Piney feed ground? We only had about an hour left of daylight. Brad and I dragged some hay bales out of the stack yard with our snow machines and fed the elk enough hay to keep them content for one night. After feeding the elk I told Brad that I wanted to leave Tim a note in his brown turd trailer house. We both entered the camp trailer. It was very cold inside. I found a piece of paper next to a pen on the small kitchen table. I wrote a note that read, "Tim, what part of don't ever double feed the elk again didn't you understand!! I signed it *Swerb* and taped it to his refrigerator door. Brad had sat down at the small table while I was writing the note. He was digging through a large plastic container of Tim's trail mix. It looked like he was picking through the trail mix and only eating the M&M's and cashews. I looked at Brad and said, "What in the hell are you doing?" He replied, "Mm...I'm hungry and these cashews taste pretty dang good." Brad then grabbed a bottle of scotch off the table and read the label on the bottle. He said, "Holy cow, this is some expensive scotch, aged for over twelve years! Maybe we should sample some of it? Brad grabbed the bottle and took a small snort. He said, "Man, that is some good stuff right there, you should try some."

I dug around in the cupboard and found a couple small blue tin cups. I took the cups outside and filled them with fresh powdered snow. I returned to the inside of the trailer and set the cups on the table. I told Brad that I preferred a scotch slushy. Brad poured each cup about half full and we sat there in the cold trailer and sipped on the tasty scotch. This was one of the most beautiful moments that I can remember. We were looking out the large front picture window of the trailer at about 450 elk eating hay right in front of us. It was snowing hard, but the huge snowflakes were slowly floating straight down to the earth with the elk in the background. I told Brad that this was a very beautiful moment and I wished that I had a camera to take some pictures of the elk. Brad looked around the inside of the trailer and spotted a VCR camera on the top bunk. He said, "Well, look here, Tim has a camera." I grabbed the camera and hit the red power button. Heck the camera was charged and ready to go. I told Brad that we should take a video for Tim of both of us eating his trail mix and drinking his high dollar Scotch whiskey. Brad laughed and thought that sounded like a good idea. He said, "You grab that camera, and I will walk out in the middle of all those elk, and you can take a video of me for Tim."

Brad headed out the door of the trailer with trail mix in one hand and a scotch in the other. I hit the red record button on the VCR camera, and we were live at Finnegan feed ground. I was narrating the video as Brad walked out into the middle of all the elk. I hit the zoom button on the camera so that Tim could see Brad eating all of his trail mix and drinking his Scotch whiskey. I was eagerly awaiting Brad to turn around and give Tim a toast in front of all the elk. Suddenly, Brad dropped his Carhartt coveralls and gave me a full moon while I was zoomed in on him. I was trying to find the stop button, but I couldn't find it because I wasn't familiar with the camera. There was a bit of a panic moment, but the full moon was now captured on film. Brad pulled up his trousers and turned around and said, "Here is to you, Baxley." As he held up the tin cup full of scotch and toasted him in front of all the elk. Brad walked back to the trailer laughing and said, "Did you get that, man?" I replied, "Oh hell, yeah!" Brad toasted me and I put the camera back up on the overhead bunk bed. We sat there for several more minutes and told a few crazy stories. I looked up and the red light was still blinking on the camera. Brad laughed and said, "Shit, how long has that camera been recording?" I replied, "I don't know but too damn long." I grabbed the camera and stepped outside the trailer to do some professional editing.

I placed the camera back where we had found it and made sure the damn thing was turned off this time. Brad and I had now eaten all of the M&M's and cashews out of Tim's trail mix and put a small dent in his bottle of scotch. Brad looked at me and said, "It will be dark soon. We need to make a mile." That meant we need to get the hell out of there before darkness set in. Brad jumped up and headed out the door of the trailer and fired up his brand-new Powder Special 600 snow machine. He flipped his visor down on his helmet and took off like a bolt of lightning. I hadn't even got my machine started yet. He was gone and disappeared into the thick patch of trees ahead. I don't think that he had had that much to drink but apparently, he was feeling invisible as he sped off. I jumped on my machine and traveled as fast as I could possibly travel without having an accident and never did catch up to him. Once I returned to our trucks, I noticed Brad was not there. I could see a single set of snow machine tracks headed west up a steep hill towards North Piney feed ground. I decided to follow the tracks in the snow. The snow conditions were very flat. I could not see very well, and it was still snowing hard out. I came across a spot where Brad had hit a large pile of dirt and became airborne for quite a distance. There were no snow machine tracks in the snow for over thirty feet. Then, I could see snow machine tracks in the snow, but it looked like the snow machine was traveling on one side with one ski in the air. I observed several divots in the snow where it looked like maybe Brad's body had landed and skipped several times like a rock. I think Brad was focused on trying to climb the steep hill and didn't see the large pile of dirt due to flat light conditions. He hit the pile of snow-covered dirt, and it launched him for a long ways. Apparently, he had survived this wreck and was still headed somewhere. I decided to follow his tracks in the snow to see if I could find him.

I followed his tracks that were headed down into a steep ravine. I decided to stay on top of the ridge to search for him. I pulled up to a steep snow cornice that was about twenty feet high and looked off the edge of it down into the ravine. There was Brad parked down in the bottom of the ravine. It looked like his head was lying on top of his handlebars. I shut my machine off and yelled at him while I was parked on top of the steep cornice. He looked up at me. I yelled, "Hey buddy, watch this!!" I fired up my machine and flipped my visor down on my helmet. I had always wanted to jump off this huge cornice before but was always too chicken to do it. Maybe the Scotch had kicked in, I don't know. I turned around and got a run at the cornice so that I could fly off of it. I hit the loud lever and away I went sailing through the air. I don't know how many feet I flew, but it was a bunch. I made a perfect landing and slid sideways right next to Brad. I was really proud of myself for what I had just accomplished. Brad didn't even see it happen. He had his head laid down on the handlebars of his snow machine groaning in pain. I said, "Hey buddy, did you see that? He just groaned and said, "Man, I had a hell of a wreck and I'm not doing so well right now." He flipped up his visor, his helmet was packed full of snow. He said, "Hey man, is my face bleeding?" I replied, "I don't think so, your helmet is full of snow though." He replied, "Oh man, I thought I was bleeding but maybe it's just the snow melting off my head." He told me about the large pile of dirt that he had hit and sailed through the air and ended up wrecking. I told him that I had followed his tracks and saw what had happened.

Brad was able to start his machine and get back to our trucks. He would later take a trip to the hospital and was diagnosed with a separated collar bone. As for Tim, I never fired him. Come to find out, he had been broken down at North Piney feed ground with no cell service and was unable to feed the elk at Finnegan. Brad and I went back up to Finnegan feed ground to help Tim feed a few weeks later. While feeding, I mentioned to Tim that I had seen a VCR camera in his trailer awhile back and wanted to know what he had been filming. He laughed and told me that he was making a video of the elk on the feed ground to send back east to his parents for a Christmas present. He said, "I should get you two assholes on the video." I laughed and replied, "I'm pretty sure you have at least one of us already." I later learned that Tim had sent the video back to his parents without editing. His parents had invited several other couples over for the exciting video of their son feeding elk in western Wyoming. Halfway through the video it shows Brad standing in the middle of 450 elk giving me the full moon. What a special moment that was for all to see. Tim told us this story at the annual Christmas party. He said that his parents and their friends were not impressed. We laughed and drank some of Tim's homemade corn. Halfway through Tim's story, he held up his hand and said, "Wait just a moment." Tim went outside and puked up some of his homemade moonshine. He quickly returned to the party and said, "OK, now where was I in my story?" He never missed a beat, he jumped right back into his story and finished telling it.

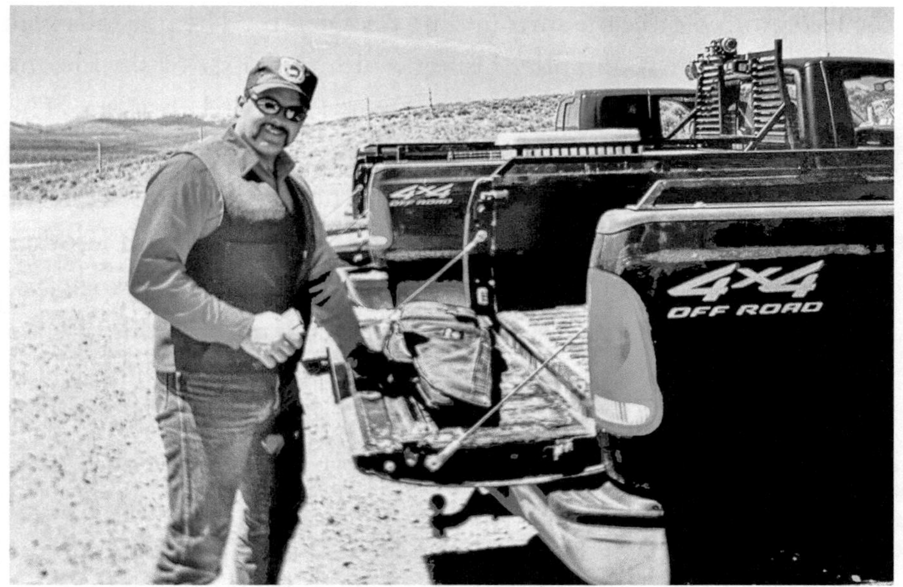

Brad Hovinga firearms qualifications

The winter was nearly over, with spring on the way. Franz elk feeder, Greg Grassell, had called me and left me a voice message. I hit the play button and the message read, "Hello Scott, this is Greg up at Franz feed ground. Hey, could you bring Robyn and myself up another harness tomorrow morning? We left it hanging on the front of the feed sled and a rag horn bull got it tangled in his antlers and took off with it somewhere. Robyn and I have looked everywhere, and we can't seem to find it?" I put the phone down and thought, *shit, that's the second one this year!* Robyn was Greg's girlfriend, and they would generally feed the elk together each day. They had a rag horn bull on the feed ground that they had named Sparky.

Sparky would clean up all the loose hay on the feed sled each day when they were done feeding. Occasionally Sparky would rub his antlers on the wooden rack on front of the hay sled where they hung their harness each day. His horns would get entangled in the harness and away he would go somewhere in the night with the harness attached to his horns. Sometimes the harness would fall off, either on the feed ground or in the surrounding trees nearby. The previous year it was reported that an antler hunter had found a set of shed horns near the Franz feed ground with a harness attached to them. The antler hunter called the game and fish office to report it. I told the antler hunter, "I bet I know where that harness came from." I guess I would be headed to Franz first thing in the morning with another new harness. At the time, a new set of harnesses were very expensive, and it was getting harder to even find them anymore. In this case we would need to also replace the lines, bridals, and bits. I think it was time to have Greg and Robyn hang their harnesses somewhere that the elk couldn't get to them.

Greg and Robyn worked hard each day. The Franz feed ground was located in deep snow country just east of Bondurant, Wyoming at the base of the Wyoming Range mountain's. There was no water at the feed ground to water the horses. The couple would fight deep snow conditions each day just getting from their house to the feed ground on snow machines. This was about a ten-mile round trip for them every day. It was too difficult to pull a heavy sled loaded with water each day all the way from their house to water the horses. It was decided that it was easier to put a large 100-gallon metal tank up at the feed ground with a propane heater mounted in the tank. After feeding, Greg and Robyn would shovel snow with a scoop shovel until the tank was full of snow each day. The heater would melt the snow into water and the horses would now be able to have a drink. If you can even imagine how much melted snow it takes to equate to about thirty gallons of water each day? It's more than you can imagine! If it didn't snow for a few days, the couple would have to haul snow in their scoop shovels for longer distances. Not only did they have to shovel snow into the water tank every day, but they also had to shovel the snow out from in front of the large Powder River gates just to be able to enter the stack yard and load up with hay. I think it is safe to say, if I had a dollar for every scoop shovel full of snow that Greg and Robyn shoveled every day, I could retire a rich man.

Greg and Robyn fed elk at this feed ground for many years both together and alone. Robyn was a tough, cute, red-headed Wyoming cowgirl. She could rope, ride, and brand with the best of them. She also broke and trained horses. I always told Greg, "You better not ever lip off to her, or she might just stuff your little ass into a post hole somewhere." Greg would just snort and giggle and say, "Yep, you're right!" Greg was short, but very tough. He was one of the best hands on a snow machine that I had ever met. He was missing some fingers on his right hand. This made it difficult for him to run the throttle on his snow machine. He would purchase a new machine and put the throttle on the left handlebar so that he could operate it better. I'm not sure I have ever met someone crazier than Greg in his day. I can guarantee you that if Grassell ever says, "That's one crazy sumbitch!" you should listen to him.

I invited Greg over to my house one night to watch the Tyson vs. Holyfield fight and have a few drinks. This was the fight when Tyson bit off part of Holyfield's ear. At the end of the evening, Grassell looked at me and drunkenly and said with a slur, "*You want to catch some big fish in the morning?"* I said, "Sure, where are we going?" Grassell responded, "*Can't tell you. Just be at the Daniel Junction at 7:00 AM. You don't need to bring anything except your fishing pole.*" He got up off the couch and walked out the front door. I was excited about this. I'm always game to go somewhere and catch big fish. I got up early the next morning, packed a lunch and grabbed my fishing pole. As I was headed out the door Lana yelled, "Where are you going fishing?" I responded, "I don't know. I will tell you when I get home tonight." Apparently, this was one of Grassell's favorite fishing spots and he didn't want anyone to know about it. I wondered if he was going to blindfold me on the trip in and then just dump me out of the truck somewhere in the mountains confused of my surroundings.

Robyn Grassell

I met Greg at 7:00 AM. He was on time and ready to go. I jumped in his truck, and he already had an open Budweiser between his legs. He smiled, snorted, and said, "Are you ready to catch some damn big fish? There is a cold beer in the cooler if you want one." I told Greg that I was fine and not much of a beer drinker, especially at 7:00 AM. He said, "You might wanna grab one, it's a long drive." I wondered where in the hell we were headed. We drove all the way to Jackson and up into the Gros Ventre mountains. Pretty quick we turned off on a rough two-track road and took that road several miles uphill and through the timber. We pulled into a camping spot right next to a lake where several of Greg's friends were camping. They had several small john boats pulled up on the shore next to their campfire. Greg's friends were excited to see him and offered him a beer. It appeared that all of his friends had started drinking beer early as well. Greg introduced his friends to me and said with a snort, "Don't be violating the law today, cuz we got a damn game warden with us!" I really didn't want anyone to know that I was a game warden. A lady standing by the campfire with a Budweiser in her hand blurted out, "Fishing with the game warden is kind of like shopping with your husband." I could sense that Greg's friends weren't really impressed with Greg for bringing a game warden into their camp.

I glanced over at the john boats and noticed that they all had motors mounted on them and none of them were registered. I also didn't observe any life jackets lying around. Wyoming law requires you to have one life jacket for each individual on the boat. Each motorized boat also needs to be registered with the state of Wyoming to be legal. I thought to myself, *Swerb, what have you got yourself into now?* Greg looked at me and yelled, "WELL, YOU GONNA STAND THERE ALL DAY WITH YOUR HANDS IN YOUR PANTS, OR ARE YOU READY TO CATCH SOME DAMN BIG TUNA? GRAB YOUR FISHING POLE AND LET'S GET AFTER IT." Greg grabbed a boat and pulled it out into the water. He said, "You sit in the front, and I will run the motor." We took the small boat all the way across the lake. The wind was blowing just slightly. Once we reached the other side of the lake, Greg shut off the motor. He grabbed a small bright pink ice fly and handed it to me. He said, "Put a little split shot about three feet up your line, tie this jig on, and add a small piece of one of these fat juicy night crawlers." As he handed me a fat squirming night crawler, he said, "Cast it out there as far as you can, and we will let the wind drift us back across the lake. Be ready to catch the biggest cutthroat you have ever caught in your life." We hadn't drifted very long, and I caught the biggest most beautiful cutthroat trout that I had ever caught in my life. The fish was 23" long. I immediately released the fish back to the water. Greg said, "What the hell did you do that for?" I explained to him that I wasn't much of a fish eater and that I really just enjoyed catching them. He replied, "Most people would mount a fish like that." As he cracked open another beer, Greg cast his line out and placed his pole in a pole holder mounted to the side of the boat. I put on another juicy night crawler and was eager to catch another beautiful cutthroat. Pretty quick, Greg had a bite. He set his beer down, grabbed his pole with both hands. As soon as his line was tight, he leaned back and set the hook with both hands. He yelled, "WHAM, TUNA ON, TUNA ON!!" Greg landed his first fish of the day and turned it back into the water. I said, "What the hell did you do that for? Most people would mount a fish like that!" Greg, just giggled and snorted and said, "Ain't this about the coolest thing you have ever done?" I replied, "If I was ever to have any more fun than this, I would probably be dead or in jail."

We continued to fish for a couple of hours. We literally caught one large cutthroat after another all morning long. It was getting close to noon time. I even started drinking some Budweiser with Greg, and I hate Budweiser! There was only one other boat on the lake. It appeared that both occupants of that boat were also fishing, just like we were, by drifting their boat across the lake. I caught another large cutthroat and returned it back to the water. I yelled at Grassell and said, "HAND ME ANOTHER ONE OF THOSE TUNA SLAYING NIGHTCRAWLERS!" Greg looked at me and said, "SHHH...Don't yell about night crawlers too loud, this lake is artificial flies and lures only." I said, "Are you shitting me right now?" Greg snorted and giggled and said, "Nope, why do you think we are catching so many big fish?" I was pissed, pissed at myself for not reading the regulations as a game warden. But I didn't even know where we were going fishing when we left the house that morning. Greg thought this was the funniest thing that he had ever seen in his life. His friends thought that it was even funnier! I plucked off the pink ice fly and threw it at Greg and said, "You're an asshole!" Greg giggled and said, "I have a panther martin lure if you want to try it, but you probably won't catch anything. I took the lure and cast it until my arm nearly fell off and never even got another bite.

We continued to drift across the lake and Greg continued to catch big fish with his secret night crawlers. As we were drifting our boat sideways and both facing the same direction, we drifted into the side of the only other boat on the lake. The occupants were looking the other direction and didn't see us coming. As we hit their boat, I heard a loud noise, BAM! Both of them reeled up their lines quickly. Grassell noticed that they were also fishing with night crawlers. He started to giggle and snort and said very loudly, "SOMEBODY DIDN'T READ THEIR REGULATIONS, ITS ARTIFICIAL FLIES AND LURES ONLY ON THIS LAKE. GOOD THING THERE AIN'T NO GAME WARDENS AROUND TODAY." The people were embarrassed and told us they were sorry. Even though we were the ones that ran into the side of their boat. We finally got some distance from their boat and Grassell looked at me and said, "Boy, we just Rocksprings the hell out of them sonsabitches!!" He giggled and snorted and nearly fell out of the boat. You would have to be from Sublette County or Wyoming to understand that phrase.

We returned home safely. I promised Grassell that I would never tell anyone where we were fishing that day, so I will stick to that promise while writing this story nearly 26 years later. As for me and

Grassell, I decided to not go fishing with him anymore to any secret places that I couldn't read up on the regulations before we left home.

It was springtime. Kathy from Fall Creek called my bag phone and told me that it was time to walk the draft horses out of the feed ground. She told me that she would walk them down the dug-way to the Fayette Ranch and meet me at the ranch headquarters if I could pick them up. I agreed to meet her the next day at noon at the headquarters. I asked her if she thought she could make it alright leading two draft horses with only one eye between the two of them. She laughed and said, "We will be just fine." It was well after noon and Kathy had not showed up yet. I was pulling a horse trailer and had no snow machine. I became concerned about her and asked the ranch manager, Chris Soderberg, if I could borrow a ranch snow machine and run up the road to check on Kathy. Chris said, "You bet, take that ol' piece of shit Polaris over there if you can get it started." I thanked him and was able to get the snow machine running. Chris and I had been playing poker together on Friday nights for several months now. I thought the world of Chris; he would help anyone, anytime, and for any reason. I headed on up the rough two-track road north of the ranch headquarters traveling on mostly dirt and mud the first few miles, due to spring snow melt. As I got higher in elevation, it was necessary to have the snow machine because the snow was getting much deeper.

I traveled through a small ranch yard with corrals. I noticed Spook, the blind draft horse, tied to a rail in one of the corrals. Kathy was not around. I thought that was kind of weird, so I continued on up the road. As I came around a sharp corner just before the dug-way, I noticed Kathy and Lucky the one-eyed draft horse lying on the ground in the road. I pulled up on my snow machine and shut it off right below Lucky and Kathy. The horse was lying on his side and Kathy was lying on top of the horse. Kathy looked at me. I could see tears in her eyes with a look of panic. Kathy said, "I don't know what happened? I was walking the horses out and Lucky just stopped. I turned around and noticed that he was sweating and breathing very hard. He had to break trail through some deep snow, but he is in great shape from feeding all winter and that shouldn't have affected him" I jumped off the snow machine and walked over to Lucky. He was breathing very shallow, lying in the middle of the road with his harness on. Kathy said, "I think he may have colic. We should call Dr. Dean and get him up here as soon as possible. This was before cell phones. My bag phone was in my truck at the ranch headquarters. I told Kathy to stay with Lucky and I would head for town to get some medication. I jumped on my snow machine and started to turn around. Kathy yelled, "SHIT, IT'S TOO LATE, I THINK HE JUST DIED!!" I got back off my snow machine and walked up to Lucky. His one good eye was glazed over and motionless. This was one of the saddest sights that I had ever seen. Kathy was crying, I was crying, and Lucky was no longer with us, just that quick. I was emotionally attached to Lucky because of everything that we had been through together.

Walking him out of North Piney feed ground with a 6" spike in his foot for nine miles. My wife Lana and I doctoring him every day for nearly three months to get him healthy again. Taking him to the vet several times when he lost his eye. Lucky and Kathy had trained and broke a completely blind draft horse that winter and now he lay there in the snow looking into the heavens with his good eye open and his harness still on. I know this sounds bad, but all I could think of is *I need to get this harness off him before he bloats and his body freezes in the night.* If you have never taken a heavy leather harness off an 1800 lb. dead draft horse lying in the deep snow, you truly haven't experienced all of life's curve balls. R.I.P. Lucky ol' Boy. Your luck finally ran out!

Chapter 7

Glendo Reservoir

It was springtime of 1999. I stopped by the regional office to catch regional supervisor Bernie Holz up on all the latest and greatest events going on with my job. During my conversation with Bernie, I learned that he was really struggling with trying to keep up with two regional offices and all the controversial issues that were going on in the Jackson Hole and Pinedale areas. Environmental groups in Jackson were making a big push to get rid of all the elk feed grounds in western Wyoming. This was nothing new for the department. We had been fighting with these groups for years. Now they were claiming that brucellosis was going to wipe out all the elk in western Wyoming if we didn't stop feeding elk. They were also worried about CWD (Chronic Wasting Disease) finding its way to western Wyoming from mule deer and infecting all the elk on feed grounds. In their eyes, feed grounds were horrible for wildlife management because it congregated elk on supplemental feed, which in turn allowed the spread of diseases to happen more rapidly among herds of elk while congregated on artificial feed. They were not wrong in their assessments. Feeding wild elk was not a good wildlife management practice. However, if we didn't short stop the elk and feed them, they would be on every cattle feedline and haystack in western Wyoming during the winter months. Not to mention, brucellosis was a real deal, and we didn't want any elk co-mingling with cattle on cattle feedlines. The only way to stop feeding the elk would be to eliminate approximately 70% of them. The public would never allow for starving elk. The outfitters and sportsmen would never agree to cut the herd back 70%. The landowners would never tolerate elk in their cattle and haystacks. This has been a problem that the department has been working on for many, many years. The National Elk Refuge in Jackson Hole Wyoming started feeding elk around 1910 after a severe winter that killed hundreds of elk from starvation the previous year.

The oil and gas industry were also starting to pick up in the Pinedale area, especially south of Pinedale on the mesa. This area was crucial winter range for hundreds, if not thousands, of mule deer. The department had just started a large-scale mule deer study to look at the effects of oil and gas development and mule deer survival rates in areas with oil and gas development. This study would involve fitting many mule deer with GPS collars and tracking their movements during winter months. The information gained would also help the department understand the long migration routes that mule deer endured each fall, moving from their summer range to their winter ranges. Some deer would migrate over 200 miles to get to their crucial winter ranges. First, the deer would have to survive the hunting season and then begin their migration during the middle of October. Then, the deer would have to navigate highways, fences, developed areas, predation, and deep snow conditions. Once the deer arrived on their winter ranges, the bucks would start to rut, and use needed fat reserves breeding does. The bucks are very vulnerable to poachers during the rut. This area has a great deal of public roads, and many people love to go out and take pictures and film large mule deer bucks. This causes constant disturbance and sometimes harassment to the mule deer when they need their fat reserves the most. Shed antler hunting had also become very popular during this time. Photographers and antler hunters would literally live daily with some of these large bucks most of the winter. They wanted a video of the deer with antlers on, and then they wanted pictures of them holding the deer's shed antlers. This caused constant harassment to some deer, especially large bucks during the winter months. At this time large brown deer antlers were worth about $10.00/lb.

After visiting with Bernie about all the large issues that were going on in the region, he told me that Wildlife Administration was discussing the idea of creating a new position for the Jackson/Pinedale region. The new position would be responsible for supervising 7 game wardens in the region. This would allow Bernie more time to deal with the bigger issues. The title of the new position would be Game Warden Supervisor. No other region in the state had a game warden supervisor. The regional wildlife supervisor supervised the wardens in each region. This would be a brand-new position in the state. They would create this position from the retirement of long-time Alpine game warden Dallas Jenkins. Bernie told me to keep this information under my hat because Wildlife Administration was only in the planning stages, and he was not sure that it would ever happen. After leaving Bernie's office and thinking about what I had just heard, I thought to myself *that sounds like a really cool job supervising the game wardens. Heck, I hadn't even become an official game warden yet with my own district, so I probably wouldn't be able to compete very well for the new position.* I really wanted to tell my buddy Brad about the new information, but I was told to keep it to myself.

Big Piney game warden Brad Hovinga and I had volunteered to assist with watercraft enforcement on Glendo Reservoir over the busy Fourth of July weekend. This would be one of the busiest weekends all year for boaters and recreationalists. Some years this reservoir would have over 30,000 people in the State Park during this weekend. A great share of these people would camp on Sandy Beach and party like there was no tomorrow. For some, there probably wasn't a tomorrow after drinking themselves to death the night before. It would be our job to patrol the Sandy Beach area and make sure nobody was operating boats while under the influence of alcohol. This activity generally occurred late at night after many drinks had been consumed.

Brad met me in Pinedale, and we hooked on to our 20' Lund patrol boat and headed for Glendo State Park. We were both excited to get out of town for a few days and see some different country and deal with some different type of people. We were travelling down the interstate between Wamsutter and Rawlins listening to music on the radio and singing along to some stupid song. I had my mobile radio turned down because I could never hear it very good anyways. I heard something muffled come over the mobile radio. Brad quickly turned down the stereo and turned up the mobile radio. He said, "Holy shit, did you hear that traffic?" I responded, "Hell no, do I ever hear it?" Brad said, "No listen, something serious is going on." Pretty quick the highway patrol dispatcher came over the radio. "Caution, we have a male subject at mile marker 198 on I-80 traveling towards oncoming traffic at a high rate of speed." I looked at the mile marker that we had just passed, and it read 197. I told Brad that whatever was going on was happening somewhere right in front of us about one mile away. We came up over a hill and I noticed a long line of semi-trucks stacked up in front of us, all in the right-hand lane and traveling about 60 mph. I pulled in behind the slow-moving semis. About that time a small SUV swerved out into the left lane in front of us to pass the semi-trucks. As soon as the car pulled out into the passing lane it was hit head-on by a small red car that was coming towards us at a high rate of speed. I heard a loud crashing noise and observed a small red car spinning to my left in circles towards the medium between the two interstates. The car that pulled out in front of us was now facing towards us in the passing lane. Both cars were absolutely demolished. There was shattered glass and pieces of car lying everywhere. I pulled off the right shoulder of the road behind a semi-truck and turned on my rear red and blue lights to warn other motorists of the wreck ahead.

Head on collision

Brad and I were both trained in First Aid and CPR. We felt like we needed to help wherever help was needed because we were at the scene and law enforcement officers. There was black smoke coming from the engine compartment of both wrecked cars. I could smell the odor of burnt rubber, oil, and gas as I walked through the shattered glass on the interstate to approach the wrecked SUV. There was no glass left in either car and both vehicles were almost unrecognizable. As I looked through the passenger side window that was broken out, I observed something that I will never forget as long as I live.

It looked like there were 4-5 people in the vehicle. Some of them were unrecognizable and I was certain that most of them were dead. I looked in the backseat and could see two young children in car seats. I didn't know where to start, I didn't know what to do!! Another woman came running up to the car and checked for a pulse on the female that was in the passenger seat. I stood back, she looked like a certified EMT with the clothes that she was wearing. She turned and looked at me while she was still checking for a pulse on the female and yelled, "Don't worry about the dead ones get the live ones out!!"

My adrenaline started to pump, and I jerked the rear passenger door open on the car to try and get the young kids out. One girl looked like she was about four years old strapped in a car seat. Her baby blue eyes were open, and she was breathing. I quickly unlatched the car seatbelt and scooped the little girl up into my arms. I didn't know if the car was going to catch on fire or not, so I was in a hurry. The next thing I knew I was standing in the middle of the interstate holding this young sweet little girl in my arms. She was limp like a dish towel and her breathing was shallow. I carried her away from the smoking car and laid her down in the grass along the highway. Her eyes locked on mine as I put her down in the grass, and then she quit breathing. I was trying to check for a pulse, I didn't know what to do. All I could think about was to get the other baby out of the car seat before the car caught on fire. As I was checking for a pulse, the female EMT looked at me and said, "If she is dead, help the others." I looked up and others including Brad were rescuing the baby out of the smoking car. I felt so helpless. Had this little girl just died in my arms? Was there anything I could do to save her? I wasn't even sure if she was actually dead.

After checking for a pulse for several minutes I could not find one. I noticed the life had gone out of the little girl's eyes and they looked glazed over and gray in color. I put my hand on her cheek, and it felt cool to the touch. I reached down and closed the little girl's eyelids with my fingers. Everything seemed like it was in slow motion. I could hear sirens in the background and sounds of police radios and people yelling. But it all sounded muffled and in slow motion. The pavement was hot. I could still smell the odor of burning rubber. I felt so helpless. I didn't even want to see the person in the other car who had hit this family head on and took their lives. None of the firemen or EMT's had even walked over to the other car sitting by itself in the medium. I looked over at the smoking car in the medium and the dead little girl lying in the grass beside the interstate and felt anger flow through my veins. I thought, *how could someone do such a horrible thing?* I looked over at Brad. We both had tears in our eyes. I said,

"Come on buddy, let's get out of here, looks like they have plenty of help now.

We jumped into my patrol truck, shut off my red and blue lights, and turned off the mobile radio. I looked over at Brad and we both just shook our heads and never said a word. It was a pretty humble and quiet trip the rest of the way to Glendo Reservoir. This shows you how quickly life can end for someone. To think that only a few minutes ago we were both singing and laughing to a song on the radio. Then having a little girl die in your arms only minutes later. I later learned from a highway patrolman that four people died in the car wreck. The only survivor was the two-year old baby who was strapped tightly in her car seat. What a horrible thing to happen. Who would raise this little girl? Everyone should count their blessings every single day.

I hadn't been to Glendo Reservoir for quite some time. I wasn't even sure where it was located or how close we were to the exit. Brad and I had hardly said a word to one another after dealing with the wreck. My brain was numb, all I could think about was the little girl dying in my arms. I looked up and read a sign that read Glendo State Park Exit 111. I just about ran off the road after reading this sign. The number 111 was the hospital room number that both my dad and grandpa had earlier died in. It was also the same number of the room where I had to meet with the psychologist Dr. Whyme to get hired with the Game and Fish Department. Now, a little girl just died in my arms and I'm turning off on Exit 111. What does this mean? Maybe it's all just a coincidence?

We arrived at Glendo Reservoir and stayed in a small camp trailer near the lake. The organizer of the law enforcement task force was the legendary Douglas game warden Rodney Leibert. Rod was a lot of fun to work with. He was a little older than Brad and I and had a lot of energy. He had a great deal of experience working watercraft patrol and had dealt with many folks in the past who were boating under the influence (BUI.) Rod was always in a great mood and had an unforgettable laugh that you could hear a mile away. He was passionate about being a game warden and worked many long hard hours during his career. Rod loved to put on a good feed and have a whiskey or two when off duty. And that we did. Rod cooked us up some tasty shish kebabs for dinner and we ate until we were as full as a tick.

Rod started laughing uncontrollably and said, "Hey, I heard a couple Cody game wardens are coming over to help because they got in trouble at a regional meeting and are being punished for their disrespectable behavior towards regional wildlife supervisor Gary Brown." Rod told us their names, I blew whiskey out of my nose and laughed out loud. These guys were veteran game wardens with 25+ years of service. They spent most of their time on horseback in the remote backcountry checking hunters. Rarely did they ever check a fisherman for their fishing license, let alone operate a boat. They were considered "High Country Rangers." Now they would have a full weekend checking boaters, drunks, and fishermen. I wondered if they would be wearing their cowboy hats while checking boaters. Rod laughed some more and said, "And guess what, Swerbe? I have assigned you to ride with them tomorrow morning on their patrol boat." I didn't even know they had a patrol boat. They must have borrowed one from another game warden. New game wardens or game warden trainees typically got assigned to work Glendo Reservoir over the Fourth of July. You were certainly being punished as a veteran game warden to get assigned to work Glendo over the Fourth. I knew both wardens well. I had worked with them in the Cody region several years ago when I started out as a Damage Technician.

Morning came and I met both veteran game wardens down at the boat ramp at about 8:00 AM. They were arguing with one another about who was going to have to sit in the boat and who was going to back the trailer down the boat ramp. They sounded like a couple of kids. I could tell neither one of them was very excited about being there for the weekend. They finally got headed backwards down the boat ramp. The trailer started heading hard to the left and the warden in the back of the boat yelled, "STOP, STOP!!" The driver mashed on the brakes and the boat came off the trailer and slid down the boat ramp and into the water. Thank God, it made it to the water, because I'm not sure how we would have loaded it back on the trailer. This was a very embarrassing moment to be wearing a redshirt among the other spectators waiting to launch their boats. Here, there were three game wardens who just unloaded a boat similar to how you would unload a dead moose out of the back of your patrol truck. Just open the tailgate, back up really fast, and mash on the brakes. Out goes the dead moose! Now, the two were yelling at each other. One of them yelled, "I didn't know you had unhooked the damn boat from the trailer!" The other one yelled back, "I wouldn't have if I would have known you couldn't back a damn trailer straight down the ramp!" If any other wardens including Rod could have seen this, they would have died laughing. Some of the best entertainment that I have ever seen in my life is watching a husband and wife try to back a boat trailer down a boat ramp and load their boat during a windstorm. Generally, the wife is trying to back the trailer down the ramp while the husband is shouting curse words, because she can't look in her mirrors and back straight. Meanwhile, the wind is blowing the boat sideways into the trailer that's only halfway on the boat ramp. By the end of it, they are both standing in water waist-deep trying to load the boat in the wind yelling and cursing at one another.

I grabbed my backpack that contained my citation book, binoculars, lunch, etc. and threw it in the boat. I then grabbed my portable radio and clipped it to my belt and hooked the mic to the collar of my shirt. We headed out across the lake and one warden yelled to the other, "STOP THE BOAT RIGHT NOW!!" The driver of the boat grabbed the throttle and jerked it back quickly. The boat came to a quick stop. The warden in the back of the boat looked at me and said to the other warden, "Look how stupid Swerb looks wearing that damn mic on his collar." He looked at the driver of the boat and asked, "Doesn't he look stupid? Swerb, put that damn radio away or we are going to have to take you back to shore and leave you there for the day." I laughed and put the radio away. I could see how my day was going to go with these two High Country Rangers.

We were soon gliding across Glendo Reservoir in our Crest Liner patrol boat that was missing about a quarter inch of fiberglass underneath from sliding backwards down the concrete boat ramp. Thank God, the engine had been in the upright position! We spotted a couple of shore fishermen up ahead. The driver of the boat gently nosed the boat into a bunch of large boulders that were on the shoreline. He looked at the veteran warden in the back and said, "Well, get out and check their licenses, that's what you are getting paid to do." The veteran warden got off the boat and headed over to check the fishermen for their licenses. As he was walking over to them the wind moved the back of the boat towards the shoreline. The driver still had the prop down and running. When the prop hit the rocks, it made a loud noise. The warden on shore looked back after hearing the loud noise and yelled, "YOU DUMBASS, YOU'RE SUPPOSED TO TAKE IT OUT OF GEAR AND RAISE THE MOTOR!!" The driver quickly shut the motor off and yelled, "QUIT YELLING AT ME IN FRONT OF THE FISHERMEN, YOU'RE HURTING MY FEELINGS!" I thought to myself, *oh dear God, this is going to be a long day.*

We headed on across the lake towards Sandy Beach. The beach had several hundred people sun tanning and drinking beer. I told the veteran game wardens that when I was on the Reservoir Crew doing watercraft enforcement, we had to write down all our contacts and write a law enforcement summary at the end of the summer. The driver of the boat replied, "Yeah, we had to do the same thing years ago, but these contacts aren't that difficult to get, watch this!!" He then honked the horn of the boat several times and waved to everyone on the beach, who were mostly pretty girls in bikinis sun tanning. He said, "Now, Swerbe, you count everyone who waves back and write that down as a contact." I was starting to see what I had to look forward to in the next 25 years.

We then headed out across the lake to check fishermen in boats. The driver of the boat looked back at me and said, "Swerbe, let me show you how to properly check a boat full of fishermen." He pulled up alongside a boat that was full of fishermen and trolling. Once the driver of the fishing boat made eye contact with him, he yelled, DO YOU ALL HAVE YOUR LIFE JACKETS AND FISHING LICENSES?" The driver of the boat yelled back "YES, SIR!" The driver of our boat looked back and said, "See, Swerb, that wasn't so hard." He mashed on the throttle and back across the lake we went back to the boat dock. He told us to back the trailer down the ramp since he was no good at it. I looked at my watch and it was almost noon, I guess we were done for the day. I decided to go back to the camp trailer and catch a nap in case Rod wanted to work all night arresting drunk boaters.

Rod put on another nice dinner and Brad decided that he and I should perform a foot patrol on Sandy Beach to make sure everyone was behaving. I was game because I had never done this before and had heard that it can be pretty entertaining. It was late at night. We were walking down the beach. Most folks had bonfires roaring and loud music playing. The Park Service had ramped up their personnel to make sure that everyone was behaving. This meant dogs on leashes and no fireworks in the State Park. I personally would never issue someone a citation for having a bonfire and shooting off fireworks over the Fourth of July. That's what the Fourth is all about! I don't think I observed anyone on the beach that wasn't drinking except Brad and me.

We walked past a camp with lots of people and a large bonfire blazing. I heard a girl yell, "HEY, ARE YOU GUYS GAME WAR-

DENS?" I looked up and noticed a beautiful blonde lady sitting in a lawn chair wearing a skimpy red, white, and blue star-spangled, banner bikini. She had a very nice figure to say the least. I replied, "Yes ma'am, we are." She said, "Why don't you guys come up and join us for a drink?" I looked at Brad and he just smiled. We both walked up the hill towards their huge bonfire. From the light of the fire, I could see that the lady was sitting next to her boyfriend and had her hand up the crotch of her boyfriend's swim trunks. We said "hi" and visited with them for a few minutes. The lady smiled and asked, "Would you game wardens like to see my boobies?" Before we could even answer, she lifted her bikini top and was proud to show us some of God's great creations. *God Bless America,* I thought to myself. I had never seen anything like that before. Brad and I stood there with our eyes wide open looking at one another. It was at this moment I observed a Park Ranger standing in the shadows of a nearby tree. He didn't look impressed. He stepped out of the shadow of the tree towards the light of the bonfire. He looked at me and said, "That is known as indecent exposure. I have been arresting people all night for this sort of activity." I replied, "It's certainly exposure, but not indecent. Are you going to arrest her?" The Park Ranger was not impressed with my comment, and I probably shouldn't have said anything. It just kind of came out. The Park Ranger smirked at me and turned and walked off into the dark of the night. I felt embarrassed. I looked at Brad and said, "I think it's time to make a mile!" He agreed. We got back in our boat and headed back across the lake for our camp trailer. The next day I heard a rumor that the Park Rangers were mad at the game wardens because all they did is walk up and down Sandy Beach and have women show them their boobies. This certainly was not true. We were just victims of an isolated instance with a pretty girl who just wanted to celebrate the Fourth of July.

The next morning, I was scheduled to ride with Rod. I had never worked with Rod in this capacity before. I had heard from other wardens that Rod was pretty gung-ho while doing watercraft enforcement. It was about 9:00 AM as we left the boat dock. Rod was operating the boat and had it running wide-open across the lake headed for Sandy Beach. We looked up and observed a jet boat traveling at a high rate of speed right next to a person on a jet-ski. The person operating the jet boat cranked the boat hard to the right to create a wake and spray the person operating the jet-ski. Rod shut our boat down quickly and grabbed his binoculars to watch the boats more closely. As he was looking through his binoculars he yelled, "That's careless operation, I bet they are BUI!!" This means (Boating Under, the Influence). Rod shoved the throttle wide-open and away we went across the lake in hot pursuit of the jet-boat. Rod kept yelling, "THAT'S CARELESS OPERATION, THAT'S CARELESS OPERATION!" as he flipped the switch to activate his sirens and red and blue lights. It took us forever to catch up to the speeding jet boat. We finally got their attention and they shut their boat down. As we approached the boat, I recognized some of the people on the boat. It was one male driver with four beautiful women wearing bikinis. One of the women was blonde-haired wearing a red, white, and blue star-spangled bikini.

We pulled alongside their boat, the blonde women smiled and yelled, "HEY, I KNOW YOU FROM LAST NIGHT!" Rod looked at me like he had just found his wife's panties in the front seat of my pick-up truck. I looked back at Rod and said, "I will tell you about it later." Rod looked at the operator of the boat and explained why we had stopped him. Rod then asked the man to remove his sunglasses. The man took off his really cool sunglasses. Both of his eyes were very blood shot. Rod asked the man if he had been drinking. The man responded, "I have only had two beers this morning." I asked the man if he got any sleep last night. He smiled and replied, "No, we actually watched the sun come up this morning." This meant to me that the man had partied all night long with no sleep and only had two beers this morning. Rod told the man that we were going to have to run some field sobriety tests on him to make sure that he was sober enough to be operating a boat. The legal limit of alcohol at that time was .10. Rod pulled out a portable breathalyzer test (PBT) and asked the man to blow into the tube as hard as he could. The man's girlfriend, who was the blonde in the red, white, and blue bikini, moved up next to her boyfriend. She put her hand up his shorts again, grabbed his crotch and said, "Just relax honey and blow into the tube." This was the damnedest thing that I had ever seen! The man took a deep breath, relaxed, and blew into the tube. He blew a .08 which was just under the legal limit of alcohol to be operating a boat.

Rod then asked the women on board if there were any of them sober enough to operate the boat safely back to shore. One girl said, "I'm sober, I have only had one beer." Rod requested the woman to operate the boat at a safe speed back to Sandy Beach. We followed the jet-boat across the lake back to their camp. Once we arrived Rod told me that he was going to sit in the back of our patrol boat and issue the man a citation for careless operation. He said, "Please keep everybody occupied and away from our boat while I issue the citation." As we approached the beach, everyone in their camp came walking over to see what was going on. I stood in the front of our patrol boat while Rod sat in the back to issue the citation. As I was standing guard, several women from camp came walking over to our boat. Two women were extremely intoxicated and blurted out with a slur, "Hey, we know you, you stopped at our camp last night." They kept asking me questions about what was going on and how much trouble their friend was in. As I was explaining things to them, several of them jumped quickly onto our boat. One of them grabbed my crotch and the other grabbed my butt as I turned around. The third woman grabbed my pen out of my front shirt pocket and waved it in front of my face. She said with a slur, "Hey, let's see if you are sober enough to be operating this boat." She started moving the pen slowly from left to right in front of my face. She said, "Now just relax and try and follow the pen with your eyes, this is called a nystagmus or horizontal gaze test." I couldn't believe what had just happened. I had quickly lost control of the situation and the women had all boarded the boat. I was spinning in circles trying to block the women from grabbing my privates. One woman slipped by me and was now in the back of the boat with Rod. Rod remained focused with his head down while writing out the citation. The woman rubbed his head with her hand and said, "How are you coming with that citation, Rodney?" I didn't want to have to physically throw the women off the boat. I finally got off the boat and they all followed me while Rodney finished writing out the citation. All I could do is laugh and apologize to Rod when it was all said and done. I laughed and thought to myself, *at least they weren't hostile*.

We ended up putting in another long day patrolling the reservoir. I was thankful that we didn't have to arrest anyone and spend the day hauling them to jail. We met back up at the camp trailer for dinner. Rod barbequed us some huge beef steaks and all the trimmings. We had just got a bonfire going and sat down to relax for the first time all day. Rod had his truck mobile radio set up so that he could hear radio traffic through his exterior siren speaker. His truck was parked near the bonfire when all of sudden a highway patrol dispatcher came across the radio and relayed, "ATTENTION, SHOTS FIRED AT GILLIGAND'S COVE ON GLENDO RESERVOIR. REPEAT, SHOTS FIRED AT GILLIGAND'S COVE ON GLENDO RESERVOIR. ALL AVAILABLE UNITS REQUESTED FOR BACK-UP." Rod jumped up out of his lawn chair, laughed and said, "Looks like it's time to roll men, let's go!" Some of us still had to put our duty belts on and prepare for the worst. Rod was in his truck and headed down the highway with lights and sirens running within seconds. I looked at Brad and said, "I don't know where we are going, but we better keep up!" Ready or not, it was time to roll. I drove as fast as I could possibly drive without running off the narrow winding highway that ran along the shore of the lake. I never caught up with Rod, but I could see him about one mile ahead of us and kept him in sight.

A short time later we rolled into Gilligand's Cove with lights and sirens blaring. I noticed a couple of highway patrolman vehicles and one State Park's law enforcement truck already in the parking lot. A short distance away, I heard shots fired and noticed a highway patrolman trying to wrestle down a large man. The man had a pistol and was firing it in the air as the patrolman was trying to wrestle his arm down and retrieve his pistol. Brad and I took off running that direction. By the time we arrived, the highway patrolman had recovered the man's pistol, and they were arguing and yelling loudly at one another. The man appeared to be intoxicated. His speech was slurred when he yelled at the patrolman, and he was having a hard time standing upright. The patrolman was pointing his finger in the man's chest and yelling loudly at him face to face causing the man to walk backwards. All the other law enforcement officers had their pistols drawn and pointed at the man. I wasn't sure what was going on. Why hadn't they arrested the man? The highway patrolman turned and walked away from the man with his fists clenched. I could tell he was very upset with the man and wanted to punch him. As the patrolman walked away from the man, the man started to charge the highway patrolman from behind. I quickly stepped in between the two men and tried to calm the man down before things got really ugly. I asked the patrolman to step back and please let me visit with the man. A couple other officers grabbed the patrolman and ushered him away from us. God had blessed me with great interpersonal skills, and it was time to use them. I looked the man in the eye and told him very calmly that I was not there to hurt or harm him, but he needed to calm down and tell me exactly what had just happened. The man started crying and told me he wanted to kick the highway patrolman's ass. I told the man that the only ass that was going to get kicked would be his, if he didn't knock his shit off. I said, "Look around, the only person who is not armed is you!" The man sat down on the ground and started crying even harder. I knelt on one knee in front of him and told him that everything was going to be alright, if he could just stay calm. Once the man had his crying under control I whispered, "Hey bud, tell me what just happened?"

The man pointed to the north and said, "See that large camp of Hispanic people over there. They moved their camp right in on top of mine. They got in late last night and kept us up all night with their loud music and partying. I asked them nicely to either move their camp or turn down their loud music. Tonight, they started playing their music loud again. I asked the man to please turn his music down. He flipped me off and yelled "F--- YOU" and turned his music on high blast. I lost my patience with them, grabbed my pistol, and fired it in the air a few times. They reported me to the cops and told them that I was trying to kill them. I would never kill anyone. I just wanted them to turn their damn music down." The man went on to say, "I was so upset that I went back to my camp and had a few drinks. I walked back over to fire my pistol in the air again when the cops all showed up. The patrolman started yelling and screaming at me to drop my pistol. I got so upset that I accidentally pulled the trigger and fired another shot or two into the air. That is when the patrolman charged me and took my pistol away." I explained to the man that I could understand why he was so upset, but there were probably some better options out there on how he could have handled the situation. The man agreed and apologized for his actions. I also told the man that he was damn lucky that he didn't get shot by law enforcement or someone from the Hispanic camp. He replied, "Yeah, I suppose that wasn't the smartest thing that I have ever done."

About that time the patrolman came walking back over to us and started yelling and screaming at the man again. The man jumped up and was on the fight again. I looked at the patrolman and asked him to please give me a moment with the man. The patrolman agreed, turned, and walked away. I finally was able to get the man calmed down again. I told the man that more than likely he would be arrested and brought in for questioning if the camp of Hispanics wanted to press charges against him. The man said, "I understand. Just keep that damn patrolman away from me." I told him that I would see what I could do. I then visited with another highway patrolman and explained the situation to him. He agreed that if the man was arrested, he would be the one to arrest him. I thanked him, shook his hand, and headed back to my patrol vehicle. As I was almost back to my truck, I stopped and turned around. I could see that the man was being arrested and he appeared to be complying with the other patrolman.

Once we returned to our camp, we stoked up the bonfire and poured a whiskey. We all sat around the fire and discussed what had just happened. Rod started laughing in a loud tone and said, "Damn Swerb, what did you say to that man to get him calmed down like that?" I smiled and replied, "I told the man that if he didn't calm down and knock his shit off, that I was going to sic the biggest, and meanest game warden in the state on him and his name was Rod Leibert. I think that was the loudest that I had ever heard Rod laugh!!

Chapter 8

Night Crawlers, Chukars, and Football

South Pinedale game warden Dennis Almquist and I were sitting in the break room at the Pinedale office enjoying a fresh cup of coffee and telling stories. Office manager Des Brunette stepped into the room and said, "I have a gentleman at the front desk who would like to speak to a game warden." Dennis kind of squinched his eyes and whispered, "What the hell does he want?" Des smiled and said, "I don't know. Why don't you go ask him?" Dennis got up slowly, as if he really didn't want to talk to anyone at that moment and headed for the front desk. The man at the front desk had a deep voice and I could overhear their conversation back in the breakroom. The man stated with a loud voice, "I would like to report some sonsabitches fishing with worms down on the state section on the New Fork River by the airport!" Heck that is right where I lived! It was tough to access the state section due to all the private property surrounding the state section. Dennis replied to the man, "Heck, that's artificial flies and lures only down in that area." The man said, "Yeah, I know. I was floating my drift boat with a client when we observed two people standing on shore fishing with worms." Dennis replied, "How in the hell did they get into that area without floating the river?" The man replied, "They landed a damn helicopter down there in the tall willers!" I thought to myself, *who in the hell would have enough money to fly their own heli-*

copter down to the New Fork River and fish with worms from the shore? This was considered a blue-ribbon fishery from local outfitters and guides, and nobody fished this stretch of water with worms!

Dennis stepped back into the break room and said, "I guess I got to run down to the New Fork River and deal with a couple guys fishing with some damn worms. Sounds like they flew a damn helicopter down there and landed in the tall willows somewhere?" I asked Dennis if he would like me to jump in my truck, follow him down there, and give him a hand. Dennis threw both his hands in the air and said, "Hell, I don't care, if you don't have anything better to do?" I told Dennis that I was headed home to eat some lunch anyways, so it wasn't out of my way. Dennis replied, "Well, I don't know what the hell we are going to find, but I guess we can run down there and check it out." I replied, "Heaven forbid someone use a damn night crawler to catch a brown trout. Maybe they will actually catch some fish!" Dennis laughed and said, "I hear ya, all these damn regulations we have to enforce, I'm surprised you can even keep a fish down there anymore. Pretty quick it will be catch and release only!" I jumped into my truck and followed Dennis down to the area. We parked on a tall hill over-looking the river. We both glassed with our binoculars for several minutes and could not locate any fishermen or a helicopter. *You would think that a person could see a helicopter parked down there in the willows somewhere*? We glassed and glassed and came up with nothing. Dennis said, "Well Hell, I guess I will put my hip waders on and head down there and see what I can find." I told Dennis that I would stay up on the high hill and watch for them. I also told him to grab his portable radio and turn it on. I would let him know if I located them.

By now it was a hot July day, and the mosquitoes were horrendous down by the river. I pulled my spotting scope out and mounted it on my driver's side window. I zoomed in and focused on Dennis walking out across a marshy bog about 200 yards away. He was madly flailing his arms at all the mosquitoes. I could hear him cursing out loud, "Damn mosquitoes, go, away!!" Now he was at a spot that would require him to walk through some open water to get near the river and willows. As I had him zoomed into my spotting scope, Dennis almost completely disappeared out of my sight. He had stepped into a deep hole in the bog and went almost out of sight under water. Pretty quick he came flailing to the surface, cursing, and swimming for the shore on the far side. I watched him frantically dog paddle before he reached the shoreline. Thank God, he made it safely, I didn't really want to have to rescue him with all the damn mosquitoes down there. Now, he was REALLY mad! I could tell that by his body language and distant cuss words.

Dennis disappeared into the tall willows and went out of my sight. About that time, I could hear a helicopter start up. It was revving its engine getting ready for take-off. The noise was loud, but I still couldn't locate the helicopter in the tall willows. The noise was coming from the area close to where Dennis had disappeared into the willows. I grabbed my shitty department binoculars and started glassing the area looking for a helicopter. Finally, I located a large spinning blade come rising out of the willows pretty close to where Dennis should have been. The helicopter was now above the willows and slowly headed north. I was really hoping that Dennis was going to catch up with them after everything he had gone through to contact them. Pretty quick, I could see a red shirt with flailing arms come busting out of the willows headed for an open meadow. It was Dennis trying to head them off and get their attention. I went back to my spotting scope and zoomed in on Dennis. *This was going to be good,* I thought to myself.

Dennis was now running full speed across a boggy meadow in his hip waders, soaking wet, covered in mosquitoes, and frantically waving his arms at the helicopter as they came straight towards him. Now, Dennis was standing in the middle of the boggy meadow with the helicopter hovering right over his head. Dennis reached up with his right hand and made several quick motions with his hand in front of his throat moving left to right. Dennis was sending a hand signal to the pilot to SHUT THE DAMN THING DOWN RIGHT NOW!! The pilot slowly sat the helicopter down in the meadow right in front of Dennis. The turbulence from the helicopter blade caused Dennis's hat to blow off. The helicopter sat there for several minutes idling down. I watched in my spotting scope as Dennis approached the pilot in the helicopter. Dennis was waving his arm at the pilot as if to say "GET OUT OF THAT SHIP, I NEED TO VISIT WITH YOU RIGHT NOW!!"

The pilot shut the helicopter completely off. Both he and the passenger exited and headed over towards Dennis. I wish I could have heard what was being said in the conversation. All I could see was Dennis's arms flailing around as he spoke to them. It looked like both men had handed Dennis their fishing licenses. It then appeared to me that Dennis was searching the helicopter for something. *Could it be night crawlers?* The contact only took several minutes, and Dennis was headed back towards my location. When Dennis arrived, he was soaking wet and had some mud on his face from falling in the bog hole. I could tell he wasn't impressed with the situation. As Dennis approached my truck I asked, "Well, how did that go?" Dennis replied, "Well, that was a complete waste of my time. They were both from California and had non-resident annual fishing licenses, and were fishing with hardware, not worms!! I searched their helicopter for night crawlers and couldn't find any. All they had was a tackle box full of black and yellow panther martin lures." That was my favorite lure! I always said, "If they aren't biting on a panther martin, you might as well go home, because they are not biting at all. I laughed and told Dennis, "Well, I bet they will never forget that contact from a Wyoming game warden, running out of the willers soaking wet in hip waders with mud on his face, waving his arms and yelling at them for fishing with worms." Dennis laughed and said, "Yeah, sonsabitches!! They will think twice about dipping a worm in my warden district. I'm going to head home and change out of my wet clothes." That said, he drained the water out of his hip waders and threw his wet portable radio on the front seat of his patrol truck.

I returned to the office. Des, our office manager, handed me a small pink slip with an address and phone number written on it. She smiled and said, "Here ya go, Swerb, got another call for you to go investigate. I replied, "What's this one regarding?" She laughed and said, "Someone just reported a game bird running around in their yard that is unable to fly. They said it looks like it may be wearing orange sunglasses or something." I blurted out, "ORANGE SUNGLASSES?" Des just smiled and said, "That's what they said." I grabbed the note with the address, shook my head and said, "Alright, I will see what I can find."

The address took me to a house in town on the edge of Pinedale. As I pulled up to the address, I noticed a man standing high up on an extension ladder painting the eve on the backside of his house. As I walked around the corner to visit with the man he said, "Oh hi, I'm the one that called the office and reported the bird in my yard. He is right over there under that pine tree." I thanked the man and told him that I would check it out. As I approached the bird, it ran away from me and hid under a thick shrub bush in the man's yard. It did look like it was wearing orange sunglasses or something. It also looked like a chukar partridge to me. The elevation in Pinedale was so high that you never observed chukar's, Hungarian partridges or pheasants. There just were not many small game birds in the area. Mostly sage grouse, ruffed grouse, and blue grouse. I also was not aware of any game bird farms in the area.

Chukar partridge with orange sunglasses

I chased the bird around the man's house twice. I nearly knocked the man off his ladder on one pass, trying to grab the bird as it ran between the house and the ladder. I hit the ladder with my shoulder as I pounced on the bird. The man yelled down to me, "CAREFUL, YOU ALMOST KNOCKED ME OFF THE LADDER!" I replied, "Sorry Sir, I got him caught though!" I looked at the small bird and it was indeed a chukar. It also had an orange piece of plastic attached to its bill that resembled sunglasses. Once I had the bird in my hand, it seemed healthy. It just couldn't fly. I didn't know what to do with the bird and I certainly didn't want to kill it. So, I carried it to the edge of the man's property and threw the bird high up into the air towards an open field to the south to see if it could fly away. The man on the ladder turned around to watch just as I released the bird into the atmosphere. The bird flew high up into the sky for about one hundred yards, then made a quick turn to the right and started flying right back towards me. The bird was losing elevation fast and was now flying towards houses in town. The man on the ladder started to get a concerned look on his face and yelled, "OH SHIT!" The chucker flew right over my head and smacked headfirst into the side of the house that the man was painting. The bird nearly knocked the man off the ladder and hit the house right next to the man's head. It hit the house so hard that it left blood and feathers stuck in the fresh paint.

I walked over to the motionless chukar hoping for the best. The chucker was dead. I picked up the dead bird and looked up at the guy on the ladder and said, "Well, that didn't work very well." The man replied, "I'm sure glad that I called for a professional who could come save the bird." I felt horrible and had no words to say to the man. I tucked the dead bird under my arm, walked back to my patrol truck, and threw it in the back. I later showed the dead chukar to another game warden. He told me that it was a pen-raised chukar and that whoever was raising them had placed what they call a "Blinder" on their beaks, so that they couldn't see anything and wouldn't fly away. Well, the "Blinder" damn sure worked, and the chukar couldn't see the house that it flew into! I guess I should have cut the blinder off before releasing the bird into the air. I returned to the office and Des smiled and said, "Well, how did that one go?" I replied, "Pretty good for about ten seconds, but apparently the bird needed glasses, because it flew into a building and killed itself." I never did find out who was illegally raising game birds in the area.

I was really glad to be back in Pinedale and have the law enforcement academy training completed and behind me. Having the academy experience would make me more qualified if a permanent warden district ever became available. At this time there were no senior game wardens retiring and the outlook for a permanent warden district looked pretty bleak. The feed ground manager position kept me plenty busy, but I was really wanting to become a permanent game warden.

Pinedale regional supervisor Bernie Holz called me into his office.

I was always nervous when I got called into his office. You never really knew if you were going to get a that-a-boy or an ass chewing, or maybe even both. Bernie asked me if I would be interested in attending an upcoming course in Casper. The course was titled Reid Interview and Interrogation. He told me that he had attended this training years ago and that he thought it was very valuable training. He told me that the course was 2-3 days long and dealt with how to interview suspects/poachers to determine deception. I told Bernie that I would be very interested in attending this training. Later that night I called my brother Wade, who had been a Deputy Sheriff for years and was now a Livestock Investigator stationed in Riverton, Wyoming. I asked Wade if he had ever attended this training. He told me that he had been through a great deal of training over the years, and this was the best training that he had ever attended. After visiting with my brother, I was very excited to attend this training.

Several weeks later I attended this training in Casper. WOW!! Is all that I can say! This training was absolutely amazing! Police officers and detectives interviewed people who had literally robbed banks and even killed people and were able to get these suspects to confess to their crimes. These weren't petty crimes. These were crimes that were going to send them to prison for a long time, and they confessed to the crimes! The process first tells the officer if the suspect is lying or not based on a few short questions. Combine answers to the questions, eye and body movement of the suspect, and you will know immediately if the suspect is being deceptive with you or not. Once you know that they are lying, you as an officer need to get them shut down from the lie and back on track with the truth. This is another process. By the end of the process, if you have done it correctly, you will get a confession and the entire truth out of the suspect. This process can take several hours based on the circumstances and the suspect whom you are interviewing. As a game warden, I will not explain this process and divulge any important information to anyone who wishes to poach animals or fish. All I can tell you is it works very well, and you should never lie to your local game warden, if you are ever in a situation of being interviewed for a game violation. Especially if the warden who is interviewing you has had this training! I couldn't wait to get home and try this on my young kids the next time I thought they may be lying to me. Hopefully I would never have to use these techniques on my wife for having an affair or something silly like that.

It was summertime. I was busy doing feed ground maintenance, purchasing hay for feed grounds, and fixing up our new home. It seemed like there was never enough time in the day to complete everything. I borrowed a friend's tractor and ditcher and dug new ditches in our nine-acre pasture so that we could irrigate and grow grass for our five horses. My property was at the end of the ditch. The previous owner never used water, so I had to fight with all my neighbors to finally get some water. I would just get all my dams set with a nice head of water and then the water would be gone. The neighbor below me was eighty years old and had been hogging all the water for many years. He drove into my yard one day and chewed my ass for messing with the head gate. I very nicely told the old man that I also had water rights and would like to irrigate my pasture and grow some grass to feed my horses. He yelled at me and said, "YOU LEAVE THE DAMN HEAD GATE ALONE, DON'T EVER TOUCH IT AGAIN!!" As he shook his pointer finger at me. I kindly told the old man that I was going to hide a spring loaded 2"x4" board in the grass next to the head gate and next time he bent over to steal my water the board was going to spring up between his legs and smack him right in the nut sack!! He looked at the ground and laughed, shook my hand, and replied, "I don't know why, but I like you! Use the damn water anytime you need some." He turned and walked back to his truck and left my property. We had an understanding after that conversation and got along fine after that.

It was Saturday morning. My son Wesley woke me up early and

asked if I would take him into town so that he could participate in the Punt, Pass, and Kick event at the high school football field in Pinedale. Wes loved to play football and was about ten years old at the time. As we were leaving the house my eight-year-old daughter Wendy yelled, "I WANT TO GO, I WANT TO GO!" This was supposed to be a father/son moment. I don't think I had ever seen my daughter even throw a football, let alone punt or kick one. She was wearing pink shorts with her cowboy boots on. I said, "Alright, if you want to go you will need to put some tennis shoes on so that you can kick the football straight and far." She looked for what seemed like forever, and she couldn't find any tennis shoes. Honestly, I don't think she even owned a pair at the time. Finally, she came running down the stairs wearing a flowery looking pair of girl shoes. The shoes looked like something you would do ballet or weed the garden in. They weren't Nike or Adidas, just flowery little garden/girl shoes. I smiled and said, "Alright, jump in the truck we are going to be late." Wendy screamed, "YEAH", as she ran 20 miles per hour towards the truck and jumped in. Wes looked at me and rolled his eyes as if to say, "REALLY DAD, we have to take my sister!" Wes was at that age where it was really important to look cool and not have his sister tagging along.

We arrived at the football field. It was full of young boys kicking and throwing the football around. I did not see any girls in Wendy's age class. We had about twenty minutes to practice, so I borrowed a football and showed Wendy how to punt the ball and kick the ball off a tee. I even spent a few minutes showing her how to properly throw a football like a man and not a girl. I had played football at the college level and even coached high school football for a few years, so I was very familiar with the art of kicking and passing a football. Wendy did really well for no more practice than she had.

It was time for the event. The sponsors lined all the ten-year-old boys up to start the competition. There were no girls, so the sponsor looked at Wendy and said, "Why don't you just line up with the boys and compete with the boys today." Wendy just smiled and jumped in at the end of the line that consisted of about ten boys. There were some really good male athletes in the competition. Wes would have to do really well if he was going to win the event. Wes had a great punt, a great kick and an awesome pass and would end up getting first place in the competition. I was very proud of him, and his total score qualified him to attend the regional competition in Longmont, Colorado. Wendy stepped up to the plate and nailed a beautiful kick off the tee. The football went end over end long and straight. She then threw a very nice spiral pass that went about twice as far as I thought she could throw. And finally, she stepped up and punted the ball. It went high and straight to my amazement. For an eight-year-old girl I was very impressed. Her total score ended up being better than most of the boys that Wes competed against. The sponsor walked up to me and shook my hand and said, "Congratulations Dad, that girl can play football." He also told me that her score was high enough to compete at the upcoming regional event in Longmont, Colorado. Both kids came home with a trophy and a blue first place ribbon. I had never seen Wendy so excited in my life. She wanted to go home and practice some more. Wes just rolled his eyes as if to say, "REALLY, now we have to take her to Longmont, Colorado."

I would spend hours each evening after work teaching Wendy and Wes proper techniques on how to properly kick, punt and pass a football. Wendy was very eager to learn and become better at every aspect of kicking and throwing a football. One evening I came home from work, and she was kicking piles of horse poop in the pasture. She completely kicked every pile of horse manure in the nine-acre pasture! Heck, I wouldn't even need to drag the fields and spread manure this year. I pulled up in my game and fish truck and rolled down the window and yelled, "WENDY, WHAT ARE YOU DOING OUT THERE?" She responded. "I'm trying to strengthen my kicking leg, Dad, by spreading horse poop!" I laughed and said, "Well be careful that you don't pull your groin muscle."

Both kids practiced every evening in our large backyard for several weeks. I really didn't want to drive to Longmont, Colorado for the next competition. But this was the first time that my kids and I had done something fun together. We were building a stronger relationship with one another all due to throwing and kicking a damn football around the yard in the evenings. The day would finally come when Wendy, Wes, and I were headed down the interstate to Longmont, Colorado. This was before GPS units and smart phones. Hell, I didn't even know where we were going, and I didn't make a room reservation for a motel room. I figured there would be plenty of available rooms in a large city.

We were cruising down the interstate in our brand-new black Ford truck with the dent in the passenger-side quarter panel from the Christmas tree excursion. We had the radio blaring with Wes sitting in the front seat and Wendy sitting in the back. Wendy would slowly sneak her hand over the back of Wes's seat and pull on his hair and ears. He would turn around quickly and yell, "WENDY, KNOCK IT OFF!" Wendy would giggle and tell him to shut up and then pull his hair again ten minutes later. They were starting to drive me nuts, but I guess that's what young kids do to their parents. We arrived in Longmont and ate dinner at McDonalds. I pulled into a gas station to fill the truck with Diesel and get directions to the high school football field. The football field was actually pretty easy to find, and I didn't have to deal with much heavy traffic. I just wanted to know where it was located because we needed to be there at 8:00 AM the next morning. We located the football field and the kids wanted to practice for a bit. It was good for them to blow off some steam after the long ride in the truck.

Now, it was time to try and find a motel room for the night. This proved to be very difficult. We stopped at about a half dozen motels and they were all full for the night. We finally found a very old three-story hotel in the downtown area that had a room available. The room cost me $40.00 for the night and the heavy-set gal working the front desk handed me a skeleton key to open the door to room 316. I hadn't seen one of these keys since I was a kid. We grabbed our duffle bags and lugged them up three flights of stairs. The stairs were made of hardwood and creaked with every step. There was no oil or stain finish left on the wooden stairs. The wood was worn down in the center of each step from where people had been walking the stairs for many years. There was also no handrail on the walls to assist you with climbing the stairs. What can one expect for only $40.00! We arrived at our room at the top of the stairway. The door was an old-style door with a single skeleton keyhole. I unlocked the door, but the door wouldn't open. After jerking on the door knob several times without success, I gave it a swift kick and the door flew open. The room was an absolute mess. There was one queen-size bed in the center of the room with a single light bulb and cord hanging above the center of the bed. The cord and lightbulb had a large spider web hanging from it. I flipped on the old-style light switch and the light actually came on. Wendy walked in the room ahead of me and screamed. She screamed so loud that it scared me. I said, "What is wrong?" She put her hand over her mouth and said, "Dad, look at the size of that cockroach on the bed." I said, "Oh Wendy, it won't take up much room." It did appear to me that nobody had stayed in this room for quite some time, or at least it hadn't been cleaned for a very long time. It also appeared to me that all three of us were going to be sleeping in one small bed.

Thank God, I had packed me a small bottle of Black Velvet. I would need something to help me sleep in this haunted house they called a hotel. We finally climbed in bed, and I clicked the single light off by pulling the cloth cord attached to the light fixture. All I could hear was heavy traffic outside and the sounds of police sirens. I heard someone pounding on a door directly below us on the second floor. I then heard loud arguing and screaming coming from people below us. I jumped out of bed and jerked open the door to our room to see what was going on. I observed a man beating the hell out of his wife/girlfriend in the hallway below us. He then grabbed her by her long air and drug her down the hardwood stairs. I could hear a loud *thump, thump* every time her head bounced off a hardwood stair. I shut the door and went back into the room and turned on the dim light. Wendy asked, "Daddy what are you doing." I responded, "Go to sleep honey, and keep the door locked until I return." I dug through my duffle bag and quickly found my .40 caliber Glock pistol and tucked it into my waist band in the small of my back. I looked at Wes as I exited the door and said, "Lock the door and don't let nobody enter, I will return shortly." Wendy started crying and said, "Daddy, I don't want to stay here anymore. Somebody might kill us in our sleep." I replied, "Don't worry honey, I will be back shortly."

I quickly ran down the wooden stairs as fast as I could. Any man that thinks it's cool to beat a woman was going to have a piece of me. I didn't care what the circumstances were! Once I reached the first floor, I noticed several police officers on top of the man with his hands behind his back and several officer's knees planted on the back of his head. The man was screaming, "F---You, you Mother F------s!" This may have resembled a George Floyd moment in time. The girl was beaten and bloody with a hotel blanket wrapped around her. I could see a female officer interviewing the woman in the background.

Apparently, this is what the police sirens were all about. Someone had already reported this man to the police. I didn't get close and didn't want to get in the way. Once I observed that he had been successfully apprehended, I turned and went back to my room. My daughter Wendy was scared as she watched me put my pistol back in my duffle bag. I explained everything to my kids and told them that the man had been arrested and would be going to jail. I told them to get a good night's rest as we had an important competition early in the morning.

We awoke early, I'm really not sure any of us actually got any sleep. All I could hear all night were the sounds of sirens in the night, dogs barking, and some roosters crowing somewhere down below us at about 5:00 AM. The kids wanted to get to the football field early and practice before the event. So, we skipped eating breakfast at a restaurant and just grabbed some McDonald's food along the way.

I watched the kids practice for nearly an hour. They were both doing very well with their punting, passing, and kicking. Wendy was doing about the best that I had ever seen her do before. The time finally came. Wendy was standing in line with about twenty other girls. Each girl would go one at a time starting with kicking the football from a tee. I was watching Wendy's competition as they all lined up to kick the ball. I knew in my heart that Wendy could out kick them all. The referee placed her ball on the tee and said, "Kick it whenever you are ready." Wendy took her time and walked around the ball on the tee several times. She then reached down and repositioned the ball to make it stand up straighter on the tee. This is what I had taught her to do. She stepped about five steps back and lined her right foot up with the ball. I looked out in the field where three referees wearing black and white shirts were standing. Their job was to mark the ball where it landed and then measure the distance of the kick. As Wendy was getting ready to kick the ball, I looked at how close all the refs were to her. I said to myself, *if you guys are going to mark her ball, you better get to backing up because she is going to kick it over all your heads.* Wendy ran forward and nailed the ball perfectly. It went high and straight into the sky end over end. I heard one of the refs yell, "OH SHIT!!" as he watched the ball fly way over his head. He turned around and ran as fast as he could to accurately spot the ball. Wendy had kicked the ball further than I had ever seen her kick it before.

Both Wes and Wendy (Audrey and Rusty from the movie Christmas Vacation, is what I had nicknamed them) did an awesome job that day in all events. I was extremely proud of both of them. Heck, Wendy ended up in first place which qualified her for State in Denver, Colorado. Wes ended up in third place and did an excellent job. Wendy (Audrey) made sure that Wes (Rusty) knew that she had won first place all the way home. She kept showing him her blue ribbon and trophy and asking him what color his ribbon was and where his trophy was? Rusty got aggravated with this behavior very quickly and the fight was on.

"YEA I KNOW YOU GOT FIRST PLACE WENDY, NOW SHUT UP AND LEAVE ME ALONE!!"

Wendy would sit back down in the back seat and hit him in the back of the head with a football until he would lose his patience again and yell, "WENDY, DANG IT! KNOCK IT OFF!!" It was a long ride back home to Pinedale, but a great trip with my kids, one that I will always cherish. Wendy was pretty proud to report to her mother Lana that she had won first place.

Shortly after returning home, I received a letter in the mail from the Punt, Pass, and Kick committee that Wendy had qualified for the State competition in Denver, Colorado. What I didn't know is that we would be receiving free tickets to attend the Bronco's VS. Chargers home game in September. Heck, I had never been to a professional football game before, and Denver was my favorite team. I told the family about it, and everyone was really excited to attend.

Wendy would continue to practice for a couple of hours every evening. One day I returned home from work and Wendy was out practicing her kick from the tee in a heavy rainstorm. She was soaking wet only wearing gym shorts and a t-shirt. She was crying and her face and legs were muddy. I asked her what was wrong. She replied, "Dad, I pulled my groin muscle kicking horse poop yesterday in the pasture and my leg is killing me. I can't even kick the ball straight, or far anymore!" I will never forget the tears streaming down her little muddy cheeks that cold rainy day. I told her to take a rest for a while and to go into the house and warm up. She just cried and said, "But Dad, I just want to win!" I told her she would be fine, but she needed to rest her injured leg.

Wendy continued practicing and practicing every night after school for several weeks. The day finally came, and we were loaded up and headed to Denver, Colorado to watch our first ever professional football game. We were even escorted into the large parking area and given a parking spot right next to the playing field. I had never seen so many tailgate parties in all my life. People painted in orange, white and blue looked like they had been drinking heavily since the early morning hours. There were little George Foreman grills flaming up everywhere cooking brats, hotdogs, and hamburgers. The smell of all the barbeque grills burning all at once was a smell to remember. It made me hungry and want to have a cold beer. We were soon escorted out onto the playing field. We got the pleasure of walking right through all of the Denver Bronco players as they were stretching and warming up. I couldn't believe how big some of these guys actually were once I was standing next to them. It was a huge honor for me to just be walking on the same field with all the professional players. The stadium was nearly empty at this time as we were there several hours early. Pretty quick a beautiful blonde women came riding up to us on her beautiful white horse. This was the Denver Broncos' mascot. The beautiful lady whom I had seen on my television screen many times at home circling the football field before each game. She observed my daughter Wendy, who was holding her Denver Bronco football. The lady smiled and asked Wendy if she was in the Punt, Pass, and Kick competition. My daughter had a huge smile and replied, "Yes I am. Nice looking horse!" The lady smiled, shook Wendy's hand from atop the horse and said, "Good Luck Girl" as she rode off through all of the players on the field.

My daughter was on cloud nine and so was I. I could envision my daughter being the next Denver Bronco mascot lady someday. She would be riding her beautiful white horse with her long thin blonde hair waving in the wind behind her, as she ran laps around the football field. About the time that I was having this daydream, Lana elbowed me in the ribs and said, "I can't believe what an ugly horse she is riding." I said, "Honey, that horse is beautiful." Lana replied, "Look how short the nose and ears are on that horse, and it kind of has a pot belly." I said, "Oh honey, you don't know what you are talking about." I think Lana did know what she was talking about. I was probably more focused on what was sitting in the saddle than the length of the horse's ears and nose.

We slowly worked our way across the football field over to an area where the kids could practice their punt, pass, and kick. Wendy was actually more focused than I thought she would be with all the distractions going on. She quickly made friends with several other girls who she would be competing against. At one point in time, I noticed that Wendy was showing another girl how to better kick the football off the tee. The girl stepped back and nailed the ball. As the ball was flying through the air, the girl gave Wendy a hug and said, "Thank you so much for all your help, Wendy, I can kick much better now." I eased over to Wendy and whispered in her ear, "Wendy, you don't need to show your competition all of your secrets." Wendy laughed and said, "Oh Yeah Dad, I didn't think about that."

The competition was about to begin. I noticed several other girls who would be very competitive against Wendy. I pulled Wendy aside and gave her a father/daughter prep talk. I told her not to be nervous even though there would be thousands of people watching her. I told her to make sure that everything was perfect before she kicked the ball from the tee. I said, "Wendy, make sure the ball is placed perfectly on the tee before you kick it, just like we trained." Wendy said, "Yes, Dad, Yes, Dad, Yes, Dad!" The time finally came, and all the girls were all in line for the competition during the half time show. The referee placed the ball on the tee for Wendy to kick. I was as nervous as a freshman boy asking a senior girl to prom in front of her parents.

Wendy stepped back to kick the ball. She started running towards the ball to kick it and suddenly stopped dead in her tracks before kicking the ball. I thought, *oh dear God, what is she doing now?* She then walked out in front of the ball about five feet and sat down Indian style on the football field and stared at the ball. She sat there for a few minutes in front of thousands of people. I thought, *that's my daughter.* She then slowly got up and walked towards the ball and moved it just a tiny little bit. She walked back out in front of the ball sat down again and stared at it. Then she got up and walked to the other side of the ball to kick it. The ref blew his whistle and Wendy ran forward and booted that ball as far as I had ever seen her kick it before. Her distance was farther than any other girl in that competition. She then stepped up and made one of the most beautiful passes that I had ever seen her throw before. The pass was a nice tight spiral that flew straight as an arrow. The crowd cheered, and cheered loud! I pulled Wendy aside and told her what a wonderful job she was doing. I also told her that she would need to punt the football farther than she had ever punted it before. I gambled and told her to kick the end of the ball and not the center of the ball. When she kicks the center of the ball it generally just goes high and not very far. She stepped up and booted the football end over end. It wasn't a beautiful spiral, but it went long and far. The crowd cheered. I think Wendy had done a fantastic job.

The judges finally got all the scores tallied. Wendy had won first place in the competition. They placed her medal around her neck on national television and announced her as Wendy Werbelow from Pinedale, Wyoming for all to see. She was even on the big overhead screen accepting her medal. This was one of my proudest father days ever. This was something that Wendy wanted to do, and she excelled at it. I think the Denver Broncos lost that day, but what else is new. Wendy's total combined score fell two inches short from qualifying her for the national punt, pass, and kick competition. This was truly a great experience for all of us and a moment that I will never forget. I still remember that Saturday morning when Wendy came running out of her bedroom wanting to go with Wes and I to the local Pinedale punt, pass, and kick competition. I could have easily told Wendy "No" that morning, that this was a father/son event. So, for you fathers out there, don't ever tell your daughter no. You never know what someone is truly capable of when they put their mind and energy into it. Thanks for such a memorable experience, Wendy.

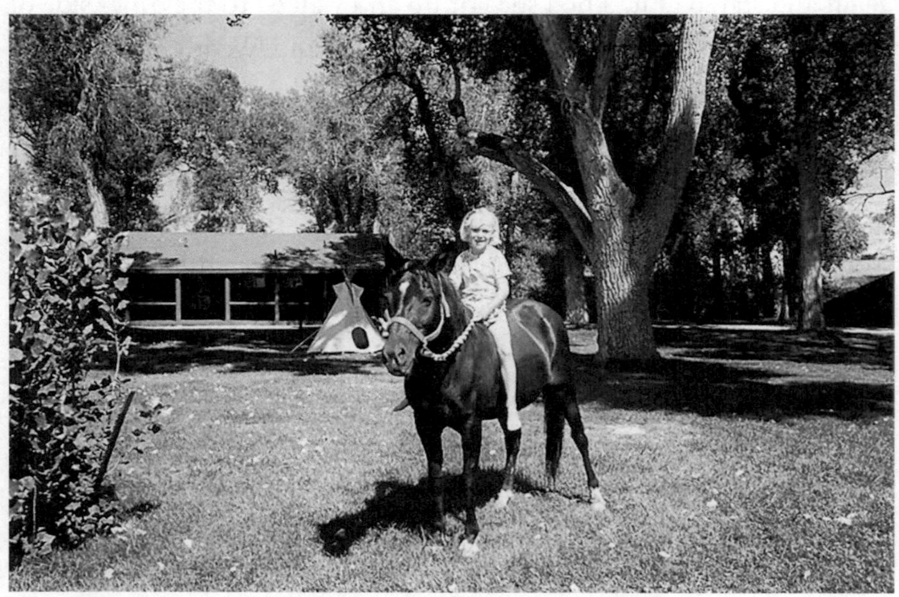

Wendy riding her favorite horse Foxy

Before I knew it, I was back in Pinedale. Back at work and dealing with the daily grind of making sure all the hay was successfully hauled into all the feed grounds prior to winter setting in. I still had many maintenance projects to complete on the feed grounds and felt like I was running behind schedule with winter fast approaching. I needed to head up to the Green River Lakes feed ground to check on the road conditions and to see if the road was smooth enough to get a semi load of hay up there. The hay haulers absolutely despised hauling hay on this road. It would become so rough that it felt like you were crossing a cattle guard for about twenty miles. The hay trucks could hardly get their speed up to hydroplane over the washboard bumps. So, it would just be a slow and very dusty trip all the way to the feed ground. The hay haulers would charge the department almost double the going rate to haul hay into this feed ground due to the rough road conditions.

I jumped into my patrol truck and headed that direction. Once I reached the dirt road at the end of the pavement at the Forest boundary, some guy flashed his lights at me in the parking lot as if he wanted to speak with me. I quickly hit my brakes and came to a screeching halt at the end of the pavement. The man jumped out of his old beat-up Ford with a rusty colored stock rack and headed over to my patrol truck. He reached out and shook my hand and introduced himself to me. I had never met this man before, but he lived nearby. He asked me if I had ever met the Crazy Mountain Man of the Upper Green River. I told the man that I had not. He laughed and shook his head and said, "Well, that's probably a good thing, the guy is bat shit crazy and lives just across the river from here." The man went on to tell me that this mountain man was known as Wild Bill to the locals. Wild Bill had apparently built his own log cabin by hand and by himself. The man cut, slid, and peeled all of the logs for his cabin in the nearby area. He evidently had a long gray beard with shoulder length gray hair and wore his hand made rawhide clothes daily. The rawhide clothes were made of deer and elk hides. The mountain man had used the brains of animals to tan his fine hides and make clothes out of them. He even made his own pair of moccasins out of rawhide and wore them daily.

I visited with the man for a while and asked him why he was telling me all this information about Wild Bill. He said, "Don't you dare ever mention my name to him or that crazy bastard will burn down my home and maybe even kill my family." He said, "The reason that I'm talking to you is that I just observed him pick up a road-kill deer and load it into his truck and haul it down to his cabin. He picks up roadkill all the time to feed to his pack of German shepherd dogs that are picketed all around his property. He doesn't have a driver's license or vehicle insurance and rarely makes it to town." I asked the man where he lived. The man smiled and said, "Right over there in that cabin across the river." The man spit some tobacco juice on the pavement next to my boots. He wiped some spit off his lips with his right hand and reached out to shake my hand. He said, "Pleasure to meet you, young man, be careful with that one!" I shook the man's spit-soaked hand and told him that it was a pleasure to meet him as well. Picking up road-kill wildlife in Wyoming was illegal at that time. I would need to investigate this further. I turned my truck around and found the Mountain Man's driveway a short distance to the south. I headed down the steep driveway to a bridge where I could see the Mountain Man's cabin.

I decided to stop and grab my shitty department binoculars to see what I could see before continuing down the road. As my binoculars slowly came into focus, I could not believe what I was seeing. The mountain man was standing out in his yard with no shirt on. He was wearing a red handkerchief wrapped around the top of his head. He had an elk ivory necklace dangling around his neck as he split his wood with a double-bladed axe. He was wearing leather pants and moccasins and had a large Bowie knife strapped to his right leg. I could see German shepherd dogs chained up all over the property.

My final count on dogs was nineteen. I also observed a dead mule deer doe hanging on the back of his woodshed. This was probably the road-kill deer that he had just picked up to feed his dogs. As I sat there in the middle of the road looking through my binoculars, the hair stood up on my backside. I was already trespassing and what if the Mountain Man looked up to see the game warden watching him from across the river? Half of me said, "Just drive down there and introduce yourself." The other half of me said, "Every one of those German shepherd dogs would rather eat a fresh warm game warden over a cold roadkill deer any day." And if the dogs didn't kill me, Wild Bill might! I decided to back out of the situation and head back towards Green River Lakes. I would meet with North Pinedale game warden, Duke Early, in the morning and see what he knew about Wild Bill the Mountain Man.

Chapter 9

Game Warden Supervisor, Wolves, and Twin Towers

It was March of 2000. Regional Wildlife Supervisor Bernie Holz had called me into his office to update him on my work with getting "No Human Presence Closures" implemented on all the elk feed grounds. I was nervous because there were several feed grounds that I was not able to get through all the governmental red tape and get actual human presence closures in place. I knocked on Bernie's door. I heard his voice say, "Enter." I opened the door and Bernie pushed his antique oak chair with steel wheels back towards the wall. He said, "Come on in, Swerb, sit down." This always made me nervous because sometimes Bernie would let you sit down and then he would just sit and stare into your eyes until you said something really stupid. Which I was really good at. I quickly updated Bernie on all of the feed ground closures. He just stared at me for several seconds and responded, "AHA." He then looked up at the ceiling and moved his eyes left and right as if he was in deep thought. I thought to myself, *Oh Boy, here we go!!* Bernie then pulled a Cuban cigar out of his left front pocket of his red shirt and licked the end of it. He placed it in his mouth and said, "Wildlife Administration has approved the Pinedale/Jackson region for a new position titled Game Warden Supervisor. This position will supervise all the game wardens in the region. We are going to start advertising for the position soon. Do you have any thoughts about this position, or who would be the best candidate for the position?"

I couldn't believe what I had just heard. The region was going to hire a new position that would supervise all the game wardens. My wheels started turning in my head. I thought to myself, *God, I wish I was qualified for this position. This would be like my dream job. I also thought, would this position also supervise myself since I was technically a feed ground manager/game warden? Would I end up with a new boss?* I thought for a few moments, I probably even looked up at the ceiling for a while with no cigar in my mouth. I responded, "Bernie, what do you think about the position and who do you think would be a good candidate?" Bernie responded, "I think it will be a useful position in the region. I currently am dealing with too many issues in the Jackson region to keep up with. This would free my schedule up more to deal with some of the bigger issues going on in Jackson. I don't have a feel for who would be the best candidate for the position, but my guess is that it will be a very popular position that will attract some very qualified candidates from across the state." I told Bernie that I agreed with him on that and that I was looking forward to working with whomever they chose to hire. We visited for a few more minutes and was interrupted by a phone call that Bernie had to take from Wildlife Administration. Bernie looked at me and said, "I better take this call, it's Cleveland. I knew any call from Cleveland was always important, so I quickly stepped out of Bernie's office and closed his door. My wheels were really spinning. I really wanted to apply for this new position, but I hadn't even become an official game warden with my own district yet. So, they probably wouldn't even consider me. *Besides I was way too young to become a supervisor this early in my career.*

Many of the wardens in the Jackson/Pinedale region were getting ready to retire at this point in their careers and didn't want to take on a supervisor's position. I did visit with South Pinedale game warden, Dennis Almquist. He told me that he had put a great deal of thought into the position and was going to apply for it. I was happy for Dennis and wished him the best of luck. He replied, "Hell that will up my retirement salary if I can handle that position for three years, but I don't know if I want to be a damn supervisor."

Time flew by quickly. The next thing I knew after reading an email one day, was that they had selected Glenrock game warden Scott Edberg for the position as the new Jackson/Pinedale game warden supervisor. Dennis was a little upset that he wasn't selected for the position, but he and Edberg were pretty good friends and Dennis was excited to work for him. I had only met Edberg at the annual Game Wardens Association banquet. He seemed like a nice guy with lots of energy. He was also very involved with the Game Wardens Association.

Edberg soon showed up and purchased a nice place out on Pole Creek. He was able to purchase this place just before the oil boom. I think this might have been the last affordable house in the county at that time. I was excited to meet Mr. Edberg and looked forward to working with him and the Jackson/Pinedale game wardens. It turned out that Feed Ground Supervisor Ron Dean would still be my official supervisor.

I showed up to work at the Pinedale office early one Monday morning and noticed Mr. Edberg had his office already set up right across from mine. As soon as I entered the building I heard a voice yell, "SWERBE", how the hell ya doing, bud?" Mr. Edberg came running out of his office and gave me a firm handshake and pat on the back. He was very friendly and talked really fast with a loud voice. I generally could not understand the first three or four words of each sentence that came out of his mouth. He talked too fast for my brain to comprehend what he was saying, and I didn't hear very well even at a young age.

After visiting with Scott for a while, I really liked him and felt like we were going to get along just fine. Scott was a very social person with a high energy level. Over a short period of time, I learned that Mr. Edberg was very organized and on top of every issue that was going on in the region. He cracked a sharp whip and had high expectations of all the wardens in the region. Some of the senior wardens that were near retirement didn't appreciate his enthusiasm as much as others.

Scott Edberg, new game warden supervisor in Pinedale

Mr. Edberg awoke very early each morning and accomplished more work in one day than most could in a week. There were days where he would check fishermen in three or four different warden districts spanning several different counties. On these days he would put several hundred miles on his patrol truck. He did everything fast, including driving his patrol truck! I always swore that he was the only guy I knew that could start his truck, put it in gear, and hit the gas pedal all in one motion.

Elk feeder Tim Baxley, who had fed for several years at Finnegan and North Piney feed ground had decided to quit feeding elk and work in the oil field for a chance to make more money. Tim was working down around Farson. I remember having a beer with Tim and asked him how his new job was going. Tim replied, "I'll tell you, boss man, I work in a place they call Farson Hole. This place sucks in the winter months and sucks in the summer months!! I'm really getting tired of working no see to no see." This meant Tim would begin his day in the oil field before daylight and not get home until after dark each night. It was good to catch up with Tim. I really missed seeing this guy and listening to all his crazy stories. I never met a man in my life that had such a happy and positive attitude about life.

2001 was a big year with lots of changes. I had replaced Tim Baxley with Corey Norby to feed Finnegan and North Piney feed grounds. In March of 1995 fourteen wolves were released into Yellowstone National Park. This was a very controversial event. Some people wanted them, many local people did not. Wolf numbers increased much faster and higher than any of the wolf experts predicted. The wolves also expanded their territories and started moving into the Pinedale area by the late nineties. As an elk feed ground manager, I was concerned how elk and wolves would interact on the elk feed grounds when the wolves showed up. The first report of wolves that I received was from elk feeder Ross Copeland on Bench Corral feed ground. Locals call this feed ground "Muddy feed ground." Ross called me one morning during a terrible blizzard. He said he arrived on the feed ground and observed three wolves (2 gray and 1 black) move approximately six hundred elk to the north. He was not sure if they had killed any elk or not as he could not see very well in the blizzard conditions. But he did say that all the elk were gone, and he was not sure where they had gone. I was concerned that the elk would end up on a private ranch to the north near Peterson Hill and would eventually end up in haystacks and cattle feedlines on the Cottonwood Ranch. I was also concerned about the elk co-mingling with cattle in the area and transmitting brucellosis to the cattle. I told Ross that I would grab my snow machine and head that way.

The blizzard conditions were horrible, I could barely see the highway between Daniel and Big Piney. I drove right by the turn off into Bench Corral. I would need to unload my snow machine near the highway and take it about four miles to the north. Once on my snow machine I was in a complete ground blizzard. I could not see the trail into the feed ground, but I knew what direction it was, so I blindly blasted through the drifted snow and headed north. Once I arrived at the feed ground, the elk were all gone but I could see a large swath of elk tracks in the snow, and they were headed north. When elk panic, they get in a tight bunch and move together in a herd. This swath of elk tracks was about thirty yards wide winding through the deep snow. The wind was blowing so hard that I could barely stay on my snow machine. What I saw next, I will never forget. I came across a dead calf elk in the swath of elk tracks. A golden eagle was feeding on the dead calf in the blizzard. As I approached the dead calf, the eagle flew off into the blizzard and disappeared. The eagle had already eaten both eyes out of the warm dead body of the dead calf. The wolves had not eaten anything on the calf. The calf was hamstrung and bit in the throat area. I could not believe that this calf had been killed in a blizzard less than thirty minutes ago and an eagle had already found it dead and had eaten its eyes out that quick.

I jumped on my snow machine and continued following the elk tracks to the north. I traveled about one hundred yards and found another dead calf. This calf had ravens and magpies feeding on it already. As I pulled up next to the calf the birds disappeared into the blizzard. I noticed they too had already eaten the eyes out of the dead calf. This calf had also been hamstrung and bit in the throat area. My guess is one wolf had a hold of the calf's hind leg while another wolf bit the calf in the throat and killed it. The wolves had not consumed any of this calf as well. What really got my attention is how these birds could find a dead animal in a blizzard that quick and eat the eyes out of them. What sense does a bird have to find a dead animal that quick in a blizzard? I continued north with hopes of seeing my first official wolf in the wild. Soon, I found wolf tracks in the deep snow, they were headed up a deep sage brush draw. I stopped my snow machine and observed the tracks in the snow. These tracks were the largest dog tracks that I had ever seen in my life. I pulled a pen out of my pocket and placed it across the wolf track. The track was wider than my pen. I left my machine and began following the wolf tracks up the draw. The snow was tough to walk through, and the wind was screaming. I walked around a corner and saw some movement in the sage brush ahead of me. Three black and gray wolves ran up the steep hill to my left. They were only about forty yards away. The thing that I will never forget about this moment was how big they were and how fast they ran up the steep hill. Imagine a Saint Bernard dog. These wolves were larger and faster. It was a sight that I will never forget for sure. After seeing the wolves, I decided to get back to my snow machine and get out of there before I got lost in the blizzard. The herd of about six hundred elk returned to the feed ground several days later.

I started receiving reports from other elk feeders about them observing three wolves on their feed grounds. What amazed me, is that the wolves wouldn't camp out on a feed ground with hundreds of elk to eat for the winter. They would chase the elk and kill a few of them and move on to the next feed ground. Sometimes they would completely consume the elk and sometimes they would consume very little if anything. The elk were used to seeing coyotes on the feed grounds but not wolves. When wolves would visit the feed grounds, the elk would get in a tight wad and leave the feed ground, sometimes running over ten miles away. The elk would always return to the feed grounds, but sometimes it took several days. Since wolves were new to feed grounds, the elk feeders would call me every time that they observed wolves on their feed ground. As near as I could tell based on calls from elk feeders, these three wolves were hitting 4-5 feed grounds in a week's time and traveling about 30-40 miles per week. They would make one big circle and return to each feed ground about once a week. Every time that wolves visited a feed ground, elk would ball up into a wad and leave the feed ground. The elk would be gone for several days and return. The wolves are opportunistic killers. Yes, they will kill the sick and wounded, but they will also kill whatever elk gives them the best chance to take down. Often, it's a calf that they can cut out of the herd and take down. Wolf kills can be very ugly, especially when a pack of wolves are involved. They typically tear the animal apart and take pieces of the elk away a short distance to feed on away from other wolves. I have seen elk legs spread out in four different directions. Typically, there will be blood and elk hair on top of the snow for about a 25-yard radius around the dead elk carcass. Coyotes are always near or on elk feed grounds. When the feeders don't see any coyotes around for several days, they know wolves are in the area. Coyotes will fall in behind the wolves and clean up the meat that the wolves didn't eat. Coyotes must make sure that the wolves have left the area, or they may be killed by the wolves.

Wolves really complicated feed ground management over time. Wolves displaced elk onto private property many times. This caused cattle producers damage to their hay and put cattle and elk together making cattle more susceptible to contracting brucellosis from elk. For many years wildlife managers tried to encourage elk to stay on native winter ranges and not end up on the elk feed grounds. Managers did this by implementing habitat improvement in areas that could hold elk off feed grounds and away from damage situations. At one point in time, many elk wintered out in the Gros Ventre Valley north of Jackson Hole and the Upper Green River areas north of Pinedale. Managers called these elk "Good Elk". Elk that spend all winter on feed grounds were considered "Bad Elk".

Over the years, interactions with wolves and elk changed on the feed grounds. Over time, elk quit leaving the feed grounds when the wolves would show up. Instead, they would find security in numbers and get in a tight ball and run circles around the feed ground. The wolves would make their kill or kills and the elk would not run off for several days and then return. After several years of wolves interacting with elk most of our "Good Elk" left native winter ranges and joined the feed ground or "Bad Elk" for security in numbers. This congregated elk even more on feed grounds, increasing the chances of elk spreading brucellosis or CWD (Chronic Wasting Disease.) There is still a huge push today from environmental groups in the Jackson area for the Department to end the feeding of elk. This is a very complicated and political situation that managers have been dealing with for nearly one hundred years.

Western Wyoming is deep snow country with very limited winter range for deer, elk, and antelope. The winter of 2022 was absolutely horrible. It devastated nearly all of the antelope herd in western Wyoming and over 85% of the deer herd killing hundreds if not thousands of animals. The elk herd did well with very little loss, due to the fact they were fed. I can only imagine how many elk would have starved and died in the winter of 2022 if the Department had not been feeding them. I can only imagine the damage situations that thousands of elk would have been in if it weren't for feeding them. Imagine that many elk co-mingling with hundreds or thousands of cattle with brucellosis concerns. I have always told myself that the only thing that will stop the feeding of elk is a disease that wipes them all out, or a federal judge who orders the Department to stop feeding. The national elk refuge in Jackson Hole Wyoming feeds 5000-10,000 elk annually right along the highway north of Jackson. If feeding of these elk were to cease, can you only imagine where all these elk would end up? Probably starving to death in the town of Jackson and surrounding sub-divisions. It would be an absolute nightmare to deal with. So, for all of you people and environmental groups out there that are opposed to feeding elk, be careful what you ask for.

The Gros Ventre Valley north of Jackson Hole has three feed grounds. These feed grounds were created years ago to prevent elk from starving and prevent elk from moving down the valley and co-mingling with domestic cattle herds. The three feed grounds allowed managers to spread the elk out each winter. Each feed ground may have nearly 1000 elk on feed each winter. Over time wolves would chase elk on these feed grounds. Elk found security in numbers and all the elk joined one feed ground. This caused the Department to have to feed over three thousand elk on one feed ground. Elk feeders could no longer spread the elk out and would run out of hay on one feed ground. They would have to move hay daily with a snow cat from one feed ground to another. This complicated feed ground management and the spread of brucellosis with congregating so many elk in one area. Wyoming game and fish personnel also spent hundreds of hours moving hay from one feed ground to another to keep elk fed daily and hold them in the Gros Ventre. Over time, the "Good Elk" that wintered out on native winter ranges in nearby areas joined the feed ground elk for security in numbers against the wolf packs. There have been some years where the wolves moved all the feed ground elk out of the Gros Ventre and elk ended up joining the elk on the NER (National Elk Refuge.) Over the years the NER has been striving to feed less elk on the refuge and eventually phase out elk feeding. Adding additional elk to the refuge has complicated their management plans over the years.

Snow cat operation hauling hay in the Gros Ventre Valley

Wolves had just recently moved the North Piney elk off the feed ground and sent approximately 600 elk to Bench Corral feed ground located over fifteen miles to the east. Again, I had to snow machine into North Piney to walk the draft horses out. This trek in the deep snow was 8.2 miles. In 2001 the wolves had also moved the Black Butte feed ground elk off the feed ground and sent them south and east onto private property causing damage to haystacks and cattle feedlines. Game and Fish personnel spent most of the winter moving approximately 600 elk through gates and jumps on an eight-foot-tall elk fence that spanned nearly thirty miles. Bait lines with alfalfa hay were often utilized to bait elk through fences and over elk jumps to get them off private property. In some cases, a helicopter was utilized to move the elk due to rocky terrain and deep snow conditions.

I had the pleasure to move these elk one cold winter morning with the legendary helicopter pilot Dave Savage from Idaho. Dave was one of the best helicopter pilots that I have ever met. We were able to get the last 150 elk out of a rock pile and head them for a gate in the elk fence. The only problem was that the gate was shut and snowed in with deep snow drifts. Dave hovered over the closed gate and told me to jump out of the helicopter and open the gate. After digging deep snow with my feet and hands for nearly thirty minutes, I was able to open the gate. I crawled up on top of the open gate and Dave hovered over the top of me and picked me up. We went back and rounded the elk back up and Dave successfully put all the elk through an eight-foot gate with the helicopter. This saved us hours of beating up our snow machines in the rock pile trying to move elk. That winter I called the head wolf biologist with the USFWS (United States Fish and Wildlife Service) and asked him if he was concerned with wolves moving brucellosis infected elk to private property and co-mingling with cattle. His response was "Scott, wolves chase and eat elk. That is what they do, and they are very proficient at it." I hung up the phone. The Feds would have no responsibility for the problems that the wolves were causing.

2001 was also a drought year. I could not find enough hay in small bales for all the feed grounds. Hay was selling for about $75.00/ton that year. I ended up in a pissing match with a local hay producer over the price of hay that year that forced me to buy hay in Idaho and the

Helicopter pilot Dave Salvage

Star Valley. I ended up purchasing 1400 tons of hay from Idaho and 600 tons from Star Valley. I had purchased literally every small bale that I could find in five counties. To completely stock all the feed grounds, I ended up buying large one-ton bales that would be fed with a tractor instead of a team of horses. This would be the first time in feed ground history that elk would be fed one-ton bales with a tractor. The large one-ton bales would be hauled to some of our mildest feed grounds that had the least amount of snow on them. These feed grounds would be Bench Corral, Soda Lake, and Muddy feed ground east of Boulder.

Muddy feed ground was located just inside of the Forest Service boundary. All hay on Forest Service Lands needed to be certified weed-free. I had met with Forest Service personnel to get permission to haul uncertified hay to the Muddy feed ground. They granted me permission to do so but misunderstood me and thought this was for the other Muddy feed ground (Bench Corral) that was located north of Big Piney on State Land. The landowner with whom I had gotten into a pissing match over hay prices, found out that I had hauled uncertified hay onto Forest Service Lands and complained to the Forest Service District Ranger. After several heated meetings, I was ordered to haul the hay out of the feed ground. This meant that I had to move 375 one-ton bales approximately 100 yards and stack them on private property with no hayshed and no stack yard fence. I would end up building a temporary stack yard fence around the haystack. At the end of the day, we still fed the elk uncertified hay on Forest Service property, as that is where the feed ground was located. I guess I should have just paid the landowner another $5.00/ton and not gone to Idaho for hay. At this point in my career, I was starting to understand politics.

Antler hunting was also becoming a bigger deal every year. The price of brown deer and elk antlers was around $10.00/lb. Antler hunters were scouring the winter ranges looking for shed antlers and moving deer around on the winter range. Many sportsmen came to the Game and Fish Department demanding that we do something about the harassment to mule deer on crucial winter ranges. I heard things like, "You guys need to have an antler hunting season. You need to have a limited quota antler hunting season. You need to charge for antler hunting permits. You need to close the winter ranges to all human presence." We had received enough pressure from the public that we had to do something. And in my opinion, it was a legitimate problem. Could we prove that antler hunters were causing deer to die from harassment? Probably not. But we knew it certainly was not helping the deer get through the winter by being constantly harassed all winter. About 50% of our constituents supported an antler hunting season and about 50% were adamantly opposed to regulating anybody or anything.

It was at this time that chief game warden Jay Lawson assigned me to an antler hunting committee to develop an antler hunting regulation. This would mean writing a proposal for an antler hunting season and taking it out to the public. Well, we did just that and the public shot us out of the water and opposed an antler hunting season. I had never been yelled at by so many people in all my life. Our committee worked on this assignment for over one year and completely got shot down by our constituents. At the end of the day, the Wyoming Game and Fish Department received an Attorney General's opinion that we had no authority to regulate shed antlers. All the work we had done seemed useless, and all we did was tick off the public.

Large replica mule deer rack at Jackson Hole's annual antler auction every May

Feed ground maintenance continued for me. Gary Hornberger had taken a job with the Construction Crew. I could not keep up with all the maintenance. It seemed like I would have it all completed for the year and a windstorm would come up and blow the roof off several hay sheds in one day. Heavy rainstorms would wash roads out, not allowing hay haulers to stock feed grounds with hay. Hay sheds, stack yards, feed sleds, feed wagons, and horse corrals were always in need of repair. I had complained enough to Bernie Holz, the regional wildlife supervisor, that they finally gave permission to hire another feed ground assistant. We also now had the new Feed Ground Management Stamp that generated nearly $200,000/year. This stamp needed to be purchased by hunters who hunted any elk that were fed on state operated feed grounds. The cost of the stamp was $10.00. We advertised for the feed ground maintenance position and interviewed several candidates. A man who had just graduated from the University of Wyoming with a Wildlife Management degree named Brian Baker received the job. I would spend the next several weeks orienting Brian to all the feed grounds and maintenance needs. It was a pleasure to have Brian working in the feed ground program and taking up some slack.

It was also at this time that we had hired an outside consultant to visit with private landowners to try and gain access on private property for hunting. We paid this man a great deal of money and nobody knew much about him. He was dark-skinned and spoke broken English. Some department employees thought he may be from India. I visited with the man several times and for me he was very hard to understand. He was a silver-tongued sort of guy who wore a suit coat and top hat. Some employees didn't care much for the man, but they didn't know much about him. He would meet with some of the larger landowners and offer them a contract and money for private land hunting access. The program would later take off and be known as the PLPW (Private Land Public Wildlife) program. This ended up being a great program for access to hunters on private property. Once we had these agreements, we could set our own hunting seasons on private property and use hunters to take care of our damage situations. Instead of us moving elk in December or January on a snow machine, we could use hunters to put pressure on the elk and move them back to the feed grounds. We would later develop walk-in areas and ranch rules for hunters. All the hunters had to do was get a permission slip to put on the front window of their vehicle and they could hunt all the land that was enrolled into the program. The landowners did not get paid much for access, but it was at least something. Many of these landowners ended up with no elk on their property causing damage to hay. This was a huge benefit in itself.

Then came a tragic day that I will never forget. The date was May 27, 2001 (Memorial Day Weekend). South Pinedale game warden, Dennis Almquist, had received a call from SALECS, our radio dispatch that a boat had capsized on Little Half Moon Reservoir. It was late in the day and Dennis was not close to Little Half Moon Reservoir, nor did he have a boat handy. The report stated that people may be drowning and need of help ASAP. Almquist quickly called game warden supervisor, Scott Edberg, to see if he was close and if he had a boat. Mr. Edberg was at his home on Pole Creek and had a small aluminum boat with a motor that was his personal boat. Mr. Edberg agreed to head to Half Moon Lake just as soon as he could get his boat hooked up.

When Edberg arrived at the lake, he noticed someone clinging to a boat while the boat was sinking. He also noticed someone clinging to a log with others assisting. He quickly reached the man clinging to the boat and rescued him. The man was very cold with hypothermia setting in. He was very close to letting go of the boat and drowning. It was later determined that Charles Tim Baxley had drowned a few minutes earlier. Apparently, Tim was on a camping trip with his mother and father-in-law and family dog over the holiday weekend. They had the boat loaded up with their camping gear and all their groceries. As they were headed across the lake to camp, the boat's motor died, causing water to come over the back of the boat. The boat started to sink. Tim jumped out of the boat and yelled, "Hold on, I'll be back in a minute." This was Tim and his "Can Do" anything positive attitude. Tim started swimming to shore and disappeared in the water about sixty feet from the shoreline. The Sublette County Sheriff's office, Tip Top Search and Rescue, Wyoming Game and Fish Department, and Forest Service officials all arrived at the scene. Tim's mother and father-in-law had been rescued, but no sign of Tim himself. Tim's body would later be found in about twelve feet of water. It was presumed that Tim locked up from hypothermia and drowned in the cold mountain water of Little Half Moon Lake. What a horrible tragedy. God took a good man that day.

Many Game and Fish Department employees attended Tim's celebration of life in Pinedale. Tim didn't want a funeral. He wanted friends and family to come celebrate his life, and celebrate we did! What a great man he was. Tim's wife, Patty, still resides in the Pinedale area today. A very sweet lady! As for Scott Edberg, he ended up receiving an award from the Coast Guard for his heroic efforts saving Tim's father-in-law on that terrible day. It just goes to show that you never know what you are going to have to deal with on any given day when you answer your phone as a law enforcement officer, or a Wyoming game warden.

I awoke early to assist Big Piney game warden Brad Hovinga with checking antelope hunters in area 88 north of Big Piney. I always looked forward to checking antelope hunters. You could actually see them miles away from a high point. As a game warden you could see who the shooter was, if they were shooting from a public road or vehicle and if they were wearing fluorescent orange clothing. You could see antelope and antelope hunters at any time of the day instead of just early morning or late evening hours. I loved early morning sunrises and the smell of sage brush, especially after a rain. I loved watching antelope in the rut. I don't think I have ever seen any other big game animal work as hard for a piece of tail, than a rutting buck antelope. I have seen them fight to their death and run does for hundreds of miles in a day, all to breed a single doe. I have seen a few men do this as well.

Tim Baxley with team of draft horses named Kent and Doug

This day was a beautiful blue-sky day out in the Badlands of Wyoming. A day where you might not ever see anyone else unless they were out hunting antelope. I had talked to Brad earlier in the morning to see where he was headed so that we didn't cover the same areas. He would be working just to the south of me. I was listening to a broken AM radio station because that's all that I could get in this remote area. I don't hear very well but I heard that an airplane had clipped the tower of a building in New York City. I thought to myself, *what a dumbass! Someone hit a tower with their airplane in New York City, it must be foggy there!* I drove a little further and a news alert came over the radio that someone had hit a second tower in New York City. I thought *holy shit, the same guy has now hit two towers with his airplane, man that dude is having a bad day!* About that time, I heard my bag phone ringing, it was Brad. I answered, "Hey ya ole Douche Bag, what's up?" Brad replied, "Have you been listening to the news?" I replied, "Yea, can you believe some dumbass has hit two different towers with his airplane in New York City?" Brad replied, "No some terrorists have just crashed a jet into the twin towers of the World Trade Center, it sounds like there are two different planes involved with two different buildings." I couldn't believe what I was hearing, my heart sank. I tuned to a different radio station that I could hear much better. As soon as that radio station came through, they were talking about another jet that had crashed in a field near Pennsylvania. Pretty quick another plane had crashed into the Pentagon in Washington DC. My heart sank, *what in the world was happening?* The date was September 11, 2001.

I listened to the radio the rest of the day and couldn't wait to get home and watch the news to see what had actually happened. After watching the videos of the towers crashing down, people jumping from the top stories of the building and people getting buried in rubble I felt very angry. *How could this have happened? How could terrorist be trained to take over huge jets and fly them into buildings in the United States? How could our security ever allow this to happen?* This event changed the world that day with trust. Look at what all of this has done to airport security even today. *Why did these terrorists do this to us, why did they kill so many innocent people that day?* This was the first day of my life that I felt so blessed that I lived in Wyoming and was out in the middle of nowhere when this occurred. If it hadn't been for the crackling AM radio station, I wouldn't have even known this had happened. God bless our firefighters, EMT's, and law enforcement personnel that had to deal with such a tragedy during those horrible days.

Chapter 10

A Dog Named Poacher

It was February of 2002. I had just returned from visiting my parents Martin and Diana Mayland in Mexico. I hadn't checked my work cell phone for messages in over a week. I turned my phone on and discovered that I had 17 voice messages. This made my heart sink to think of how much work I was going to have ahead of me after being away for two weeks. I clicked on the first voice message that went something like this. "Hi, Swerb, this is Hall Sawyer. Hey just wanted to let you know that while flying for a mule deer survey today on the Mesa south of Pinedale I observed some suspicious activity. I observed an older model yellow Chevy pick-up parked on a two-track road. There were two male looking individuals walking around out in the sage brush carrying military type assault rifles. I did not see any dead deer or birds in the area but wanted to let you know. The truck looked like a late 70's model Chevy. Thanks, call me if you need any more information." I looked at the date and time of the message. Shit, this message was left almost ten days ago. I felt horrible that I had missed that call. I called Hall immediately to get more information. Hall was doing a mule deer study on the Mesa to determine the effects of oil and gas development with mule deer migrations and numbers. Hall spent a great deal of time flying in a fixed wing aircraft counting and documenting mule deer locations in the Pinedale area. He was a great source of information and our eyes in the sky for poachers.

We had started a mule deer winter range task force in 1998 to try and catch poachers on the winter range in the Pinedale areas. This task force gathered game wardens from all over the state. We made sure that we had a warden patrolling the winter range every day of the month starting in November and ending in January. This was in addition to the Pinedale and Jackson wardens that also patrolled the area. At the time we were documenting around a dozen deer a winter that had been shot needlessly and their heads cut off for their large racks. Typically, these deer were poached in November while they were in the rut. The bucks were huge and dumb while in the rut. This area had a great deal of vehicle access on the winter ranges. Poachers could get in a remote area, roll down their window and drop a huge buck in a matter of seconds. Catching them was very difficult. Some poachers would drop a large buck in a remote area and drive off returning in the spring to cut off the head and bring it into the office for a Wyoming Interstate Game Tag. Once tagged the deer was legal for them to possess. They would claim that they were out antler hunting in the spring and found a winter kill buck. It would be up to us to prove that it had been poached. This is difficult after the dead deer had been lying dead on the landscape for several months and scavenged by predators. When a poacher shoots a large buck from their vehicle and drives off, there are no foot tracks in the snow and no empty shell casings to collect for evidence. At this point we had not caught any poachers while utilizing our statewide task force.

I drove to Pinedale to meet with Mr. Edberg to see if he had heard the report from Hall Sawyer. He had not heard anything about the suspicious people or vehicle from two weeks ago. We called Hall and received the exact location of where he had seen these people earlier. We thanked Hall for his information and jumped in Mr. Edberg's truck to try and find the location of where the older model yellow Chevy had been pulled off a two-track road. Even though this information was two weeks old Edberg drove like an asshole out to the location. I don't generally wear a seatbelt but decided to buckle up. We slid around every corner and as soon as the truck would straighten out Edberg would give it the onion again and mash the gas pedal to the floor. We arrived at the location. Thankfully it hadn't snowed much during that two-week period, and we were able to still see the tracks in the snow where the truck had pulled off the road. We attempted to find foot tracks in the snow but that was difficult because the snow had melted off causing bare ground in many areas. After looking around in the immediate area for some time we located two spent shell casings. I carefully looked at the base of the empty shell casing and discovered that it had been fired from a .223 rifle. This was probably the military style rifle that Hall had seen from the air. Questions starting racing through my head. Did these people actually shoot an animal or were they just out shooting their rifles? Heck, maybe they were just shooting coyotes, cottontails, or jack rabbits, which would be legal. We made a large circle and walked several hundred yards from where their vehicle had pulled off the road. I found an area that had more snow than the other areas. I was hoping to find some drag marks or blood in the area that still had snow. After carefully watching the ground in front of me I discovered something very interesting.

I noticed some small broken branches in a small sage brush plant. The closer I looked I observed a couple pieces of deer hair on the broken branches. I then observed some grass that had been trampled down. The closer I looked I could determine drag marks in the snow and dirt. After following the drag marks for a while, I found more blood and hair from a mule deer. Edberg and I spent several hours combing the area. We found more .223 shell casings, an empty Coors Light can, and some old foot tracks left in some mud. We also determined that at least two deer had been shot and drug whole to their truck. There was no evidence of birds scavenging on dead deer in the area or any deer carcasses or gut piles. I sat back and scratched my head and thought to myself, *these sonsabitches poached at least two deer and loaded them whole into their truck and drove off leaving no other evidence of a dead deer.* When you have no evidence of a dead deer, you have no bullet and no way of gathering a tissue sample for DNA testing. You also have no birds in the area indicating to game wardens that something is dead. I call these magpies, ravens, and eagles deputy game wardens because they show us where dead animals are. *Were these guys this smart? Did they kill large bucks and haul the entire carcass off? Where would they dispose of the carcasses? Would they gut the animals somewhere else to avoid detection?* These were some of the questions running through my head. I became very angry and could feel my blood start to boil. These poachers were the worst out there in my opinion. They were shooting large bucks on the winter range when the deer were the most vulnerable. Absolutely no sport or fair chase in what they had done. I was so mad at myself for missing Hall's call that day. Maybe I shouldn't have gone to Mexico taking time off from my job? Would we ever catch these guys?

Once we determined that deer had been poached, game warden supervisor Scott Edberg sent an email out to all personnel in the Jackson/Pinedale region to be on the lookout for an older model yellow Chevy truck. About two weeks later we got a lead that there was an older model yellow Chevy parked in a garage in Big Piney, Wyoming. I contacted Big Piney game warden Brad Hovinga and we agreed to meet and go look at this vehicle. This may be tricky to look into someone's garage without a search warrant and we certainly didn't have enough probable cause for a judge to sign off on a search warrant with the information that we had at the time. Brad and I finally found the reported garage with the yellow Chevy truck parked inside. The only way to look through the small window on the backside of the garage was to enter a yard with a tall wooden fence around it occupied by a large ferocious German Shepard dog. The large dog was barking uncontrollably and jumping up and down on the fence as Brad and I got close to the garage. This place was located in the middle of town. Neighbors would be wondering what the dog was excited about and see Brad and myself trying to peek through the window of the garage on private property.

I had an idea, I told Brad that I would move over on the other side of the garage and distract the dog while he snuck through the gate to look through the window. Brad looked at me kind of cross-eyed as if to say, "OH THE HELL, YA SAY!!" I said, "Come on! We have to move quickly." I ran around to the other side of the garage and pulled myself up on top of the fence to look into the yard. Once up there I yelled "HEY DOG!!" The ferocious dog came around the corner, located me and came at a full run barking and snarling as he jumped up on the fence nearly taking my nose off. I quickly jumped off the fence as the angry dog jumped up and down trying to clear the fence and eat my ass off. I was pretty sure if I aggravated the dog anymore that he would clear the fence and I would have to shoot an innocent dog in self-defense trying to protect his owner's property. This would make the newspaper and possibly get me fired. Not to mention I would have to write a report to my supervisor explain why we were trespassing in the first place.

I backed off from the fence and snuck around the backside of the garage to see Brad hauling ass back through the gate with an angry dog right on his ass. He slammed the gate shut just as the dog nearly bit him. Brad looked at me with wide open eyes and said, "Son of a bitch that was close!!" I replied, "Good job, is this our truck?" Brad replied, "I don't think so, it's too clean and it doesn't look like it has been running for several years, the tires are all low. Besides, I recognize the truck and it belongs to the mayor of Big Piney!!" I replied, "OH SHIT...THE MAYOR! Let's get the hell out of here!" So, I guess we struck out on that lead.

We had recently hired a new Damage Technician named Ty Huffman. Ty was a young strong man and dearly strove to be a game warden someday. He assisted us with moving elk to feed grounds on snow machines. Or hauling fence materials to landowners with damage problems from elk, or just whatever we needed on a daily basis. Several weeks had passed since we entered the mayor's yard looking for the old yellow truck. I had actually kind of forgotten about the case and had moved on to other things. Ty had been over in the Big Piney area moving elk off private property. He was traveling on his way home in the night after a long day when he noticed something interesting. There was an older yellow Chevy pick-up parked in front of a gas station in Marbleton getting gas. Ty immediately called me on the radio to tell me what he had seen. I requested him to turn around quickly and try and look into the back of the truck for deer hair or blood while they were paying for their gas. Ty said, "10-4, I'll see what I can do." I was excited, *could this actually be the truck and people responsible for poaching deer over a month ago?* I sat patiently in the driveway of my home waiting for a response from Ty on the radio. "GF-84, GF-116," I grabbed the mic and responded, "Go ahead." "GF-84 hey man, I was able to peek in the back of that truck and it's covered with deer hair and blood, over." I replied, "Copy, can you get a plate number and follow that vehicle from a distance to try and see where they are living?" "GF-84 copy that man! I got a look at the guys, and they look pretty shady. I'll see what I can learn." I sat patiently in my truck in the dark waiting for another call. It was about 8:00 PM now when the radio sounded, "GF-84, GF-116 this vehicle traveled south of Big Piney, and it looks like maybe they are living in a trailer court. I got their address and license plate number on the truck, over." I replied, "10-4, good work, let's meet at the office in the morning." Ty replied as if he was almost laughing, "10-4 Man, see you then."

I was so excited that we may finally have our culprits located. I called Mr. Edberg and told him the news. He was very excited and said, "Awesome, lets meet up in the morning and we can meet with the County Attorney and get a search warrant." I thought, *SEARCH*

WARRANT, I have never done one of those before, this could get exciting.

I could hardly sleep that night thinking about everything. How would we prove the case? We had no dead deer, no bullet, and no good tire or foot tracks! All we had was blood and hair in the back of some old yellow Chevy pickup truck. Hell, this could have been from a deer that they legally harvested during the fall hunting season. Ty did say that they looked shady, and there was two of them matching what Hall had told us earlier. We could take a DNA sample of the deer blood and hair in back of the truck, but we had nothing to match it to because I was too stupid to collect hair samples at the kill site. Now I would have to write up a detailed CMS (Case Management System) report for the County Attorney and try and convince him that we had enough for a search warrant. How would I remember all the details of the case since it had been going on for over a month? Mr. Edberg agreed to assist me with the report, and I was thankful for that. I hadn't dealt with a case like this before and had no experience with search warrants.

It took several days before we could get a meeting with the County Attorney. Edberg and I hiked up the flight of stairs to the top floor of the courthouse to meet with the man. I had never met him before and was kind of nervous to be honest with you. His cute receptionist looked up at me and said, "How may I help you guys today?" I replied, "We are here to see the County Attorney regarding a poaching case." She responded, "What is your name, and do you have an appointment?" I told her our names and stated that "Yes, we did have an appointment for 2:00 PM." She had a confused look on her face as she got up and knocked on the man's office door. She slowly opened the door and whispered, "I have a couple red shirts out here to see you regarding a poaching case. Do you have time to meet with them?" The man got up and greeted us at the door. He was a tall man wearing a nice suit and tie. He looked very professional except his gray hair was standing straight on end as if he had been running his fingers through it all day in a stressful situation. We shook hands and introduced ourselves. He invited us into his office to sit down. His office was cluttered with stacks of paper and law books stacked everywhere. There was barely any room for more than a cup of coffee on his desk. His eyes were blood shot and he looked stressed out to me.

We explained our case over and over to him and he acted like he was just not getting it. I explained that we wanted to search all outbuildings and vehicles. He ran his fingers through his hair and looked at the ceiling and said, "Help me understand, why, do you guys want to search the vehicles and outbuildings?" I responded with a frustrated tone in my voice, "Because they poached two deer, and they may have hidden the antlers in the outbuilding or trunk of the car that was parked in the driveway the night that Ty observed them pull into their driveway." He kept running his fingers through his hair and looking at the ceiling. Now, he had closed his eyes while rubbing his fingers through his greasy hair and said, "How do you guys know this is their address and not a friend's house? How do you know if the plate number comes back to who was driving the truck that night. It could just be the registered owner of the truck?" I assured him that there were some things that we didn't know but we were going to find out. I also assured him that we would not serve the search warrant if we got involved and felt like we had the wrong guys. He didn't want to hear any of this but eventually agreed to write one up and see if the judge would sign it. Edberg and I left his office feeling unsure about the whole situation. It was like he just didn't grasp what was going on. Maybe he had never worked wildlife cases before? We jumped in Edberg's truck, and I looked over at him and said, "I always thought you had to be pretty smart to be a County Attorney, but apparently not?" Edberg just smiled and had no response.

The judge did sign off on the search warrant. The next thing I knew Edberg and I were on our way to the trailer court south of Big

Piney. Our goal was to arrive at their house trailer at about 5:00 PM and catch them coming home from work. We didn't even know if they had jobs or not. It was nearly dark as we drove through the trailer park. It was eerie as we passed by all the different trailers. Most of them had broken down cars parked in front of them. Many of them had cars up on blocks with their hoods propped open. There were people peeking through their curtains watching our law enforcement truck drive by their house. They would peek and then quickly close their blinds or shut the door. This was definitely a low-income housing trailer park. Many places had large guard dogs like pit bulls and Rottweilers chained up with logging chains in front of their trailer. Dogs barked and hit the end of their chains as we drove by. Edberg didn't seem nervous at all. This was probably just another day for an experienced game warden and now a supervisor.

We pulled up in front of the trailer and the yellow Chevy truck was not there. *How long would we have to sit in front of their trailer before they returned home? Did we have the right guys? How would we confront them when they showed up to see a game warden's truck at their residence? Were they dangerous people? Did they have any warrants?* These were questions that were running through my head. I started thinking about my law enforcement training utilizing the Reid Interview and Interrogation tactics. *Would these people lie to us, and would we have an opportunity to utilize this great training?* We only had one name to go from and that was the registered owner of the yellow truck's license plate. I looked at Edberg and said, "Well, how do you want to deal with this situation?" Edberg looked at me and said very quickly, "Oh shit, they are pulling up right now." I looked to my left. They had parked right next to my patrol truck and were getting out of their truck and headed for the trailer. I jumped out of my truck and walked in front of the guy in the lead before he could enter the trailer. I didn't know what to say or how to start the conversation, so I said, "I guess you know why we are here?" The man dropped his head and quietly said, "Yes, we poached some deer." I about crapped my pants. We had the right guys and he just admitted that they had shot some deer. Meanwhile, Edberg had the other guy and was asking him questions. I could overhear the conversation and the man was lying to Edberg about knowing anything about a poached deer. I looked at Edberg and whispered, "These are our guys he already admitted to me that they had poached some deer." Edberg looked at me with a short smile and raised his eyebrows as if to say, "Oh really!"

I asked the man if we could go in the trailer and discuss things out of the cold. The man agreed and we followed him in the trailer. What I saw next, I will never forget. There were deer parts and quarters of deer meat hanging up on the walls all around the living room of the trailer. The walls were the old dark wood paneling with orange shag carpet flooring. As I tripped over dogs trying to get through the front door, I counted 9 dogs in the trailer house. Two adults and seven puppies. The two men had gutted the deer out on their living room floor for Christ's sake. The dogs had been feeding on the guts and other deer parts for quite some time. It felt like it was over ninety degrees in the trailer. The dogs had been shitting and peeing on the floor. There was dog shit everywhere and the trailer smelled absolutely horrible between the dog shit and deer parts. I started to gag and could feel my head start to sweat. As I walked through the front door I struggled to not step on a puppy or a pile of dog shit. There was a young pregnant lady sitting in a recliner in the corner of the room. She had a 2–3-year-old girl sitting on her lap crying. I made my way into the kitchen stepping on puppies with every step. What I saw next made me gag again. There were deer legs and deer parts lying on the kitchen counter next to several spent .223 shell casings. The kitchen sink was completely full of coagulated blood, deer hair and water. They had tried to process the deer inside the trailer and their water lines froze not allowing the coagulated blood and water to drain. This water had been in the sink for nearly a month. I looked at Edberg and whispered, "I think we got the right poachers." With a serious look on his face, Edberg opened the door on the freezer to find it full of boned-out unwrapped deer meat. He then opened the door on the refrigerator. There was nothing in the refrigerator except deer meat. These people didn't have ketchup, milk, mustard, or nothing, except deer meat.

Pieces of poached deer and blood in the kitchen sink

The two men were in their late twenties. Their hair and hands were greasy from whatever job they had been working. One man asked me if he could take his shirt off because he was hot. I agreed and both men took their shirts off. They were covered in tattoos and piercings. I sat the men down on the couch and asked the one man to tell me what had happened with the deer poaching. I was going to hang these guys if they were killing big bucks. The man admitted to me that they had killed two doe deer because they were starving to death. He showed us the heads of the doe deer that were still in the trailer behind the recliner with the pregnant lady sitting in. About that time another young female child came out from a bedroom and crawled on her mom's lap crying. I think the young girl had been sleeping in a nearby bedroom. Everybody in the trailer was now crying including the puppies. Even the dogs were hungry! The two men told the whole story from start to finish and it matched up with what little evidence we had. I believed they were telling the truth. These people were hungry and that's why they were poaching. They had loaded the deer whole into their truck so that they wouldn't get caught and so they could feed their dogs. Both men had jobs and worked at a metal salvage yard in Big Piney. Neither man had a driver's license. One man had just been pulled over by the cops and received over seven hundred dollars in fines. He was fined for not having vehicle insurance or a valid driver's license. All because he needed to drive himself and his friend to work each day. The one man said, "Man, I can't believe we got caught, how, did you guys know it was us?" I replied, "Maybe you should have washed the deer hair and blood out of the back of your truck over a month ago."

Deer hide on living room floor

I visited for a minute with the young pregnant lady who was still crying. I asked her if either man in the trailer was the father of her kids. She looked down at the floor, closed her eyes, and shook her head no. I could see huge tears streaming down her cheeks. I thought to myself *what a damn mess*! I said, "Madam, you need to get rid of these dogs, you can't even feed yourselves." She cried and said, "I have been trying to, but nobody will take them." I looked down and one of the puppies was trying to crawl up my pant leg as it was whimpering. I looked at the lady and said, "What about this one, can I adopt this one?" the lady cried and said, "Yes, please take her home with you." I thanked the lady and gave her a twenty-dollar bill to purchase a bag of dog food for the other dogs. The puppy was a Border collie mix with long brown and white hair.

Deer blood on wood paneling wall

We ended up seizing the man's rifle and issued one man a citation for taking a deer out of season. I told them that we would show up in court and testify to the judge that they had poached because they were hungry. The judge ended up charging them thirty dollars in court costs and their .223 caliber assault rifle was returned to them. This case showed me that there are people in this world with a hell of a lot more problems than I have. Be blessed every day for what you do have. As for the puppy, I named her Poacher. She was one of the best and loyal dogs I have ever owned. A short time after bringing her home my neighbor accidentally ran over her breaking her hind leg. I was not home at the time, so my neighbor did the right thing and took her to the local vet. He told the vet, "I don't care what it costs or what you have to do, please fix my neighbor's dog." The vet fixed her alright and I received a bill for $1500 dollars. So much for the free dog!

Poacher lived to be twelve years old. She likely died of heat exhaustion or a heart attack while on a horseback ride one hot summer day in the Little Buffalo Basin near Meeteetse, Wyoming. My wife Lana and I had taken a ride that day across the Basin. It was a hot day and the dog fell behind and never returned. We searched and searched for Poacher but could not find her. I was on a hike nearly a year later and found her decayed body and red collar underneath a juniper tree approximately two hundred yards from where we had last seen her. The tag on the collar read 'Poacher'. Rest in Peace, sweet girl, and thanks for your companionship for all those years!!

The next winter, Scott Edberg would break his leg while getting out of his patrol truck in front of the game and fish regional office in Pinedale. I investigated the scene of the accident. It appeared to me that Mr. Edberg had exited his truck before the truck had come to a complete stop in front of the office. I noticed fresh skid marks on the ice underneath the snow. I then noticed the exact spot where Mr. Edberg had slipped and fell on the ice. It appeared that the truck was still moving when Mr. Edberg exited the truck. As is foot tracks on the ice were behind the driver's door several feet when the truck finally came to a stop. Mr. Edberg showed back up to the office later that day with a cast on his leg and crutches. Our Damage Technician Ty Huffman walked through the front door and observed Mr. Edberg standing at the front office with crutches. Ty said "Damn, what did you do to yourself Edberg?" Edberg replied, I slipped on the ice early this morning and broke my leg." I said, "Yea, it appeared to me that he jumped out of his patrol truck before it came to a complete stop." Ty laughed and said, "DAMN "SPEEDBERG" YOU NEED TO SLOW DOWN." From that moment on the nickname "SPEEDBERG" stuck and is still used today.

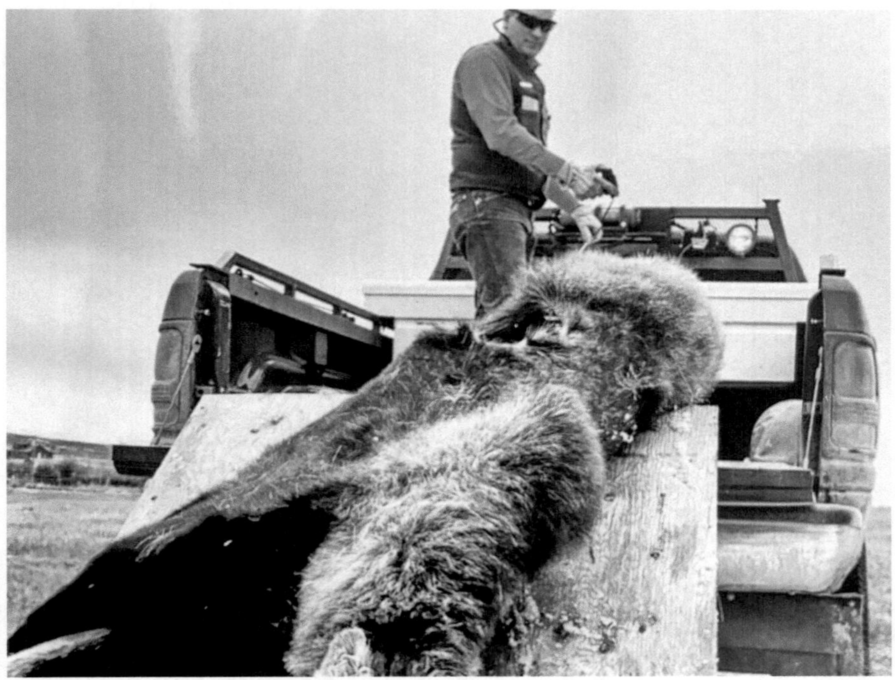

Scott Edberg loading dead moose

Chapter 11

Mule Deer and Moonshine

It was summertime 2002. I had received a report from a little old lady that she had a blind deer in her yard in Pinedale. Upon looking at the deer I was able to determine that the deer was not blind, it was just very tame and not afraid of people. Someone had likely raised this deer when it was a fawn. The deer was eating the lady's flowers and she asked me if I could remove the deer from her yard. I had a friend who lived next door who owned a horse trailer. He gave me permission to borrow his horse trailer and a bag of grain. I hooked onto the man's four horse bumper pull trailer and pulled it up in front of the lady's house. I poured grain into a bucket and shook the bucket. The small buck deer immediately headed my direction to get a taste of the grain. I simply walked into the horse trailer shaking the bucket and the deer followed. I closed the door on the trailer and the deer was caught. The lady smiled and said, "Wow that was easy." I nodded my head, smiled, and replied, "I'm a trained professional ma'am." I wasn't sure what I was going to do with the deer, but I needed to get it out of town. I decided that there was a nice place to release the deer south of Pinedale on a state section of land next to the New Fork River. This was the area where south Pinedale game warden had directed the helicopter to land when suspected of fishing with worms on the river.

I ended up dropping off a very steep and rough road to get down next to the creek. I was hoping that I could get back up the steep hill with the horse trailer. It would be rough and slick with small rocks, but I should be fine. Once down by the creek I unloaded the deer, scratched it on the head and said my goodbyes. I jumped in my game and fish truck and headed back towards town. I looked in my rearview mirror and the deer was running behind my truck like a pet dog. I sped up as fast as I could safely drive on the rough road. I finally got some distance between me and the deer with the steep hill coming up. The hill slowed me down and the deer again caught up with me. I then tried to outrun the deer for about one mile through a subdivision. Nope, the deer was not going to let me get out of its sight. Now I'm back at the main highway stopped at a stop sign with the deer standing behind the horse trailer. I'm afraid if I pull out on the busy highway the deer may get ran over by on-coming traffic. I decided to load the deer back up and take him back down to the river. It was getting late in the evening and my trailer lights didn't work on my borrowed trailer. I unloaded the deer again and hauled ass out of the area nearly totaling my buddy's horse trailer on the rough steep hill. Nope, I could not outrun the damn deer again! What seemed like a simple job was now turning into a pain in my ass.

I loaded the deer a third time and took it back down by the river. This time I put my dog's collar on the deer and tied it to a tree with some bailing twine. I hauled ass back to Pinedale and dropped my friend's trailer off before dark. I then returned to my home, which was only about two miles from where the deer was tethered to a tree. I jumped on my dirt bike and raced down to the river. The deer was still happily tied to the tree, and happy to see me. I took the collar off the deer and placed it in my coat pocket and hauled ass out of there on my dirt bike as fast as I could go. The poor deer tried his damnedest to keep up, but I got him on the steep hill. I hope nobody was watching all of this unfold, because I dang near wrecked my bike on the hill getting away from the deer. I don't know where I ended up losing the deer as I was driving too fast to look behind me. I showed up back home and no deer in sight. I had ditched the deer, but I knew I would get more calls on this deer because he was not going to stay down by the river and do what normal deer do.

Sure enough I received a call early the next morning from my neighbor to the south. He was complaining that he had a deer in his tree nursery causing damage by eating young trees and rubbing his antlers on his mature trees. He told me he thought the deer may be blind. I replied, "No, the deer is not blind, he is just very friendly." I told him that I would come down and get the deer. This time I loaded up the deer in my department horse trailer and hauled the deer up to Scab Creek feed ground. I figured if I got the deer away from civilization that maybe he would stay out of trouble. I locked the deer in the horse corral at the feed ground and drove the truck and trailer out of the immediate area. I hiked back to the horse corral and poured some grain on the ground for the deer to eat. The deer was busy eating while I snuck out the gate and hauled ass over the hill back to my truck and trailer. Down the road I went with no deer in my rearview mirror. The transplant was a success.

About one week later I received information that the young buck deer was seen in the Boulder Bar. It was reported that the deer had been observed eating popcorn and potato chips and watching Monday night football with local patrons. The next Tuesday morning I had a meeting in Pinedale with several big wigs from Cheyenne headquarters. The Director of the department reported that he observed a young buck deer standing in the middle of the highway near the Boulder Bar. The deer had cars backed up and was last seen standing by the driver's side door of a sports car eating something through the window. I acted surprised when the director told me this information. I replied, "Really, that seems odd, must be someone's pet deer." I was ready to drive down and shoot the damn deer! I was tired of dealing with it. Days later I heard rumor that one of my elk feeders hauled the deer out of the Boulder Bar and took it back up into the mountains. I thanked the man and shook his hand for taking care of the problem.

Later that fall I checked a hunting camp near Scab Creek feed ground. A lady approached me and said, "I have to tell you a funny story that happened last night. My husband and I were sitting by our campfire having a drink and some snacks. This buck deer came out of the trees and started eating snacks from our hand. When we quit giving the deer snacks it became aggressive. It jumped up on my husband's chest while he was sitting in his lawn chair and tipped him over backwards. My husband was lying on his back with his legs in the air and the damn deer tried to mount him." I replied. "I know that deer very well, did your husband smoke a cigarette afterwards?" The lady laughed so hard I thought she was going to cry. That was the last time I heard any more stories about that deer. It was probably hanging on some non-resident's meat pole somewhere.

It was mid-July and the Pinedale rendezvous annual Mountain Man celebration had just ended. Outfitter Todd Stevie (Roundy) came blowing through the front doors of the Pinedale game and fish office. Todd was pretty upset. His face was red and the veins on the side of his neck looked like small garden hoses. He reported that there were a bunch of crazy ass mountain men camped up between lower and upper Green River Lakes right along the main horse trail. He said that he rode through the area with some guests earlier in the day, and several guests nearly got bucked off their horses. He said they were dressed like mountain men in loin clothes and had their faces and horses painted. They apparently fired some black power rifles near his guests and horses started bucking and grabbing their asses. Roundy was fired up, "He said "If I hadn't had to take care of my guests, I would have gotten off my horse and kicked the shit out of all of them." I asked Roundy, "How many mountain men were in the camp?" Roundy replied, "Hell, I don't know-maybe 20-30 of them!" I replied, "That's a lot of asses to whoop!" Todd was mad and wanted something done about it. He claimed that they were camped right along the main trail in violation of Forest Service regulations, and he was certain that they didn't have a livestock permit to have that many animals on the Forest. He said he was headed over to the Forest Service office next to tell them about it. Out the door he went. I wasn't sure that I could do anything to help him because we didn't have any authority to enforce Forest Service regulations.

It was right at 5:00 PM when the Forest Service LEO (Law Enforcement Officer) stopped by the game and fish office. He asked if he could borrow our patrol boat to run up to Green River Lakes and check out some mountain men that might be illegally camping in the area. I told him that I had just talked with Todd Stevie and was aware of the situation. Our patrol boat was kind of temperamental and I didn't want to take the time to explain all the details on how to run the boat, so I agreed to run up there with him. We hooked onto the boat and headed some forty miles up a nasty rough road pulling the boat. We wanted to get there before night fall, so that we could navigate across lower Green River Lakes in the daylight. It would also be a short hike to where they were camped. It ended up being two Forest Service LEO's and myself who hiked into the area. The clouds above were dark black with lightning and white streaks of hail and heavy rain running through them. It was kind of eerie hiking into the area while it was nearly dark. It looked like we were about to get really wet.

I detected campfire smoke rolling above the tall pine trees to the north. I knew we were getting close. We approached the first camp of mountain men. About five men were dressed in rawhide and loin clothes with their faces painted like Indians. They each had a Bowie knife on their side and a pistol. I could see black powder rifles leaning on the trees near their lean-to. I approached the men and none of them would even acknowledge my presence. I just stood there next to their campfire watching them cook a full rib cage of what looked like an elk to me. I finally stepped up and asked, "How are you guys doing this evening?" One man replied without even looking at me, "Good, as long as you are not here to harass us." I replied, "We don't wish to harass anyone, but we received a complaint today from a local outfitter claiming you guys spooked their horses and are camped too close to the main horse trail." The Forest Service LEO stepped up and asked, "Do you guys have a wilderness permit for all your horses?" The same guy responded, "I don't know, they are not mine." After that, the men would not look at us and they were done talking to us.

We left that camp and started walking through the trees to visit other camps. It was eerie. There were people dressed like mountain men running from camp to camp and hiding from us under their lean-tos. Nobody wanted to talk to us. Finally, I got some man to tell me who was in charge of the horses. He pointed to the north and said, "That man, sitting over there under the tree owns all the horses." I looked over and there was a bearded man sitting Indian style by himself in the middle of a small grassy meadow underneath a small pine tree. I headed towards the man and introduced myself. He looked at me and stated, "I'm responsible for this camp and the horses. If you need to issue any citations, issue them to me." He dropped his head and held out his hands in the air and started saying some prayer to the spirits. The Forest Service guys jumped on this opportunity and asked him for his driver's license so they could issue him a citation. I began to feel the hair stand up on my back. I slowly turned around and we were being surrounded by almost everyone in camp. They formed a large circle around us and started chanting something. Every one of them was armed.

The man sitting Indian style told everyone to bow down. He made a motion with his hands as if to say sit down and be quiet. The Forest Service LEO's were telling the man that everyone in camp would need to move their camps 100 feet from the main trail. The man sitting Indian style explained to the group that they would all need to move their camps 100 feet from the main trail, or they would be cited. Most of the people took off and started moving their camps. About that time, it started to rain harder than I have ever seen it rain before. These poor people were soaking wet trying to move their camps to be in compliance with Forest Service regulations. After about twenty minutes one of the Forest Service guys starting pacing off distances from the main trail to several camps that had already moved. He demanded that they move their camps again as he had paced off the distance with his feet and they were still not 100 feet from the main trail. They started yelling at him and he started yelling back to show his authority. He told them that he had a 40 inch inseam and they needed to take larger strides to measure the distance more accurately. Things were starting to go south in a hurry. Tempers were flaring up and many people were soaking wet. They did not appreciate the government over-reach. They had tried to comply, and it was not good enough. I felt sorry for the people and wished I hadn't even been there. These Forest Service guys may get all of us killed, and for what?

About that time the leader of the mountain man group approached me. He looked me in the eye with pouring down rain and said, "These Forest Service guys are being a couple of dicks. If they don't leave now, I'm afraid someone is going to get badly hurt." He pulled his Bowie knife out of his sheath and ran it by his throat as if to say, "Someone is going to get their throat cut." I felt it was time to step up to the plate. I jumped up and yelled, "EVERYONE LISTEN UP FOR A MINUTE. WE ARE NOT HERE TO HARASS YOU. WE RESPECT YOUR WAY OF LIFE AND WHAT YOU ARE DOING HERE TODAY. I RESPECT YOUR WAY OF LIFE. PLEASE DO THE BEST THAT YOU CAN TO GET YOUR CAMPS AT LEAST 100 FEET FROM THE TRAIL, SO THAT WE CAN LEAVE YOU BE AND YOU CAN ALL TAKE SHELTER FROM THE HEAVY RAINS." I looked at the Forest Service guy that was being a dick and said, "Please help these guys move their camps so we can get out of here alive." He knew that I was serious, and he knew that I knew something that he didn't.

About that time a beautiful young woman approached me and gave me a hug. She was wearing only a loin cloth and had long beautiful black hair all the way down to her lower back. She smiled and said, "Thank you, sir. Please drink with me. It is my birthday." As she stepped back from me, I noticed she had a large knife in one hand and a small wooden whiskey barrel with a cork in it tucked under her other arm. I couldn't believe that I had just let her hug me and didn't see the damn knife! She placed the knife in the small of her back and held out the wooden bottle of whiskey offering me a drink. She had the most beautiful breasts that I think I had ever seen in my life. (Except for my wife's, of course) I said, "Thank you ma'am. Happy birthday to you. Thank you for the offer of sharing your whiskey with me, but I'm on duty right now." She smiled, gave me another hug and a kiss on the cheek and said, "Why don't you take that red shirt off and celebrate with me for a while. Please, it's my birthday!!" I didn't know what to say. There was finally peace in the camp and this young girl had been drinking heavily. If I denied her, would she turn into a hot mess? She smiled again and took a drink out of the wooden whiskey barrel. She held it up to my face and said, "Try some, its homemade corn." Man, did I want to stay and take in some culture, but I knew I must stay strong and not bow down to some half naked beautiful woman with moonshine.

I was without words when the leader of the camp approached me. He asked the young lady to please give him a minute with me. He put his arm around me and said, "Sir, I want you to understand something here. We camp in the mountains once a year somewhere. We want our camp to resemble pre- 1840 mountain men. The people here in this camp have traveled from all over the world to be right here tonight in these beautiful mountains. Nobody is allowed to take a motor vehicle to this area. They must walk, ride a horse, or come by boat to be in this camp. Some of these people have been traveling all year to get to this rendezvous site. This is a very special moment for all of us and we don't wish to be harassed." I replied, "I respect your way of life and what you are doing. If I was not working, I would take my badge off and join you. You must also respect my position as a game warden and know that my job is to enforce our regulations and protect wildlife." He said, "Sir, follow me. I would like to show you something." He took me down by the river and showed me three of the most beautiful handmade canoes that I had ever seen in my life. They were made of wood covered in stretched rawhide. He said, "Check these canoes out. Each one of them has three life jackets in them so that we are legal." He then showed me a fishing pole that had sinew for line. The hook was made of bone. He said, "We fish with these poles for food. Let me show you my fishing license." The man pulled a fishing license out of a pocket in his loin cloth. I looked at the license. His name was Dennis from Jackson Hole, Wyoming. I said, "Jackson Hole, huh?" He replied, "Yeah, I live in Jackson Hole, not sure I want to admit that." I replied great for you, what, do you do in Jackson Hole for a living?" he responded, "I'm a Dentist."

He then walked me through the entire camp, keep in mind it is pouring rain with nasty lightning and thunder. I'm not sure what the Forest Service guys were up to, but I hoped they were both still alive. He took me to the camp that was cooking an entire rib cage over a fire on a rotisserie and introduced me to the guys. I noticed the head of bull elk leaning against a tree in the darkness near the fire. I asked them what they were cooking. A huge man dressed in leather with elk ivories hanging around his neck replied, "It's an elk, we came across a dead elk the other day and salvaged what we could of it, looks like maybe wolves had killed it, the head is leaning against that tree over there." He pointed back in the timber. I wasn't sure how to deal with this one. They were eating what was left from a wolf kill? Or maybe they were lying and had killed the elk themselves. I looked at the elk's head closer and noticed that it was not fresh, and predators had eaten about half the hair off the elk skull indicating that more than likely they had found the elk dead and it had been dead for a while. I couldn't believe that they were eating the meat from this thing. I looked at the head and explained the law to them. I told them that they needed to have a Wyoming Interstate Game Tag in order to legally possess or transport the head. The large, bearded guy stood up, he had to be 6'-5" or better and weighed well over 300 lbs. He said, "Where do I get one of those tags?" I foolishly said, "Oh, just bring it by the office in Pinedale next time you are in town, and we will get you fixed up with a tag and make it legal." The large man shook my hand and said, "Consider it done! Sorry we didn't know any better." These guys didn't even have vehicles, how were they going to get this elk head to Pinedale for a stupid eight-dollar interstate game tag?

The Forest Service guys showed up. We were all soaking wet. The half-naked girl showed up again and tried to get me to drink some of her homemade corn. She gave me another hug. The Forest Service guys looked at me cross-eyed, like what the hell was that all about. They didn't like the Bowie knife tucked away in her loin cloth. I looked at the wet Forest Service guys and said, "I think it's time to make a mile, men" They issued the leader of the camp a citation for not having a wilderness permit for the horses. I also told the leader of the camp to be sure and not fire any muskets in the air when Roundy the outfitter rolled through their camp next time, or there would be hell to pay. He shook my hand and assured me there would be no more problems.

We walked out of there in the dark with dead flashlights. We didn't need any light to see with all the lightning in the sky that night. This was one of the weirdest nights that I had ever encountered in my life. It was also one of the worst lightning storms that I had ever seen. We arrived at our boat shortly after midnight and took it across lower Green River lakes in the dark. The lake was white capping with deep swells. I was never so happy to get back to shore in all my life. For years I cursed Roundy for getting me involved with that mission. About one week after this happened, I was in the Pinedale office. I heard office manager Des Brunette yell, "SWERB, PLEASE COME TO THE FRONT DESK. THERE IS A VERY SCARY MAN ENTERING THE OFFICE!" I jumped out of my chair and observed a huge mountain man carrying a bull elk head through the front door of the regional office. He walked up to the front desk and said to Des, "We need to get a Wyoming Interstate Game Tag for this elk head according to Scott Werbelow." I walked out of my office and shook the giant man's hand and thanked him for complying with the law. I would have never guessed that I would ever see this man again, but he wanted to be legal, and he had given me his word on that rainy night. I walked out of my office and watched the man load the elk head on his pack horse and ride out of town.

Chapter 12

LOTS OF CHANGE

There had been some changes in personnel over the year. My feed ground maintenance man Brian Baker had received a call from Casper regional wildlife supervisor Terry Cleveland offering him a job on the Reservoir Crew. Brian had only worked for me for a short time and was excited to begin his new career as a game warden. I was excited for Brian but bummed that I had lost another helper in the feed ground program. I would later end up interviewing and hiring Mark Pearson of Pinedale. I had heard a lot of great things about Mark from locals that he had worked for over the years. Mark had a strong background with carpentry skills, guiding hunters and fishermen, and working with horses. He seemed like a perfect fit for the position. Mark had a positive attitude and a strong work ethic. I really looked forward to working with him in the future.

I would also need to hire new elk feeders for Fall Creek, Finnegan, and North Piney feed grounds. Kathy would be leaving us at Fall Creek. This was a sad day for me and the department. Kathy had done a wonderful job feeding elk for nearly ten years. She would be missed, and her shoes would be hard to fill. I ended up hiring Mike Schaffer from LaBarge to feed Finnegan and North Piney. I would also hire JJ Butner from the Douglas area to feed at Fall Creek. JJ was the young cowboy type full of piss and vinegar. He would be living in the cabin at Fall Creek that Gary Hornberger and I built for Kathy the previous year. JJ would end up being an elk feeder by day and a bartender at the GRB (Green River Bar) by night. He was a handsome and charismatic man and had no problems finding a girlfriend.

I also received word that longtime north Pinedale game warden Duke Early would be retiring sometime near October 2002. I would miss Duke and could only hope that we would get a good replacement to fill his shoes. The public in the Pinedale area loved Duke. He had such a friendly demeanor and great personality. Duke and I had developed a great working relationship over the years. I don't know how many elk we moved together to feed grounds over the past seven years, but it was a bunch. We even caught some bad guys along the way. I will never forget the case when Duke and I ended up hiding behind a dead pine tree waiting for the poachers to return to their illegally taken elk. Duke was lying on top of me so that we could hide behind a fallen pine tree. Another hunter walked up on us as Duke was lying on top of me in his red shirt. The hunter later admitted that he thought his hunting buddy had killed us and stacked us up like cord wood behind the dead tree. After seeing that we were alive he then thought that maybe we were gay. Funny stories!! You will be greatly missed Duke Early, thanks for all your dedicated years of service to the Wyoming Game and Fish Department.

I had also received word that one of my longtime hay producers in Idaho had wrecked his airplane and was killed. Apparently, he was flying low over a bible school camp, and something went wrong, and he crashed and burned in front of family and friends that knew him well. I had bought hay from him and his wife for several years but had never met them. We did business over the phone and the hay would get delivered sometime each fall. The hay was always good quality and reasonably priced. I would receive an invoice in the mail each year and pay the man.

His wife Cindy called me one night crying and told me about the horrible accident. She was a mess after just losing her husband. But she wanted me to know that they still planned on fulfilling their contract and delivering 300 ton of hay to Jewett feed ground sometime in the fall. I felt horrible for Cindy. She didn't even know where the feed ground was located as she had never been there. I had done business with them for several years and never met them. I felt obligated to meet Cindy and show her where the feed ground was located so that she could get the hay delivered. I offered to meet her in Pinedale and buy her lunch. We would then head up to Jewett feed ground so that I could show her how to find it. At this point in our conversation, she was still crying but agreed to meet me for lunch in Pinedale. We picked a date and put it on the calendar.

The day came soon, and I met Cindy in Pinedale for lunch. We had a wonderful lunch and visited about what a great man her husband was. I felt horrible for the poor lady losing her husband so tragically.

She broke down crying several times during our conversation. We then headed up to Jewett feed ground. The clouds in the sky were black near the feed ground area. It looked like we might get some rain. I was alright with that because it had been a dry summer. I was driving a brand-new Ford one-ton truck with a V-10 engine. The truck didn't have many miles on it at all. I pulled up to the feed ground and showed her everything that she needed to know to deliver hay to this location. As we were walking back to the truck it began to rain hard and lightning. As we neared my truck, I noticed the right rear tire was completely flat. I told Cindy, "It looks like I have a flat tire, why don't you jump in the truck and stay dry while I change it quick." She agreed and jumped in the cab of the truck. I have changed hundreds of flat tires in my life, this should only take a few minutes.

At this point I don't think it could have rained any harder, even if God had been pissed at me for months! And it looked like a storm that wasn't passing anytime soon. Pretty quick here came the hail and lightning. I discovered that I needed a key to unlock the hole that some long rod is supposed to travel through to lower the tire down on the ground. I could not find the special key, so I got a large screwdriver and claw hammer out of my toolbox and ripped the lock mechanism completely out of the bumper. I threw it as far as I could, I never wanted to see it again! I couldn't find the long rod and jack anywhere. I finally jumped into the regular cab truck soaking wet and found the owner's manual in the glove box. It showed that the rod and jack were neatly hid in the engine compartment of the truck. I was excited, now I could go to work changing the tire. I put the rod together, it was now about eight feet long. I ran the rod through the hole in the bumper and twisted it and nothing happened. After about a half hour of twisting this damn rod, it became apparent to me that something wasn't working right. I pulled the rod out and held it in the air and noticed the square end of the rod was stripped out, now it was kind of a rounded. About that time a bolt of lightning hit the metal hay shed roof right next to me, while I was holding the lightning rod eight feet into the air. My hair was standing on end, and I could feel my head buzzing. I quickly grabbed the end of the lightning rod, spun my body completely around twice like an Olympic shot-put thrower and flung that damn lightning rod as far as I could throw it. I did not ever want to see it again. *Oh Shit, I thought. I'm going to need the end of that rod to screw up this tiny chicken shit jack if I ever do get the spare tire lowered down.* I was hoping that Cindy had not seen my childish fit in the rainstorm. I had also said a few choice curse words.

I crawled under the truck to see what I needed to do to lower the tire down. This was kind of nice. I was finally out of the rain. While lying on my back scooting around to find the tire I could smell something horrible. I discovered that I had just laid in a pile of wet green slimy cow shit. There was wet cow shit everywhere under my truck. It was like I had parked over the top of the only cow shit in the area. The grass was lush, green, and tall and I had not noticed it. It was all over my legs, arms and back. *I thought NICE, my blood pressure was starting to boil.* I crawled out from under the truck and rolled around in the wet grass trying to get all the cow shit off of me before I jumped back in the truck with Cindy. The only way that I was going to get the spare tire down is to reach up in there with something and cut the cable. I could not find anything to cut the cable with. I walked over to the passenger side of truck and tapped on the window. I told Cindy to hold tight that I would have to hike down to Antelope Run Ranch and borrow some tools. The ranch headquarters was about three miles away. I know I had green cow shit on my cheek and one ear when I spoke with Cindy. She said, "No problem, I'm fine,"

I started the three-mile hike in the pouring rain. I was hoping the ranch manager Charlie was around to give me a ride back to the feed ground. I had developed a good relationship with Charlie over the years. He was the type of guy who would do anything to help someone out. To my luck, Charlie was not around. *Hell, Charlie is never gone from the ranch.* I entered the large five bay shop and headed for the large red toolbox near the work bench. Charlie had every tool you could imagine. He was a pretty good heavy equipment mechanic and loved working on car and truck engines. Charlie could fix or repair anything. I dug through the toolbox and found several tools that may be useful in cutting a heavy steel cable. I even grabbed a hacksaw. Back up the hill I went loaded with tools in the rainstorm. This little trip took me over an hour.

I lay back down in the cow shit. The only tool that I could finagle up in the tight spot was the hacksaw. Except I could only take very short strokes with the hacksaw. Like one inch back and forth at a time. This took forever and my hand was starting to cramp up from being all cockeyed reaching up over the spare tire. Finally, without any prior notice the sixty-pound muddy tire dropped right on my head. It hurt, but I was relieved that I now had a spare tire. I crawled out from underneath the truck soaking wet and covered in green cow shit. At least it matched the color of my game and fish issued coat. I had to walk over the hill to retrieve the eight-foot lightning rod so that I could use the end of it to hook onto the cheesy ass jack and raise up the truck. I used my hammer to smash the end of the rod back into a square shape to fit on the jack. The jack ended up sinking into the soft ground. It was fully extended and hadn't even begun to raise the truck up yet. By now I was sweating from twisting on the jack handle for nearly fifteen minutes. I would need to find a large block of wood somewhere to raise the jack off the soft ground.

I headed down off the hill to the little elk feeder cabin down in the draw and gathered up an arm full of split firewood. Once strategically placed I was winding on the small jack again. The truck was starting to rise. I decided I better loosen the lug nuts before the tire was off the ground. This is when I discovered that you need a special lug wrench to loosen one lug to pull the plastic hub cab off and get to the real lug nuts. My patience meter was pegged, I grabbed my claw hammer and beat the plastic hub cab off the wheel. I thought to myself, *what in the hell has the world come to? This is all about TRUST. Engineers apparently think that someone is going to steal your spare tire, so you need a special lock. Someone may steal your hubcap, so you need a special tool to remove that. And now you need a special lug nut that takes a special key so that someone doesn't steal your damn tire.* At this point in my day, I was really wanting to meet the engineer that so cheerfully and brilliantly invented this stupid ass idea. If I could find that guy I would shake his hand, ask him to bend over slightly at the waist and spread his legs. I would then repeatedly kick him in the nuts!! Sorry I went off on a little tangent there.

It took me over two hours to change this damn flat tire in pouring down rain. I was wet, my hands were cut up, and I had a gash on my head covered with cow shit. I no longer had anything left to change another tire because I had thrown all the shit that didn't work down the hill. Heck, I can remember when all you needed was a bumper jack and a star wrench and you could change any tire in about fifteen minutes. I jumped back in my truck madder than a midget handcuffed to a treadmill! Cindy looked over at me and asked, "Haven't you ever changed a flat tire before?" That was the icing on the cake!! I kept my composure and replied, "Apparently Not!!" That was the last time that I had ever seen or talked to Cindy again.

I felt obligated to drive back up to the Antelope Run Ranch and thank Charlie for the use of his tools. This large ranch was gorgeous and owned by some really wealthy people. Charlie was a great guy and we had developed a good relationship over the past several years. Charlie fit the mold of a typical Wyoming cowboy. He had a dark handlebar mustache and always wore a black cowboy hat. He was double tough and didn't put up with any bullshit from anyone except the owners of the ranch. He was originally hired as a bodyguard to protect the owner of the property. He always packed a .40 caliber Glock pistol inside of his vest. The owners each had their own Lear jet. There was a runway on the property that was longer than both Pinedale and Jackson Hole to land their jets. There was a 13,000 square foot house that sat high up on a hill with an awesome view. It was called the "Hill House". Charlie called it the "Hell" house due to all the upkeep and repairs that it needed. The house had bullet proof glass windows all around the house that were nearly three inches thick. They were allegedly the thickest windows made in the world. Each room had a security system installed. There was also a large vault that the owner could lock himself in if someone ever tried to kill him. The owner had allegedly stolen the patent to a new and very successful heart staple that was used all around the world in open heart surgeries. He had had several attempts on his life from some environmentalist. Over the years Charlie was now responsible for everything on the ranch. He was no longer just a bodyguard. The ranch also had a three-to-four-million-dollar indoor riding arena. It was built out of huge logs with special horse stalls that had rubber floors and running water. The ranch almost reminded me of the "Yellowstone" ranch in Montana. As I drove into the ranch, I noticed 10-15 expensive good looking quarter horses standing in the corral next to the indoor riding arena. I thought to myself, *this would be a dream job for my wife Lana to work up at this beautiful ranch in this beautiful indoor arena. This would be something that I could never afford to build for Lana.*

I met Charlie in the front yard of the ranch house that he and his wife lived in. This was also a gorgeous log home with a beautiful yard. He greeted me with a firm hand shake as always. He said, "Come on in Big Guy." Charlie had a very pretty wife and daughter. They had very bubbly personalities and were fun to visit with. Both girls were Wyoming tough and knew how to survive. Charlie would offer me a whiskey on the rocks or a cup of coffee depending on what time of the day that I would stop by. This was evening so I took him up on a Crown Royal on the rocks. We visited for quite some time. I finally asked Charlie if the ranch ever hired anyone to train and ride all of the high dollar horses. He said, "Yes occasionally, why do you ask?" I told him that my wife Lana would love a job like that and that she was very good at training horses. I said, "Charlie, you need my wife up here riding and training horses, you just don't know it yet." He said, "Have her give me a call or come up and I will see what I can do." I was so excited for Lana. This would be her dream job for sure. I couldn't wait to get home and tell Lana the news. She was still working for Kathy Miller out on Horse Creek.

Lana was excited about the news. She drove up to the ranch and met Charlie and his wife in person. He hired her on the spot and gave her a ranch truck to drive since the commute was over sixty miles a day. I don't think I had ever seen Lana this happy. She was now working seven days a week on the ranch because she loved it so much. I was also working nearly seven days a week because I enjoyed my job so much as well. So, I knew what it was like to love your job and supported her for all the long hours that she worked.

Lana also drew a limited quota and very coveted mule deer license that fall. The license was valid in the Upper Green River area. This area was known for large buck mule deer. We didn't get much time to hunt with her and my busy work schedule during hunting season. But I did get to take her out on the last day of October, which was also the last day of her season. We spotted a 180 class mule deer right before dark. Lana made a beautiful shot on the deer. This was the largest body mule deer that I had ever seen. It was all that the two of us could do to load this deer in the back of my new Ford truck with the dent from the Christmas tree excursion. The deer would end up weighing 297 pounds on the rack with its head and legs cut off. We also decided to have the deer mounted with a shoulder mount since it was such a beautiful buck. I couldn't wait to get it back from the taxidermist. Lana was very excited. This was only the third deer that she had ever harvested.

We had the deer loaded in the back of the truck and were now hauling ass to a department Halloween party in Pinedale with blood on our hands and clothes. I told Lana, "Hell, let's just dress up as a couple Wisconsin pumpkin heads. I have some stupid looking orange hats in the back of the truck." So that we did. I loved the game and fish employees in Pinedale. We had a party to celebrate whatever we could think of. Game warden supervisor Scott Edberg had actually set up a party room in his new house. He had ice hockey, a ping pong table, electronic dart board, and a big screen projection TV that he had just purchased for $2000 dollars at Faler's General Store. Scott was the man and had the biggest television in the county. I was excited to watch Monday night football on his new television. We ended up helping Edberg move it into his house. It weighed as much as a Volkswagen bug and was just as big.

We had a great time at the Halloween party and showed off Lana's big buck deer. We had celebrated a little too much on a school night and it was time to drive home. Lana drove and said, "Let's stop and get the mail in town before we go home." I still had my goofy Wisconsin deer hunting hat on with blood on my clothes as I entered the lit-up post office in Pinedale. I went through the mail and noticed a Manila envelope addressed to me that had been sent certified from the Pinedale Airport Board. I thought to myself, *I wonder what this is all about, we did live near the airport south of Pinedale.*

We arrived home a little after midnight. I still had to hang the deer in the garage half drunk. Lana went to bed. It was way past her bedtime, and she had to get up early and go work at the ranch. I finally made it into the kitchen and opened the large Manila envelope. It was a contract from the Pinedale Airport Board offering me $1500.00 for my airspace above my house. I could sure use that money right now, but damn sure didn't want to get deprived of my air space. I read the fine print. If I accepted the money, I would have no rights if a plane crashed into my house or dropped a load of fuel on me. They had decided in the offer that they would pay me 10% of what my property was worth to fly over less than a half an acre of my property for their air space easement. I thought that was bullshit, because they were flying over my entire ten acres of property daily and not just a small fraction of it. If you did the same math for ten acres, the amount would come to about $10,000 dollars. I was tired and needed some rest. I would think about it more in the morning.

The next morning, I showed the contract to a couple of my good friends who I knew were much smarter than me. Both of them said that I shouldn't sign the contract because I would waive all my rights if something bad were to happen to my house. I would end up meeting the president of the Airport Board. I'm sorry readers, but this lady looked and acted just like Nancy Pelosi. This scared the hell out of me. She had no common sense and was all business to get whatever the Board wanted. I told her I would agree to $10,000 for the easement and not $1500.00. She said, "Sorry, the board simply can't agree to that." I got mad and said, "Well, why don't you consider buying my whole damn property. You are extending the runway towards my house right now making my property worth less every day!" She smiled and said, "Well, we didn't realize you would be a willing seller." I replied, "I will only be a willing seller if you are fair with me and my family." She smiled and told me that she would discuss it with the board and get back to me. Little did I know at the time, this would be the beginning of a very long journey, only because I was hardheaded and would not settle for their first offer, which was not fair! If I had to replace my log home with ten acres, it would be very difficult to find comparable property in the area. House prices were going way up compared to when I had purchased the property back in 1998.

The Airport Board hired a local appraiser out of the area. The man showed up to appraise my house and we did not hit it off at all. I told the man to make sure that he included the newly planted trees that I planted and all the new post and pole fence that I had spent the entire summer building around the perimeter of the property. I also told him that I had just re-stained and chinked the entire house and put new carpet throughout the entire house. He looked at me and said, "None of this is going to increase the value of your property, these are all things that your property should already have." He even said it with a nasty tone, as if to say, "Leave me the hell alone and shut up." His final appraisal ended up being $250,000. At the time you simply could not replace what I had for that amount. I went online and learned what the FAA (Federal Aviation Association) had to do to buy me out and relocate me. I'm glad that I read all this information, it was nearly two hundred pages. I learned that the Airport Board had to hire an appraiser with a long list of special qualifications that the guy they hired didn't have. I also learned that they had to relocate my family and buy comparable property. I advised the Airport Board that I was not happy with the appraisal, and that the man that they hired did not meet the qualifications for this sort of appraisal. They actually agreed with me and agreed to find another appraiser.

This time they hired the best appraiser in the state. He was considered the preacher of appraisals. This man did a very thorough job, a job that would stand up in court. His appraisal came in at $235,000. How did that work out for me, not very good. Now I was $15,000 less than the guy that I didn't like. I should have shut my mouth.

The reason they were trying to low ball me was because there were three other houses in the area that the extended runway was going to affect. Whatever the Board paid me for my property would set a precedence for the other three landowners. They did not want to come in high with an offer to me. I also learned that they paid the first appraiser $600.00 and the second appraiser $15,000. How ironic was it that the second appraiser came in $15K less. I became increasingly difficult to deal with and told them that I was done dealing with them. The next thing I knew, a man by the name of Darvin Dietz from Cody, Wyoming called me. He said he worked for Dietz and Associates in Cody. He wanted to take me to dinner and discuss the sale of my home to the Airport Board. I met Darvin at the Stockman's Bar in Pinedale. We both ordered a steak and a whiskey. Darvin told me that he had been hired by the Airport Board as a consultant/negotiator to deal with me since I had been so difficult for the Board to deal with. He also told me that I was only to talk to him, and he was only to talk to me. Darvin was a straight shooter and I really respected that.

Several weeks had gone by and Darvin and I had met for dinner several times. We really enjoyed our company together and had lots of things in common. Darvin was big into horses and so was my wife, Lana. He loved talking to Lana about horses. Darvin and I went out to dinner again one night. The whiskey was going down smooth for both of us. Darvin asked me about my job. I told him that I really loved interviewing and interrogating people and that I had been through a great deal of training to tell when someone was lying to me or not. Darvin was very enthused about this conversation. He asked me how I could tell when someone was lying. I explained some of my tactics to him and he was very interested in the conversation. I then said, "Darvin with that said, you have not been honest with me in our negotiations." Darvin dropped his head and put his hands over his face. He looked up and looked me right in the eye and said, "You are right, Scott, you and Lana are good people, and I won't allow you folks to be taken advantage of by any government entity. I will help you kids in every way I can."

The whole process took over two years to complete. Darvin made sure everything was done by the book. He made sure that we got everything that we were entitled to through the FAA relocation program. He even stood up for me to the Airport Board and fought for me at every turn in the road. At the end of the day Lana and I bought a beautiful two-story log house with ten acres in Daniel, Wyoming. The property had outbuildings, a barn, a small trapper's cabin, beautiful trees, and willows with a small fishing pond. This was a dream home for me and my family and worth much more than the airport property because it was not near an airport. I had more than tripled my money on the airport property in four years. This turned out to be a great investment for us. It took nearly another eight months to get moved into the new property as the previous owner of the property needed time to build himself a new home. We were soon moved into our new home. Lana was closer to her job on the ranch and Brad was closer to come watch Monday night football. As for me, I headed down to Faler's General Store and bought me a brand-new projection TV. I was now keeping up with the Joneses and Edberg. He even helped me unload the monster and get it set up.

I only tell this story because Darvin became a great friend of mine and deeply influenced my life for years to come. He introduced me to friends of his that became friends of mine still to this day. There are stories that I can't tell at this time, but they will come out another time. Darvin went through a divorce recently after we had met. He then came down with cancer, and later took his own life. What a great man he was. I will always be in debt to this fine man. God bless Darvin Dietz, rest in peace my friend. It just goes to show you that you can meet someone on any given day that can change your life forever. Darvin was that man for me.

As for Mark Pearson, he was doing an awesome job assisting with feed ground maintenance. He would work hard all day and sometimes ride his horse all night taking clients and gear into the high mountain lakes in the Wind River Mountains. The guy had an incredible work ethic. He was also raising his young children while his wife attended law school. Mark would come into my office once a week and tell me everything that he had done and everything that he was going to do. He never once asked me what needed to be done. He recognized it and did it. There were days that he rode with me in my truck to attend a meeting or drive into a feed ground. Mark would wash the inside of my windows with window cleaner while I drove. He tried to be productive with every part of his day.

Game and fish personnel outgrew the old Pinedale office. We needed more office space and had no money budgeted for a renovation. Mark volunteered to build new office space in the garage in an area that was currently being used for storage. Mark spent over a month building two new offices in his spare time. The offices turned out nicer and larger than any other office in the building. Mark always had a smile and a great attitude. Thanks for all your great work, Mark.

The date was August 29, 2002. The new north Pinedale game warden Herbert Frank Haley III A.K.A. “Bubba” had officially moved into the warden station in the little red brick building across from the regional office. Welcome to Pinedale, Bubba Haley.

Mark Pearson on Darby Mountain

Chapter 13

Texas Hunters, Moose and Bigfoot

It was fall of 2002. I received a report from Outfitter Todd Stevie (Roundy) that a hunter from Texas had pulled a gun on him. Roundy was pretty upset and wanted me to come up to his camp and visit with him about it. I arrived at Todd's outfitter camp, and he was still shaking mad. He claimed that he was driving up the Green River Lakes Road and met a vehicle coming towards him. The man driving the vehicle was an elderly man from Texas who had been camping and hunting in the area for years. Roundy and this man didn't get along well at all. They had had previous confrontations in the past. Roundy realized who it was coming towards him and decided to be nice for once in his life and actually wave at the guy as they passed one another. The old man did not except the gesture of being waved at and flipped Roundy off as they passed. Roundy drove on down the road and thought about it for a second. He then became agitated that this ol" bastard gave him the bird, especially after he was trying to be nice. Roundy flipped the truck around and chased the old man down flashing his lights. The old man quickly pulled over off the edge of the road. Roundy exited his vehicle and approached the driver of the vehicle. The old man rolled his window down to talk to Roundy. Roundy yelled at him and said, "IF YOU WEREN'T SUCH AN OLD CROTCHETY BASTARD, I WOULD PULL YOU

THROUGH THIS WINDOW RIP YOUR HEAD OFF AND SHIT DOWN YOUR WINDPIPE!" The old man calmly reached over, grabbed a pistol next to his right leg, cocked it and pointed it right in Roundy's face and said, 'Do you want some of this?" Roundy had met his match. He decided to back off and report the incident.

After interviewing Roundy in his camp and drinking a cup of coffee that his wife Bev had served me, I decided to go visit with the Texas hunter in his camp. The Texas hunter had the same story, except he told me that Roundy had also pulled a knife on him during the confrontation. In my line of work, I have learned over the years that there were always two sides to a story and the truth is generally somewhere in the middle. I told the old man that he and Roundy needed to knock their shit off or they were both going to jail. I then drove back down to Roundy's camp to visit with him again. I drove into his camp and rolled my window down as Roundy approached my vehicle. Roundy said, "Well, what did you learn, from that old bastard?" I looked at Roundy and replied, "What I learned is that you left a key piece of information out of your story. You pulled a knife on the man and that's why he pulled his pistol on you." Roundy laughed out loud and said, "Oh, Christ are you kidding me right now!" I said, "Nope that's what he claimed." Roundy started some deep thinking about the whole situation and replied, "Oh Christ, I pulled my pocketknife out of my jean pocket and was cleaning my fingernails while I chewed the old man's ass. If you call that pulling a knife on someone, then yes, I guess I did." I also told Roundy that he needed to knock his shit off and that if he wanted me to push it any farther that both of them may end up going to jail. Roundy agreed to back off and try and get along in the future.

Roundy and I had become good friends over the years. You never wondered what was on his mind because he would tell you, and he never sugar coated anything or held back any cuss words. At the end of every conversation, you knew exactly where Roundy was coming from. We became such good friends that Roundy would let me stay in his outfitter camp. He and his wonderful wife Bev would feed me well and give me a place to sleep. There were several times that Roundy would report a violation to me. He would call me from his satellite phone and say, "Swerb, we have poachers on the knob. Just get your ass up here and I will have a horse saddled for you. Bring your damn ticket book and we will go get them."

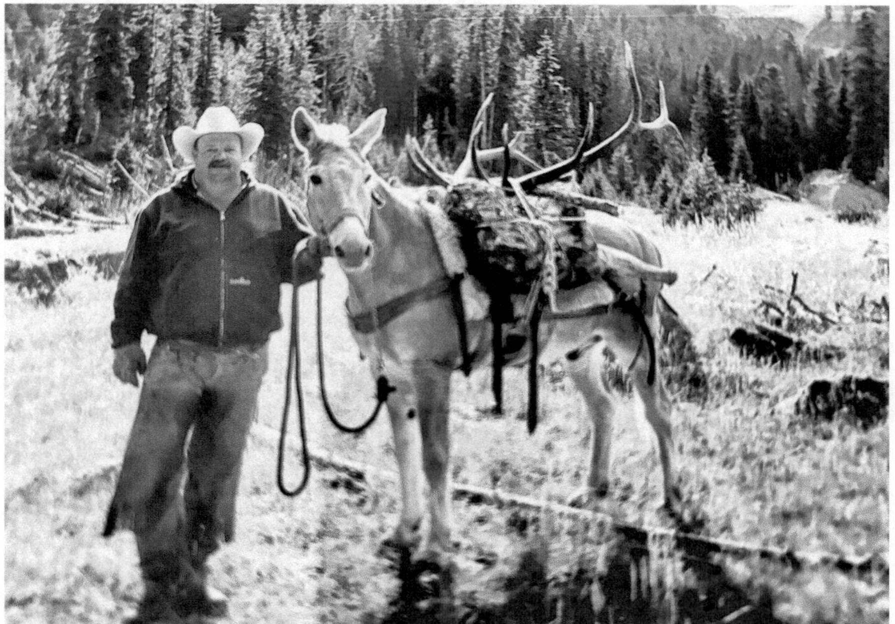

Todd (Roundy) Stevie

He certainly had a horse saddled for me alright. It was a half blind horse named "One Eye." One Eye was a great horse but he was missing his right eye and could not see anything on his right side. There were several times that I ended up on a steep narrow trail with One Eye. If he ever missed one step both of us were going to die. It would be straight down to my right for hundreds of yards. If One Eye missed a step, I would hold the right rein tight against his neck trying to keep him to the left. He would take small steps and look hard to his right with his left eye to keep from falling off the trail. We only fell once rolling down a steep embankment. Neither of us got hurt, but it scared the hell out me. I would cuss Roundy for giving me a blind horse. Roundy would just laugh and say, "A real high-country ranger wouldn't let a half blind horse slow him down none."

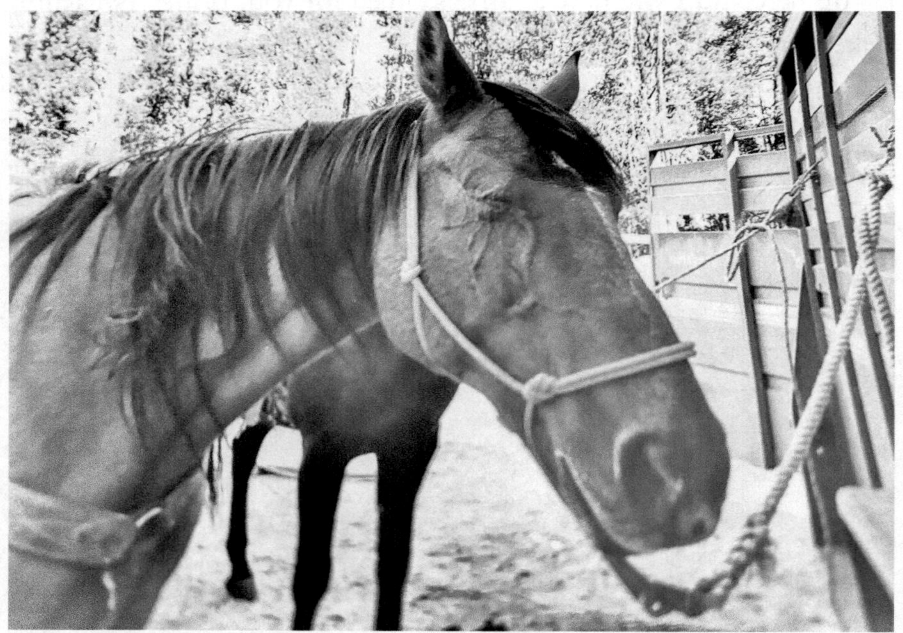

One-Eye

Roundy reported to me that he thought there was some illegal outfitting (Scab Outfitting) going on in the Upper Green. I decided to grab a couple horses and spend a few days patrolling the area. Roundy told me that I was welcome to stay in his spike camp up in Porcupine Creek. He told me that his brother Mike Stevie (One Beer) would be up there guiding some hunters and may be in the area, and that I was welcome to stay in their camp. This offer was awesome, because it saved me from having to pack a camp and set one up. I learned over time as a game warden that it was a lot of work going on pack trips by yourself. It seemed like all you did is set up camp, take care of horses, cook meals, build fires, take down camp, and move to another area. This made it more difficult to spend time patrolling and checking hunters. Having a camp jack would sure be nice, but we never had this luxury.

I grabbed my best horse Champ and my little black pack horse Spook and headed for Upper Green River Lakes. I had bought Champ at an auction for $150.00. He was the last horse to go through the auction that day. He had a four-year-old girl riding him and was very thin. The auctioneer said that the horse had been in a horse trailer wreck and had broken out his front teeth and couldn't eat very well. He said the horse was nine years old and well broke. Do you ever notice that every well broke horse at an auction is about nine years old? I thought any horse that can carry a four-year-old girl through an auction was probably pretty well broke. I started the bid at $150.00 and that was the only bid. *Shit,* I thought to myself, *I just bought another horse that I don't need, and he doesn't even have any teeth, Lana is going to kick my ass!"* After getting the horse home and looking him over a little closer, I determined that his teeth were fine. He had been on dry pasture all winter with no feed and was starving. My wife Lana and I gave him extra grain and good feed and he gained weight quickly. This would be one of the best horses that I had ever owned. His only quirk is that he didn't like a lead rope under his tail up his ass. If this ever happened, the rider was coming off. Don't ask me how I know this.

Soon, Spook was packed, and we were headed up the trail between Upper and Lower Green River Lakes. We came to the small patch of timber where the Mountain Men had their rendezvous earlier. I was riding Champ on the trail through the trees reminiscing about the beautiful half-naked mountain girl that kissed me and wanted me to join her on her birthday and drink some homemade moonshine. About that time, I looked up and observed a nice bull moose coming down the trail towards me. I thought this was pretty cool to get to see such a large bull moose up and close. The bull was not afraid of us and kept coming towards us. I pulled out my 35-millimeter camera from my saddle bag to try and get a good picture of the moose. I aimed the camera between my horse's ears and took the picture of the moose approximately ten yards from us. The picture would show my horses head and ears with the moose coming right towards us in the same picture. *I thought, what a cool picture this will be.* About that time, my horse became nervous and started raring up and prancing around. My horse nervously stepped off the trail and let the large bull walk past us. I could have literally reached out and touched the bull's horns as he moved by us. As soon as the bull passed, I kicked my horse to go and guided him to get back on the horse trail. I heard my pack horse squeal and felt the lead rope get tight. I turned around to see that the large bull was trying to mount my black pack horse Spook. Spook grabbed her ass to throw the bull-moose off her and lunged forward towards me. The lead rope went under Champ's tail and the rodeo was on. I was in the middle of getting bucked off and the moose was in the middle of my pack horse trying to get lucky. I hit the ground hard and Spook double-barreled the moose in the chest with both hind feet. All this sudden commotion scared the bull-moose off, thank God! Luckily Champ bucked me off but didn't run off and leave me with the moose. I slowly crawled back on Champ whispering in his ear, *Whoa buddy, Whoa buddy, it's going to be alright.* I got in the saddle, Champ grabbed his ass, and away we went through the trees. Champ was alright once we got out of the trees. Spook on the other hand never fully recovered from that tragic moment in her life. Every year for several years when we would ride through that spot in the trees, Spook would grab her ass as if the moose was still there.

I headed on up the steep and muddy trail. My horses were tired now and lining out well. I think the bugs had been worked out of them for a while. I arrived in camp at Porcupine Creek. One Beer was in camp and wouldn't have any hunters until the next day. I was relieved to make it to camp safely. I never did fully trust horses. I have learned in life that there are no perfect women or horses! You just have to decide what you are willing to tolerate. A sheepherder once told me when I was a young boy. "Son, you will only have one perfect horse, dog, and woman in your life and that's the truth." Well, I think I have had the perfect dog and am still waiting on the rest.

One Beer was happy to see me. He helped me unpack Spook and I told him the story about the moose on the trail. He said, "Oh yeah, you gotta watch them crazy bastards when they are in the rut." I took my horses out into a beautiful meadow full of tall grass with a babbling brook running through it. I put hobbles on them and returned to camp to build a bonfire. One Beer had cooked dinner and handed me a bottle of whiskey. This would be the part of a pack trip that I enjoyed the most. Good food, good drink, and good friends. Especially, with a view of a lifetime.

Swerb resting with a bottle of trail shortner

The whiskey was going down smooth, and the bonfire was getting larger. One Beer and I told stories for several hours. One Beer had some great stories of all his hunting and guiding clients over the years. I really respected One Beer. He was a hand at everything he did and knew the mountains well. At some point in the night One Beer said, "Man, Swerb, I hate this canyon we are in." I said, "What the hell are you talking about One Beer? This canyon is absolutely beautiful." One Beer replied, "Yeah, it's beautiful alright, but Bigfoot lives in this canyon," I laughed so hard I blew whiskey out of my nose. One Beer said, "Laugh all you want, I'm not shitting you, I know Bigfoot lives up here. I have heard him scream in the night. I have heard sounds in the night that I can't even explain. This canyon scares the shit out of me at night." One beer was completely serious. I did not believe in Bigfoot myself but respected what he was telling me because I respected the man so much.

One Beer had the hair standing up on my back telling me Bigfoot stories. I looked over to our right and there was something huge and dark walking right by us in the night. I could barely see a large dark shadow going by the campfire. One Beer hadn't seen it yet and was still telling Bigfoot stories. I didn't say anything to One Beer, I just motioned with my eyes for him to look to his right. One Beer looked to his right and whispered, "Oh f---k! It's a grizzly bear headed for the horses on the highline. I'll be right back. I need to grab my rifle and my headlamp." One Beer had a lot of energy. He returned to the fire with his 30-30 rifle and headlamp in all of about three seconds. He yelled, "LET'S GO, IM GOING TO SHOOT THAT BASTARD BEFORE HE HARMS THEM HORSES." I jumped up chasing after One Beer in the night with his headlamp on. Hell, I couldn't see anything trying to follow him in the night. As I was running through the tall grass trying to keep up, I thought to myself *I'm a drunk game warden chasing after One Beer and a grizzly bear in the night that is about to get its ass shot off. I need to take control of this situation before it escalates.* I yelled and said, “STOP, ONE BEER, DON’T SHOOT ANYTHING UNTIL WE KNOW EXACTLY WHAT IT IS AND WHAT IT’S DOING!” One Beer stopped and shined his lights towards the horses on the highline. He said, “It’s that same f--ing bull moose trying to mount Spook on the highline.” I thought to myself, *poor dang horse, she is never going to be the same again.* One Beer yelled at the moose and threw some large sticks at it. The moose moved off into the dark timber. I really do think it was the same damn bull-moose that tried to mount Spook earlier in the day. Now that the excitement was over with, we returned to the fire and added more wood and poured another whiskey and commenced to solving the rest of the world’s problems.

Horny bull moose

Morning came early. I saddled up Champ and packed Spook lightly just to get her used to a pack saddle. I decided to go to an area that I had never been before. One Beer was going to meet some clients later in the day and take them elk hunting somewhere. I told One Beer that I was headed up to Twin Lakes. One Beer said, "Ok, be careful, there is a lot of down-fall on that trail and it's steep in places." I thanked One Beer for his hospitality and told him that I might catch up with him later in the day.

We finally arrived at Twin lakes. The trail was horrible with some downed trees in bad/steep spots in the trail. What a beautiful place this was. I hobbled the horses and let them get some good feed. The lakes were so beautiful I just wanted to take my clothes off and go for a swim in the clear blue water, but the water was way too damn cold for me. I ate my lunch and even took a small safety nap. I called them a safety nap because you never knew when you might need the extra sleep. One Beer and I didn't get much sleep the night before and I had a bit of a headache going on. I searched the area for illegal outfitters but did not find a single person in the area. I decided to mount up and make a mile.

I rode down the trail a short distance and ran into One Beer with his hunters. They had about six mules with them in the trail. I visited with One Beer for a while. His hunters knew I was a game warden, and I checked their hunting licenses and conservation stamps. They also needed the feed ground stamp. But they didn't know that One Beer and I were good friends. One Beer asked me if I wouldn't mind ponying his mules back to their spike camp so that they could hunt the large ridge back down to camp in the evening. I was nervous about this because I didn't know anything about mules, and I didn't trust them. I had to uphold my high-country ranger image, so I said, "Sure, pigtail them all up and I will take them to camp for you guys." One Beer thanked me and handed me the lead rope to the string of six mules and my pack horse Spook. He said, "Be careful. That trail is a real son of a bitch in spots." I was nervous as I left the hunters. I worried about the bad spots in the trail. There were a couple places where you had to ride around dead trees that crossed the trail. In these places it was very steep to go up and around the trees. In some places it would be straight down and very rocky.

I maneuvered through the bad spots and down the trail without a single incident. These mules knew the drill and the trail better than I did. I soon arrived at the spike camp. As I was riding into camp, I think Champ was sound asleep. He looked up and saw a blue tarp flapping off the wall tent and thought something was going to eat his ass. He lunged hard to his left, which got me out of my saddle. The lead rope ran up his ass under his tail. He thought whatever was going to get him had just got him. Once he felt that lead rope underneath his tail he went to bucking. I was already out of the saddle and starting to come off before he started bucking. As I was headed for the ground, I could feel my right foot get tight in the stirrup. It all happened so fast, but I felt like my foot was going to hang up in the stirrup. This would not be good at all. Sure enough, I hit the ground hard on my right-side landing on my pistol. Shit, my right foot was hung up in the stirrup!! The next thing I knew I was dragging on my belly with my head dragging right next to the hind foot of Champ that was stomping the ground hard with every buck. His hooves were missing my head by inches as he dragged me through the meadow. I tucked my arms in underneath my body and tried to grab handfuls of grass or anything that would allow me to pull my foot out of the stirrup. I had a dream one night that I was being drug to death by a horse. This would be my worst nightmare and now it was happening.

Champ was now dragging me across a nearby creek. I was able to get a handful of willow bushes and freed my foot from the stirrup. Thank God for the small willow bushes along the creek. Once my foot came out of the stirrup in the creek, seven pack animals ran right over the top of me. F--k that hurt! I remember lying in the creek and looking up. Champ and seven horses were happily running through a meadow and were on the trail headed for home. The lead rope was still stuck-up Champ's ass under his tail, and he was not happy! The dust was still lingering in the air from the horse wreck. I was thankful to be alive and was afraid to even move because I hurt so badly. I was sure I had broken bones but didn't want to know about them yet. My ankle felt like it was broken, and my hip was in throbbing pain from landing directly on my duty pistol. I got up and watched the horses disappear into the timber headed home. All I could think was, *you really screwed up this time, Swerb. Now we are all stuck in the mountains with no dang horses, including paying clients. One Beer would be pissed at me! Someone would have to hike the eight miles out to gather horses and bring them back. Hopefully none of the horses would hurt themselves trying to keep up with Champ on the bad trail out.* It would be embarrassing for me to explain to One Beer and his hunters that I had screwed up and now we have no transportation in the mountains.

I hobbled back to camp. I don't think my ankle was broken, but damn did it hurt badly. I sat down on a log next to the fire pit and assessed my injuries. There was a bottle of whiskey resting on a nearby tree from the night before. I grabbed it and took a deep long pull off the bottle. I was pretty sure this would make my pain go away. I referred to this bottle of whiskey as my First Aid Kit. I heard a noise and looked up. Here came Champ back across the meadow still dragging the pack string. He ran right into camp next to the campfire and stopped. His nostrils were both flared out and he was still snorting. Both of his reins were busted off and only about six inches long from Champ stepping on them while running. Why he ever came back I have no idea to this day? I hobbled over to him and whispered, "*Whoa Boy, Whoa Boy, Easy Boy.*" as I grabbed the broken rein on his bridle. The problem I had was the rein was so short that I couldn't hold the rein and reach around to pull the lead rope out of his ass without making him turn in a circle and feel the pressure of the lead rope under his tail. Whenever he felt this pressure, he just wanted to run off again. I finally let go of his reins and gambled. I walked behind him and grabbed the lead rope and jerked it out from underneath his tail. He just stood there, thank God!

Mountain first aid kit

I grabbed all the other mules and put them on picket ropes and hobbles out in the meadow. It was getting dark now. I built a bonfire and poured a stout whiskey. I didn't have any ice for my drink but was able to pack some snow in a cut-off Gator-Aid bottle and have a (Lord Calvert Slushy.) One Beer arrived with his hunters as I was lying by the fire. He smiled and said, "How did it go, Swerb?" I smiled, took a sip of whiskey, and replied, "Couldn't have gone any smoother." I never did tell anyone what really had happened. That might have tarnished my high-country ranger image that I had tried so hard to build and maintain over the years.

All the horses and mules were out grazing peacefully. It was a beautiful evening with a gorgeous sunset. One Beer was just gathering the lead ropes to go out and catch the mules and put them up for the night. About that time, I heard a mule braying, bucking, and farting. I looked up and every mule in the pasture was headed home with hobbles and picket ropes. I don't know what spooked them, but it didn't take them long to be completely out of our sight. One Beer yelled at a young wrangler who was sitting on a log drinking whiskey next to me. He yelled, "GO CATCH THEM DAMN MULES BEFORE IT GETS

DARK." The young wrangler threw his cup of whiskey in the air and grabbed a handful of lead ropes and took off into the trees at a full run. I looked out into the meadow and my two horses were the only ones standing in the meadow. They didn't even look up from feeding. The young wrangler returned well after dark with the string of mules. He high lined all of them and came back to the fire and poured himself another whiskey while breathing heavily. He looked at me and said, "Are those your damn horses that stayed in the meadow?" I replied, "Yes, Sir." He toasted my cup of whiskey with his and said, "Those are some damn fine horses, don't ever sell them."

I would end up sitting around the campfire smoking good cigars and drinking cheap whiskey with the non-resident hunters all night. Man did we have some laughs and some great stories. I think they enjoyed having a Wyoming game warden in their hunting camp for the night. The last story of the night ended with me saying, "And be careful out there, Bigfoot will eat your asses off!"

Porcupine Creek, home of Bigfoot

I got up early the next morning to make a mile. I was saddled and headed back down the trail at daylight. A short time after leaving camp, Champ humped up and got all nervous. I felt like he was going to buck me off for no apparent reason. I could just feel his tension between my legs. He stopped and would not go down the trail. He was sniffing and snorting and looking down the trail ahead of us. I noticed a large pine tree that had tipped over and brought its root system up in the air. The root system was dark in color and standing about six feet tall right next to the trail ahead of us. This dark root system created a dark shadow along the trail. I thought to myself, *this is what is spooking Champ.* I kicked Champ in the ribs and said, "Come on dammit, it's just a dead tree along the trail." Champ trusted me and we cautiously headed for the dead tree. He was snorting and walking sideways, Spook was acting up as well. I was starting to lose my patience with horses and was not in the mood to get bucked off again. Hell, I could barely get in the saddle this morning with my badly twisted ankle. As we approached the dead tree with the root system standing tall in the air, I looked over it and observed a bull-moose standing right next to the trail behind the dead tree. It was the same damn bull that had tried to mount Spook twice now. The horses could not see the moose, thank God! It was hidden behind the tall root system. Champ could smell the moose and that's why he didn't want to go down the trail. I rode right by the large bull-moose and said, "Easy buddy, easy buddy!" If Champ would have seen that moose, he would have unloaded my ass again with everything that had happened over the past few days.

I would head out of the mountains with no illegal outfitting detected. I met up with recently retired north Pinedale game warden Duke Early for a cup of coffee at the Wrangler Café. Duke said, "Oh, by the way, you asked me about the crazy mountain man in the Upper Green named Wild Bill. Wild Bill is crazy, and I wouldn't trust him with anything. He collects roadkill animals to feed his German shepherd dogs. I have never confronted him about this, but I have received several complaints over the years. Watch your back with this guy!"

Chapter 14

Red-Shirted Bastards

Pinedale office manager Des Brunette received a call one Friday afternoon from a man by the name of Paul from Bondurant. Paul was drunk and complaining about an angry cow moose that was chasing him into his house each night. He said with a slur, "*If you don't get one of your red shirts down here to take care of this angry moose, I'm going to shoot the ol' bitch myself, I'm tired of her chasing me into my house at night.*" Paul was an outfitter, tough as nails, drank a lot, and didn't care for red-shirted game wardens. Des gave the message to warden supervisor Scott Edberg. Scott talked to Paul on the phone and determined that the moose was eating some alfalfa hay that Paul had purchased and stacked in his lean-to barn next to the house. Edberg loaded up some 9'x4' steel hog panels and headed that way. Edberg explained to Paul that the moose was only interested in the alfalfa hay stacked in the building next to his house. They agreed to put up the nine-foot-tall hog panels and fence off the front of the lean-to building. If the cow moose couldn't get a food reward, she would move on down the nearby willow bottom and leave the area.

This idea seemed to work for a couple of weeks as we did not hear back from Paul. Big Piney game warden Brad Hovinga and I and others were moving elk from the Braun Place to Franz feed ground one day when our portable radio sounded. It was office manager Des

Brunette trying to get a hold of any game warden that she could. Brad answered the radio, "GF-36 go ahead." Des responded, "I have a Paul on the phone from Bondurant. He claims he has a cow moose locked inside his barn and he is going to kill the son of a bitch if he can't get a game warden out there soon." I couldn't believe that Des had said "Son of a bitch" over the radio. She was such a sweet gal and I had never heard her say a cuss word before. This situation must be bad. I looked at Brad and said, "Looks like we better get these elk moved to the Franz feed ground and get to Bondurant sooner than later." Brad replied to Des, "We are moving elk, but will head that way ASAP." Des responded, "10-4, hurry I think this is very serious."

Brad and I arrived at Paul's property just before dark. I noticed a very angry moose locked inside Paul's lean-to barn. They had stood the tall nine-foot hog panels on end to close off the entrance to the building to prevent the moose from getting into the hay. Over the past few weeks Paul had plowed snow up against the hog panels about six feet tall. The snow had thawed during the day and re-froze hard at night. The cow moose couldn't enter the building, so she climbed up the frozen snowbank and jumped up on top of the lean-to's roof to try and get to the fresh alfalfa hay. The metal roof gave away and the moose fell through the roof and ended up trapped in the barn. There was absolutely no way to get her out because the only entrance to the building had frozen snow plowed up against it about six feet tall.

There were chickens in the building flying everywhere and squawking uncontrollably. There was also a boat and a motorcycle in the building. The cow moose saw Brad and me. She laid her ears back and charged the hog panel fence several times, hitting it hard. She stepped back away from the hog panels and gritted her teeth. The hair on her hump was standing up and all you could see were the whites of her eyes. This moose was pissed and possibly crazy. I looked at Brad and said, "You figure out how to get this moose out of the barn and I will go talk to Paul." Brad agreed, I think he was good with the arrangement, because it was not going to be pretty trying to talk to Paul. Paul was a heavy drinker, and it was evening time. There was a story about Paul walking naked into the Elk Horn Bar in Bondurant one night. He had nothing on but his cowboy hat. He sat at the bar and ordered a drink. He told the bartender that the drink better be on the house because it was his birthday, and he was wearing his birthday suit. As I stated before he was double tough, and nobody messed with him. He smoked hand-rolled cigarettes, the weathered wrinkles and scars on his face showed a long hard tough life.

I walked up on his porch and nervously knocked on his front door. Paul answered the door and stepped out and put me in a headlock. He held my head tight as he drug me across his porch. I couldn't believe what was happening. He yelled, "WHICH ONE OF YOU RED-SHIRTED CHICKEN-SHITTED BASTARDS IS GOING TO GET THAT DAMN MOOSE OUT OF MY BARN?" Please excuse my French but this is what was actually said. He was dragging a law enforcement officer, a Wyoming game warden across his porch in a headlock. I had wrestled for many years and was pretty tough myself. I was not afraid of Paul even though he was a tough bastard. I grabbed his elbow and pushed it up freeing my head from his grip. I read him perfectly and said, "Paul, are you afraid of a little ol' cow moose? I thought you were tougher that that!" Paul started walking down the driveway drunk towards the barn yelling, "I'm not afraid of no F-----g cow moose, I'm not afraid of no F-----g cow moose!"

We all ended up back at the barn. Brad had his pepper spray in one hand and his pistol in the other. Paul crawled through a small ground level window well and entered the barn. Brad said, "What the hell is he doing? There is no way to get the moose out? That moose is going to kill him!" The cow moose had been standing behind the haystack between the hay and the back side of the barn. Paul rolled through the window and stood up and walked towards the haystack. He was yelling, "I'm not afraid of no F----g cow moose." The moose heard him and came running around the corner towards him. Paul jumped up on the side of the haystack and started climbing to the top. The cow moose stood on her hind legs and kicked him on the back and head with both feet as he struggled to get to the top of the haystack. This would have killed most people. Paul got to the top of the haystack and walked over to the edge and yelled, "I'm not afraid of no F-----g cow moose. Paul shuffled his way over to the edge of the haystack and was looking down at the cow and yelling obscenities. He got too close to the edge and fell off the haystack landing flat on his back. This knocked the wind out of him, and the cow came around the corner of the haystack and began kicking the shit out of him. Paul rolled over and slowly climbed back up the haystack all the while the cow moose was kicking him in the back of the head and back. He reached the top again with a bloody nose and lip. This time he grabbed the rafters above his head and walked out to the edge of the haystack still holding on. There was one bale on top of the haystack that had no strings on it to hold it together. Paul climbed up on the loose bale of hay holding onto the rafters and yelled, "YOU OLD BITCH, I'm not afraid of no damn moose."

Paul slipped on the broken hay bale and fell again. How he survived I will never know. The cow moose kicked the shit out of him again as he crawled towards the window well. Brad had his pistol drawn and so did I. I yelled, "PAUL GET THE HELL OUT OF THERE BEFORE THAT MOOSE KILLS YOU!" Paul yelled back as the moose was kicking the shit out of him, "I'M NOT AFRAID OF NO F---G COW MOOSE!" Paul made it out of the building alive. He was bleeding and his clothes were full of dirt and hay leaves.

I looked the situation over and devised a plan. I told Brad that when the cow moose goes back over between the haystack and barn wall, I will sneak in there and cave off two rows of hay on her and try and trap her against the back wall of the barn. Brad looked at me like he had just found his wife's panties in the front seat of my pick-up and said, “Good luck with that buddy.” I told Brad that once she was pinned between the wall and the hayshed to take the boards off the back of the barn and let her out. I snuck back in the barn through the small window opening and pushed the outside two rows of hay as hard as I could. The hay came toppling down and pinned the cow moose against the outside wall. I went outside and helped Brad and Paul take the boards off the back of the barn. The boards were 1”x10” rough cut lumber. Paul and Brad pulled several boards off and the cow moose came out pissed off. She immediately charged Brad. He drew his pistol and shot her between the eyes three times as she charged him. The moose lay dead at Brad’s feet. Paul screamed, **“That’s the best damn thing I have ever seen a damn game warden do in my life, you chicken-shitted red-shirted bastards should have done that months ago**!” Paul shook our hands and helped us load the dead cow moose onto Brad’s snow machine trailer with the winch on his camo painted Dodge truck. While doing so, Paul’s wife jumped in her car and sped out of the driveway. Paul took off running down the highway yelling “WHERE IN THE HELL ARE YOU GOING? WHERE IN THE HELL ARE YOU GOING?” I think his wife saw an opportunity to leave the property.

I don’t know what it was with moose, but I had my fair share of challenges with moose over the years. I have a great deal of respect for moose, especially cow moose protecting their calf/calves. Their hooves are very sharp, and they can move very fast when they decide to charge.

I was in the process of closing on our new log home in Daniel. The previous owner had just moved out of the house to move into his new house across the road. He called me out of the blue one day. I was hoping that there weren’t any problems with getting closed on the house deal. His voice sounded kind of crackly as if he was nervous. He said, “Hello Scott, this is Jim. Hey, just wanted to report that my son just killed a bull moose in your new yard. He was only trying to scare it out of the horse hay with my .22 caliber rifle. He accidently hit it and killed it. I told him to call you and report it, but I don't know if you will hear from him or not, so I wanted to let you know. I hope this doesn't affect our closing on the house." I replied, "I appreciate the heads up. This may be a conflict of interest so I will have another warden go out and investigate the situation." Jim replied, "Thanks, I appreciate that and I'm sorry for my kid's actions. The bull is lying dead by the barn out back." I thanked Jim for the phone call and told him that I was excited on getting closed on the house and getting my family moved in.

Poached Bull Moose.

I then called south Pinedale game warden Dennis Almquist and asked him if he could handle the situation. I also told Dennis my conflict of interest with the situation. Dennis replied, "No problem, Swerb, I will head out right now and take care of the unfortunate situation. Dennis arrived at the property and found no evidence of a dead bull moose at the barn. What he did find were tracks in the snow of a bobcat skid-steer and a blood trail running down the middle of the road headed towards the neighbor's new house. Dennis followed the tracks and blood trail over to the neighbors. He found a spot back behind some willows where the son had dumped the moose carcass with an effort to hide it. Dennis called me and said, “Swerb, I want to be fair with the boy. But he hauled the carcass off with an attempt to hide it, and he never did call anyone to report what he had done.” I replied, “Thanks Dennis for your help. Handle the situation however you deem necessary, new neighbor or not!” Boy, I was not starting out very well with my new neighbors. The son was cited for taking a moose out of season.

We eventually got moved into our new home. I was very excited about this place. It was going to be a great deal of work, but I was anxious to get started. The property had a small one room cabin out back. I would completely remodel this cabin and make a Friday night poker room out of it. It would also serve as a spare bedroom if we had company. I would need to put new siding on the exterior and interior of the barn. The entire property fence would need replaced over time. There was also a concrete pad with some redwood 4x4’s planted in the concrete. Jim was in the process of making a dog kennel. I would turn this into my tool shed over time. That way I could warm it in the winter months and make projects and restore antique furniture. There was also an old, dilapidated house on the property that was about 25’x25.’ It would cost too much to restore this house and would be a huge amount of work. I would end up giving this house to a friend who promised to haul it off. I would then build a man-cave garage with two large barn-style sliding garage door on the existing foundation. The front yard had a beautiful fishing pond surrounded by aspen trees. The house had a large deck with an awning on the front and back. I was really looking forward to spending some time relaxing on the deck with a cold beverage after work each day. We had moose right in our yard year around because we were right next to the Green River with vast valleys of willows, small creeks, and natural springs. This place was beautiful, and I loved it. However, we would end up burning between 10-15 cords of firewood each year to stay warm. Our wood stove was our only source of heat, and it would run 24/7 for about nine months out of the year. The average growing season in this area was twenty-eight days. Mama wouldn't be growing any tomatoes here!

Infamous poker cabin

New garage

Cow moose in front yard

Charging cow moose in front yard

I would eventually meet all my neighbors. They were all great people and one of them was a taxidermist who was mounting Lana's buck deer from last fall. A younger couple had just moved in down the road. He worked as a supervisor in the oil field, and she was an attractive stay at home mom with two young kids. All our neighbors were the type of people who would do anything for you, if in need. Our kids would go to school in Pinedale which was located about fifteen miles away.

It was a Monday morning. I was attending an important meeting in Pinedale at the regional office. Office Manager Des Brunette interrupted the meeting by poking her head into the meeting room and whispered, "Swerb, I have an important call on line one for you." I jumped out of my chair and thought to myself, *hopefully this is an important call, and I can get out of this damn meeting.* I went into my office, picked up the phone, and tapped the blinking light on line one. "This is Scott, how may I help you today?" It was a lady's voice. I couldn't understand her because she was sobbing, and her voice was broken. After several minutes of listening carefully I determined that it was my new neighbor just down the road from me who had recently moved in with her husband and two children. I could not hear her well at all, as I don't hear well, especially on the phone. What I did hear is that she was my neighbor and had accidentally shot a moose, but she thought it was a pelican? I thought to myself, *Swerb you are not hearing this conversation at all, you need to get off the phone and go meet with her at her house.* I replied, "I'm sorry to hear that ma'am, can I meet with you at your house in about twenty minutes?" The lady replied, "Yes, sir, that would be good, thank you, I'm so sorry!" I told her that I would be headed that way and hung up the phone. I was confused, did she shoot a moose or a pelican? They certainly didn't look alike.

I soon arrived at her house. She was a very attractive young blonde-haired lady standing in her driveway sobbing. I asked her what had happened. She responded, "Can you come in the house please, this is very embarrassing." I agreed and followed her through the front door of their beautiful home. She explained to me that on Friday night her kids had a sleep over with other children at the house. She was getting ready to turn off the outside porch light when she noticed a cow moose eating her horse hay next to the house. She grabbed what she thought was a pellet gun (not pelican) to scare off the moose. She aimed what she thought was the pellet gun at the moose's hind end and pulled the trigger. She had accidently grabbed a .22 caliber chipmunk rifle that had been leaning next to the pellet gun. The .22 caliber rifle went "BANG" instead of "PSST" She then realized that she had grabbed the wrong rifle and shot the moose in the ass with a .22 caliber instead of a pellet gun. The cow moose walked about twenty feet and tipped over dead in her yard. She had hit the femoral artery in the rump of the cow moose and killed it. She was embarrassed and didn't want her children, their friends, or her husband to know what had happened. So, she snuck out in the night after everyone was sound asleep and dragged the dead moose with her husband's ATV into their two-car garage nearby.

I thought to myself, *Good Lord, this is the second moose that has been killed with a .22 caliber rifle in my neighborhood since I moved in.* The lady offered to take me into the garage and show me the dead moose. I opened the garage door and couldn't believe my eyes. The moose had been dead since Friday, and this was Monday. The moose was lying on its back bloated with all four legs stuck straight in the air. Man, did it stink, and her husband's lariat rope was still around the cow's neck. The lady hugged me and started sobbing again. She repeated, "I'm so sorry, I'm so sorry! My husband doesn't even know about this yet." I assured the lady that she was not going to prison and that she was not a hardened criminal for killing the moose. I told her that I would attempt to load the moose in the back of my truck and get it out of her garage. I also told her that I was going to cite her for taking a moose out of season and that it was up to her to tell her husband or not. I stated, "But, if it were me, I would tell your husband before he reads about it in the local newspaper, or a friend tells him about it at work." She sobbed more and shook her head yes, as if she agreed. I backed my patrol truck up to the garage door and loaded the huge, bloated cow moose with a come-along one click at a time. While doing so, I ended up with stinky moose snot (moose juice) all over the front of my red shirt and pants. Man, did I stink, and I still had a meeting to get back to in Pinedale. I wrote the lady a citation and tried to tuck the cow moose down in the bed of my truck as much as possible to save her embarrassment from any neighbors who might drive by.

I jumped in my truck. Man, did I stink! I thought, *I just live down the road a short distance, I'm going home to change my stinky clothes.* I pulled into my driveway and walked up to the front door of my house. As I went to enter the house the front door was locked. That was weird. I have never locked the door on my house, ever! I remembered that my young daughter Wendy had stayed home sick from school that day. I don't think she was sick; she was just having vision problems. She couldn't *envision* herself going to school that day. I banged loudly on the door with my fist. My daughter came to the front door wrapped in a towel with her hair wet, also wrapped in a towel. I asked, "How come the damn door is locked?" as I walked into the house. My daughter replied, "Dad, there has been a crazy lady running around the house all morning pounding on the doors and the windows." I walked into the kitchen and observed my scoped 30.06 rifle lying on the kitchen counter with a shell in the chamber. I said, "Wendy, what in the hell are you doing with my rifle loaded on the kitchen counter?" Wendy replied, "Dad, this lady is fricken crazy and I didn't know if I was going to have to shoot her or not! I was afraid she might break a window and come into the house." I asked her what the lady looked like. Wendy replied, she was short, had blonde hair, and was crying." I finally figured it out. This was the same lady that had killed the cow moose. She had come over to my house earlier to find me before she called the office looking for me. I looked at my daughter and said, "I don't know, but I think there are some crazy ass women in this neighborhood." I changed my clothes and made it back to the meeting just as it was ending.

Chapter 15

Memories of a Lifetime

My son Wesley had just turned twelve and was legal to hunt big game animals. He also drew a limited quota deer tag and a limited quota elk tag in the Upper Green River area. This is some of the most awesome country that Wyoming has to offer with both huge buck deer and bull elk. I took my son on several deer hunts and showed him buck deer that were larger than I had ever harvested before. He was not experienced or confident in his shooting as he had never harvested anything before. Sometimes with large buck mule deer you only have a split second to get your shot off as they are running away or disappearing into the timber. We just couldn't quite get it done on several large bucks. They outsmarted us you might say. I was proud of my son for never hurrying his shots and always making sure he could make the shot before he took it. I taught him how to be a responsible hunter and that he was responsible to make sure that he made a clean shot and did not injure an animal because he didn't have time for a good shot placement. I was always busy checking hunters during the hunting season and rarely ever got much time to spend hunting for myself or the family.

It was the last day of deer season and nearly dark. We had spotted a group of seven buck deer on the ridge above us. They were all standing on the skyline with a beautiful sunset in the background. They were all mature mule deer bucks. The distance was about three hundred yards and daylight was disappearing fast. I told Wes to lay down and put his bi-pod out and find the deer in his scope. The deer were feeding on a bare ridge. The sage brush was very tall just below them and where we were lying down. Wes was having a hard time finding the deer in his scope due to the high sage brush in front of us and the fact that he would be shooting straight up above us. He was shooting a .243 rifle that my dad had given to me for my fourteenth birthday. This rifle meant a great deal to me as my dad died when I was seventeen years old. This rifle had a beautiful wooden stock and didn't have a scratch on it anywhere. Wes took very good care of this rifle and knew what it meant to me. I knew the distance of this shot would be pushing it for the rifle and Wes.

Most of the deer had now fed out of sight over the tall ridge above us. There was one buck left standing broadside on the skyline above us. He looked like a nice 4x4 buck. Wes was finally able to find the deer in his scope. I told him to take a deep breath and relax. I also told him to slowly squeeze, not pull the trigger. "The gun should surprise you when it fires." I whispered to him. BOOM!! The gun went off and the deer jumped straight into the air. I was watching the deer through my spotting scope. He had hit the deer low in the front leg. The deer took off down-hill towards us into the tall sage brush. I thought *shit the deer is wounded, it is getting dark, and it will be tough for Wes to find it in the tall sage brush.* If there were ever a time that I wanted to finish off Wes's deer for him, this was one of them! But that would be illegal, and I'm a game warden! I told Wes that he needed to quickly find the deer in his scope and make a killing shot as we were running out of daylight. I could see the deer standing in the high sage brush with a broadside shot. But Wesley could not find the deer in his scope due to the tall sagebrush in front of him. I whispered, "Hurry up and shoot while he is standing broadside." Wes, said with a frustrated tone, "Dad, I can't see the buck anywhere." I said, "Wes, calm down and find the deer now and shoot him!" Man did I want to grab the rifle and shoot the wounded buck. I did not want to lose a wounded buck in the night and have to come back in the morning only to find the meat spoiled. If we could even find him the next day. But no, my son needed to be responsible and take the buck without help. And I didn't want to violate the law.

As I was looking for the deer again in my spotting scope, I heard BOOM. Wes replied, "Dad, I got him, he dropped right in his tracks." I didn't even see the deer. Wes had just made one heck of a shot in a difficult situation. We high fived one another and hiked up the hill. It took us awhile to finally find the buck lying in the tall sagebrush. Wes had hit the deer right behind the shoulder at about two hundred and fifty yards away. It was almost dark. I told Wes to fill out his hunting license before we dressed the animal. Wes got a weird look on his face and said, "Dad my license is back in the truck." This disappointed me, I said, "Wes, you can't legally leave the site of kill without filling out your license first. You run back to the truck and get your license and I will dress out your deer for you." This would be a lesson that Wes would never forget as the truck was several miles away and we didn't have a flashlight. I couldn't believe how quick Wes had returned with his license. He must have run the entire distance there and back. I was just getting done with cleaning out the deer. It was a long and tough drag back to the truck. Thankfully it was mostly downhill all the way.

We loaded the deer into the back of the truck. I shook Wes's hand and congratulated him on his first trophy buck deer. I told Wes that we needed to celebrate the father/son moment and have a shot of Black Velvet. I poured Wes a shot in the cap of the bottle and handed it to him. We toasted and we both threw down a shot of whiskey. Wes blew the shot back out of his nose and mouth and yelled, "HOW CAN YOU DRINK THAT SHIT DAD?" I replied, "I don't know son, it must be an acquired taste." I was proud of the shot that Wes made and glad we didn't have to spend all night and the next day searching for a wounded deer. I was also proud of myself for not finishing the deer off for him and doing something illegal, just not wanting to lose the wounded deer in the night.

Wes with his first deer

I visited with Roundy about my son Wes having a bull elk tag valid in the Upper Green River. Roundy told me that we were welcome to come stay with him and his hunters in their spike camp in Porcupine Creek. I was really excited about this as I loved that drainage, and it had some trophy bull elk in it. Wes had never harvested an elk before and we hadn't been on a father/son pack trip yet. My plan was to call it work and check hunters in the backcountry while Wes hunted elk. Wildlife administration was always supportive of this, as game wardens rarely ever got any time off to hunt! They would rather have wardens in the backcountry checking hunters rather than taking a week off during hunting season to go hunting for yourself. I asked Roundy what I could bring. He said, "Just bring yourselves and whatever you need to hunt with. We will already have food up there and camp is already set up. I was really excited about this. Wes and I wouldn't have to hardly pack anything, and camp was already there and set up. We agreed to meet at the Green River Lakes parking lot on September 30, at 10:00 AM. Opening day for elk season was October 1st. Roundy had hunters who would be packing in, and we would all go in together.

The day finally came, and man was it raining out. I don't think I had ever seen it rain any harder. It had been raining non-stop for three days. Wes and I arrived at the parking lot and Roundy was nowhere to be found. I figured he was running late so I unloaded our horses and started packing them in the rain. We had just finished packing them when Roundy showed up in his brand new four-door dually pick-up. He rolled down his electric window and said, "Sorry, but I don't think we are going anywhere in this shit, it's just too damn wet out." I replied, "That's fine, we are already packed so I think we are going to head in without you," Roundy replied, "Camp is set up, just take the new stove out and burn the new paint off the stove pipe before you light it in the wall tent. Good luck Wes. You guys have a safe trip. I will be up in a few days with my hunters." I thanked Roundy for everything. As he was leaving the parking lot, he backed up the truck and rolled down the window and said, "Oh shit, I told you we would have food up there for you guys. We never made it back up there to pack in any food." I replied, "That's alright, we have trail mix and some beef jerky, we will be fine." Roundy said, "NO, dammit, I told you I would have food up there and this is my fault. I will go back down to my base camp and get you guys some food to eat for Christ Sake. Hold tight, I will be right back." Wes and I crawled back in the truck to get out of the rain waiting for Roundy to return with food. Roundy soon returned and handed me a family pack of hotdogs. He said, "Here ya go, it ain't much but it will make a turd." I thanked Roundy and threw the hotdogs in my saddle bag.

My wife Lana had sent us with one of her most gentle horses from her parent's guest ranch in Shell. The horse had hauled hundreds of dudes for miles over the years. She said Chief would also make a good pack horse if Wes were to kill an elk. I tied a scabbard to Chief and put Wes's rifle in it. I helped Wes get on Chief and we were now officially headed on our first father/son pack trip in pouring rain. Wes didn't look all that impressed at the moment. I was riding Champ and had packed Spook very lightly. Mostly with whiskey, hobbles, trail mix, some clothes, and hunting gear. I also threw in my ticket book in case I ran into any hunters violating the law in the backcountry. The plan was, if Wes harvested an elk, we would pack the elk out on Spook and Chief and Wes would walk out leading Chief with the elk.

We were lined out and headed down the trail. We started walking through the patch of timber that the moose tried to mount Spook in last fall. Spook all of sudden grabbed her ass and ran up next to me. Wes said, "What got into her, Dad?" I replied, "Oh not much son, she got mounted by a moose right here last year and has not forgotten about it yet." Wes didn't say much to that, but I could tell his wheels were spinning. We finally got into the thick trees out of the rain a bit. The trail was muddy and steep. The horses were spinning out trying to gain traction and keep moving uphill without falling. I was having a hard time keeping my horse upright when I heard Wes, yell, "DAD, DAD!" This scared the heck out of me. I had never heard Wes yell like this before. I turned around to see Wes hanging off the side of his saddle. The saddle had slid sideways on Chief. I yelled at Wes, "GET YOUR DAMN FOOT OUT OF THE STIRRUP AND GET OFF THE HORSE!" Wes yelled back, "I CAN'T, MY FOOT IS STUCK IN THE STIRRUP!" Wes was wearing heavy hiking boots that were too large for the stirrups.

I panicked and jumped off my horse and tied Champ to a large tree the best I could. I yelled at Wes, "DON'T MOVE, I'M COMING!" Wes yelled, "DAD, I CAN'T HANG ON ANY LONGER." I yelled back, "DAMMIT, HANG ON! IF YOU FALL THAT HORSE MAY SPOOK AND DRAG YOU TO DEATH." I quickly made it down the slippery trail in the mud. The first thing I did was prop Wes up with my shoulder and pull his stuck foot out of the stirrup. I then helped him slowly get off the horse. The rifle in the scabbard was now between Chief's front legs. Thank God Chief was bulletproof, or we may have had one hell of a horse wreck. I straightened the saddle out and tightened the cinch. It was hard for Wes to get back on the horse because the trail was so steep and slippery. Once in the saddle, I told Wes to only put his toes in the stirrups in case this were to ever happen again. This scared me probably more than Wes. His mother would never forgive me, and I would never forgive myself. If something horrible had happened to Wes just trying to harvest his first elk.

We finally arrived at the spike camp in Porcupine Creek. The wall tent was nearly collapsed from the heavy rain. Both Wes and I were soaked to the bone. We unpacked the horses and took care of them. The new wood stove was put together in the wall tent but had never been used before. Roundy told me to take it outside and light it for the first time to burn the paint off the new pipe. The hell with that idea, it was raining worse than a cow peeing on a flat rock out there and we needed a fire to get dry and warm. I opened the door on the stove and noticed about three inches of water in the bottom of the stove. Water was coming down the stovepipe. I cleaned out the water the best that I could. There was nothing dry to start a fire with anywhere. I hiked back in the heavy timber and found some pine needles underneath some low hanging pine branches. I had to dig down about eight inches to find dry matter. I filled my hat with small twigs and pine needles and hauled them back to the wall tent. Wes was starting to shake. I said, "Don't worry son, your father is a trained professional and a high-country ranger and will have a blazing fire before you know it."

It took nearly an hour to get the fire started due to the fact that there was so much rainwater coming down the stovepipe. Thank God I had packed a cigarette lighter to light my expensive cigar that Brad Hovinga had given me several months back because there were no other matches in camp. It took forever for the tent to finally warm up. There was just no dry wood anywhere. The horses were high lined in the trees but still getting plenty wet and cold. Wes was starting to warm up and said, “Dad, I’m kind of hungry, what do we have to eat?” I replied, “Well Rusty, (his nickname) let’s see what I can find.” I went outside and grabbed the family pack of hotdogs out of my saddle bag. I brought them in the wall tent and tossed the package over to him. I said, “There ya go, Rusty, don’t eat too many of them. That’s all we got.” Rusty didn’t want to complain but had a concerned look on his twelve-year old dirty face. He said, “Are there any buns or ketchup?” I replied, “Nope, you can warm them on top of the stove or eat them cold, whichever you prefer.” I did have some trail mix and beef jerky, but we would have to ration that out. By now, the stove pipe had heated up and the new paint was burning off the new stove pipe. We could hardly breathe or see one another in the tent, due to the heavy smoke that was burning off the pipe. I cracked the flap on the front door of the tent to let some of the smoke out. The nasty fumes from this father/son moment probably affected both of us, even today.

I had hunted this area twice before with great success. There was an area that Roundy called “the trap” It was called the trap because once elk got into the steep narrow canyon, they were essentially trapped if you were hunting the entrance below the canyon. I had been to the trap twice before but had never been there at first light. I always wanted to be there at first light thinking that would be the best time of the day to hunt it. The canyon had open hill sides and lots of timber. It would be good to catch the elk out in the open while they were feeding in the early morning hours. The trail into the trap was very steep and rugged. It would be difficult for me to find it in the dark, as I had only been in there twice before in the daylight. There were areas where the horse trail disappeared in the heavy downfall timber, and you would have to pick your way through. Once you got within a mile of the trap, the horse trail turned into a small game trail that was difficult to see at times. We would also need to cross a creek three different times to get into the trap. My plan was to leave the horses in camp and hike into the trap in the dark before sunrise. The hike would likely take a couple of hours. I wasn't sure because I had never hiked in there before on foot, I always was riding a horse. Rusty had no idea what he was in for in the morning, but it was definitely going to be an adventure for sure. I just hoped that it would stop raining.

We crawled into our bedrolls. The tent was now comfortable and warm. I knew the warmth wouldn't last long and we would be freezing our asses off by morning. I set my wind-up alarm clock for 5:00 AM. Our backpacks were loaded and ready to go with everything that we would need to harvest an elk, including our family pack of hotdogs. If Wes killed an elk, we would quarter the elk and come back and get the horses to pack it out.

I felt like I had slept pretty well, but for some reason I was wide awake at 3:00 AM. I wasn't sure how long it would take us to hike into the trap to be there at first light. I decided to get up and make a mile. I slapped Rusty's sleeping bag with my hand and said, "Time to get up and go hunting." Rusty slowly opened his eyes and said, "What time is it, Dad?" I replied, "It's time to go kill a trophy bull elk, son." I turned my flashlight on, so that we could see to get dressed in the dark tent. It was colder than my first prom date in that wall tent! We could see our breath in the light of the flashlight. I opened the front flap of the wall tent and stepped outside. It was darker than the inside of a black cow and drizzling rain. Thank God it wasn't pouring rain. I made sure Rusty had his rifle, bullets, knife, saw, binoculars, hunting license, water, and hotdogs. I had just purchased a brand-new elk bugle at Faler's general store in Pinedale. I had used them before and was excited to try and call a bull elk in for Wes to shoot. I shoved the elk call in my backpack along with a few other things that might be important, like toilet paper. Rusty said, "What's for breakfast, Dad?" I handed Rusty a small zip lock bag full of trail mix and a bottle of Gatorade. He asked, "That's it?" I replied, "Yup, if you kill an elk, we can have back-straps for dinner tonight."

We loaded up and left camp. I had a flashlight but did not want to waste the battery power unless we really needed it. I turned the light on to cross the first creek crossing right outside of camp. The water was deeper than I thought. We both got our feet wet. We had crossed the creek for the last time and were headed up a steep hill on a horse trail. Both of us were wet up to our knees. I figured we could always build a fire later in the day and dry our shoes and socks out. It was so dark that I had lost the trail in front of me. I stopped and turned my flashlight on. I was surprised to see that we were still on the trail. I was also surprised to see a grizzly bear track in the mud about twelve inches long. For some reason, a large grizzly bear track in the mud is really illuminated by a flashlight. Rusty walked up next to me and said, "Dad, is that a grizzly bear track?" I replied, "Yes son, it is," as I turned off the flashlight and continued up the steep trail. At this point I noticed that Rusty was nearly stepping on my heels as I walked. He was like a magnet stuck to my back. I think the bear track scared him a bit.

We finally reached the area where I wanted to be at first light. Except first light wouldn't be coming for at least another hour. Let's just say we were plenty early. It was cold and drizzling rain. You could see your breath. I was excited to finally be in this area at daylight. That alone was quite an accomplishment. I heard an elk bugle right across the small canyon in front of us. The bull sounded like he was mature and maybe five hundred yards away. I grabbed my brand-new elk bugle out of my backpack. I would need to install the small elastic diaphragm over the end of the call. I pulled it out of the bag, and it rolled up like a condom in the cold. I struggled for several minutes trying to get it to roll out and fit properly. I finally got frustrated with my cold hands and pulled a little too hard and tore the elastic that fits at the tip of the call. It didn't look too bad, and I was sure the call would still work.

There is nothing better than hearing a bull elk bugle in a cold clear crisp morning. It is like there is complete silence and then this huge scream that makes the hair on your back stand up. It was starting to get daylight. I could see about five cows on the edge of the trees across the canyon. If I could call the bugling bull out of the trees, Wes would have about a three-hundred-yard shot. The bull was right on the edge of the trees bugling. It was light enough to shoot. I looked at Rusty and said, "Lean over that log and get a good steady rest with your rifle. I'm going to try and call that bull out of the trees. If he comes out wait until you have a good standing broadside shot and gently squeeze the trigger." Rusty's eyes got big. I could tell he was really excited. He was shooting a .280 Ruger. A rifle that was dead on and one that I had harvested many big game animals with over the years.

I looked at Rusty who was lying on the ground in front of me and whispered, "Are you ready?" He nodded his head yes. I grabbed the call and blew as hard as I could. You can't ease into these calls you have to give it the onion or they don't work very well. I could not believe my ears. This call made the loudest horrible screech that I have ever heard in my life! It sounded like air whistling out of a semi tire as it goes flat from a puncture wound. The bull elk ran out of the trees, gathered his five cows, and herded them back into the trees. Rusty turned around and looked at me and whispered, "What in the hell did you do that for, Dad?" I told Rusty that I was sorry that I screwed everything up and explained the torn diaphragm to him. We waited there about another hour and never heard the elk again. I later saw them running over the top of the mountain about one mile from us. I looked at Rusty and said, “Well son, we are done hunting this area. Sorry that I screwed it all up for you.” Rusty was disappointed but he understood that sometimes things just don’t work out the way you would like them to. It was just disappointing because we had worked so hard to get to this area by daylight. Now we were soaking wet and cold and would need to hike back to camp.

Hot dog cooker

We returned to camp. It had stopped raining and it looked like the sun was trying to peek out through the high mountain clouds. This was actually very beautiful to see the rays of the sunshine blasting through the broken-up clouds. I was so ready for some sunshine and warmth. I built a fire near the wall tent in the fire pit. The same fire pit that One Beer and I sat by and told Bigfoot stories the previous fall. I cut some pine sticks and sharpened them so that we could cook our hotdogs over some hot coals. I loaded up Rusty's stick with a hotdog and told him to enjoy as I handed it over to him. Rusty caught his hotdog on fire and just let it burn in the fire pit. I said, "Hey Rusty, your hotdog is on fire you better move it." He responded, "I know, Dad, I want to burn it and give it a crisp charcoaled coating to taste since we don't have any ketchup or mustard." I tried it myself. They actually did taste better burnt.

We finished lunch, dried out and put the horses out on hobbles for a while to feed out in the meadow. Once the horses were taken care of, Rusty and I took a nap in the wall tent. We were tired from getting up at 3:00 AM.

Porcupine Creek Meadow

It was now late afternoon. We decided to take a hike south of camp to look for elk. This was also a very good spot and much easier to get to. We had hiked approximately two miles south and ended up in a large canyon. This canyon had open grassy meadows and timber.

I heard an elk bugle way high up on the mountain. Rusty and I grabbed our binoculars and started glassing up high. I spotted the elk, and they were on the highest mountain peak in the area and a long ways away. I could tell that the bull looked pretty nice. He was a mature six-point bull, near as I could tell. It was getting late in the evening. Rusty wanted to hike up there and try and harvest the bull. I told Rusty that it was a heck of a lot further up there than it looked. I also told him that we would hunt this area first thing in the morning and maybe the elk would come down to water and be much closer to camp and the horse trail. We returned to camp right at dark and built another large bonfire. As we were sitting by the fire roasting another hotdog, Rusty looked up at me and said, "You know, Dad, we could be eating elk back straps right now if you hadn't screwed all that up." I replied, "Quiet Rusty, eat your hotdog and be thankful." Rusty laughed and said, "I didn't ever think that I could eat my body weight in hotdogs." I had to admit, I was ready for some real food myself.

Daylight came early. We awoke and ate some more trail mix and jerky. We swigged down another bottle of Gatorade and headed south to see if we could get on the elk that we had spotted yesterday evening. We arrived at that location and again heard a bull elk bugling. I glassed at the very top of the mountain and the elk were still in the same spot as they were yesterday. I was hoping that they would come down to water in the nearby creek. The last thing that I wanted to do was hike clear to the top of that steep mountain and harvest an elk. I was already getting too old for that crap. But Rusty was young, full of piss and vinegar, and had never killed a bull elk before. As I was glassing the elk, I said, "I don't know, Rusty, what do, you think?" Rusty replied, "Let's go get him, Dad." This was the last thing that I wanted to hear. Heck, I don't think I would have hiked that high to kill a bighorn sheep. And there was dang sure some of those up there at that elevation as well. I replied, "Well, if you think we can get all the way up there and pack a bull elk back to camp, let's go." Rusty looked at me excited and said, "Come on, Dad, we can do it." Up the mountain we went.

It was a grueling climb to say the least. I thought I was going to puke up a lung. Rusty was tired but not near as tired as I was. We climbed and climbed and climbed some more. We were nearly to the top of the mountain, and I heard the bull bugle again. I looked up and spotted the bull on top of the mountain about 300 yards away. I looked at Rusty and said, "Do you think you can hit that bull from here, or do you want to try and get closer?" Rusty said, "I think I can hit him from here." Rusty laid down on the ground and leaned over a dead tree for a steady rest. I was hoping he would miss, and we could go home, but I was also thinking about back straps for dinner! Rusty slowly pulled the trigger and BANG went the gun. The bull elk hunched up and ran into some thick jack pines out of sight. I high fived Rusty and said, "Nice shot son, you hit him." The bull was only about 300 yards away, but it took us nearly two hours to hike up to the area where he had hit him. Every step was grueling, one step forward and two steps back sliding in the loose rocks. Most areas had large cliffs and you couldn't even think about getting up any of them.

We finally arrived in the area where I thought he had hit the bull. I couldn't find any blood but wasn't even sure we were in the exact location where he had hit him. I walked over to some thick jack pines and started wading through them. There were no trails, making it difficult to get through them. We searched the area for nearly thirty minutes. I was starting to think that maybe the bull had run off and we might not find him. I had searched the thick patch of timber that I had seen him last go into very thoroughly and no bull elk. I walked through the thick patch of timber and was looking for blood or elk tracks in the grass, to see if the bull had made it through the trees and went somewhere else. I walked back down the ridge and looked back up at the thick patch of timber. While glassing, I thought I could see something that looked like a tan elk hide. It was behind some trees and hanging off a cliff. Not a likely spot for this elk to be, but I thought I had better go check it out. It was a steep climb to get up to the area where I thought I could see the tan elk hide. Once in the area, I spotted it. I couldn't believe my eyes. The bull elk was hanging off a cliff with his horns stuck between two small trees. I was excited and so was Rusty. But how would we deal with this situation? I wanted to get some good pictures of Rusty with his first bull elk, but we couldn't because the bull was hanging off a cliff and you couldn't get near him for a photo.

I decided to pull out my small brand-new Gerber saw. I had never used it before, but it looked very sharp. My idea was to saw the skull plate off the bull and let the bull drop down into the canyon below. I sawed what seemed like an hour and was only about halfway through the skull plate. I had blisters on both hands from gripping the saw so tight. The weight of the elk kept putting the saw in a bind. This idea was not working well at all. I now had sweat dripping off my head and was breathing hard and we hadn't even done any hard work yet. I decided that it may be easier to saw off one of the small trees and let the entire bull roll down the canyon. So that is what I did. What happened next, Rusty and I will never forget. The bull elk dropped off the cliff and landed hard in the canyon below. When the bull hit the ground the 6x6 antlers busted off the elk's skull and flew at least thirty feet in the air and down the canyon. The elk rack landed way out in front of the still-rolling bull elk. The bull elk rolled over the antlers and went out of sight over another cliff and down another canyon. At least we were getting closer to the horse trail with the bull elk and the meat would now be tenderized.

Rusty and I worked our way down the canyon and picked up the elk antlers. I didn't even want to look off the next cliff to see where the bull may have ended up. We peeked over the edge. I observed the bull lodged between two boulders the size of a Volkswagen straight below us about 300 yards away. We had to walk around the cliff and head down the mountain and then back up the canyon to get to the bull. We finally arrived. The bull was wedged tight between the two boulders. We would have to bone the elk out right where he lay. We had game bags in our backpacks. It took us about two hours to bone the elk out and fill the game bags with boned out meat. We now had two backpacks, one rifle, one 6x6 elk rack, and an entire boned-out elk in game bags. I told Rusty that we were only making one trip and I was not hiking back up the steep damn mountain for another trip with meat. We both had two large bags filled with meat that we tied together and draped around our necks. We also both carried two large bags of boned-out meat. The mountain was very steep, but at least it was straight downhill. We took our time and dragged bags of meat on the ground with many resting stops along the way.

It was nearly dark before we reached the horse trail in the bottom of the canyon where we had started from around 7:00 AM that morning. I was never so exhausted and happy in all my life. We had finally made it to where the horses could pack the meat the rest of the way out. I took my backpack off and washed my hands in the creek. I was soaking wet from sweating so much. I sat down on the trail with my back against a tree to finally rest for a minute. Rusty was just as tired. Suddenly, my heart sank, I had a horrible thought in my head. I looked at Rusty and said, "Did you happen to cut those beautiful ivories out of the bull." Rusty looked at me and replied, "No, I thought you got them." I responded, "Shit Rusty, those were beautiful ivories and your first bull. I will hike back up there and get them while you rest for a while." The second trip nearly killed me. I don't even know how I made it to be honest. I finally reached the bull, cut the ivories out and headed back off the mountain. By the time I arrived back at the meat, it was dark. We still had about two miles to hike back to camp. Rusty didn't want to leave his elk rack with the meat, but we were completely exhausted by now. We hung the boned out elk meat high up in a pine tree so that the grizzly bears couldn't eat it during the night.

Wes's first 6X6 bull elk

We slowly walked back to camp dragging our legs with every step. I started a fire and poured a stiff whiskey. Rusty even had a small shot and didn't blow it out of his nose this time. I sat down on a stump and took a sip of whiskey. I looked at Rusty and said, "Shit, I forgot to carve off some back straps for dinner tonight." Rusty smiled and reached into his backpack. He pulled out a large chunk of back strap and said, "I was one step ahead of you, Dad, when you hiked back up to get my ivories, I remembered to grab some back straps for dinner tonight. Besides, I don't think I could eat another damn hotdog as long as I live." I could have just hugged him, heck maybe I did. We placed a grill over the hot fire and cooked up some fresh elk back straps for dinner. This may have been the best tasting back straps that I had ever eaten. We celebrated around the fire and told father/son stories. We also talked about our day and how exciting it was to finally find the bull elk dead hanging off the cliff. I didn't think we were going to find it at all. Rusty had made a great shot and hit the bull right behind the shoulder. We were both very excited and tired. The whiskey went down pretty smooth that night and we both slept like a baby.

We slept in the next morning and had back straps for breakfast. The morning sun was high and starting to throw off some warmth. The sun felt good and the canyon that we were camped in was absolutely beautiful. All we had to do today was go pack out the elk meat and head back home. I had tied Chief to a tree close to camp so that I could saddle him up. I had him saddled and went to throw the saddle panniers on him. He didn't want anything to do with the saddle panniers. He reared back hard on the lead rope, dug his hind feet into the ground and pulled as hard as he could. The lead rope broke in half and Chief went over backwards right into the side of Roundy's wall tent. The horse was lying on top of the tent. Rusty looked at me from the campfire and said, "Dad, I don't think that horse is going to be

Our home before Chief destroyed it

worth a damn at packing an elk." Thank God the tent collapsed, and Chief didn't tear a hole in the tent. This spooked him even more and he had a walleyed bucking fit right through camp and out into the meadow. He finally calmed down and let me catch him. This horse was supposed to be bullet proof and able to pack. He didn't want anything to do with the saddle panniers. I ended up hobbling him out in the meadow and sacked him out with the saddle panniers until he was used to them and allowed me to put them over the saddle. I wasn't very optimistic that Chief was going to let us put any fresh elk meat on him after seeing this behavior.

We reached the area where the elk meat was hanging. I approached Chief with a game bag full of boned-out elk meat. He snorted and blew sideways. This was not going to be easy to get him packed and hopefully nobody would get hurt in doing so. He would not stand still. Rusty was trying to hang onto the lead rope but wasn't strong enough. I was afraid Rusty was going to get hurt so I hobbled the horse and tied him to a tree. I was still struggling trying to load the meat on him when I heard a voice in the trees above us. The voice said, "How's it going down there?" I looked up and, thank God, it was Roundy riding a draft horse. I replied, "Going pretty good if we could get the elk meat on this damn horse." Roundy tied up and came down to help us. Roundy was a very skilled horse packer, and he didn't put up with any shit from any horse or mule. I actually observed him belly-kick a mule one day to get it to pack out a bull elk. I would have never believed it, but it damn sure worked. Roundy grabbed Chief by the lead rope, stared into his eyes, and yelled, "KNOCK YOU'RE SHIT OFF, DAMMIT!" That damn horse never moved while I loaded the boned-out meat on him. Once the meat was loaded, we tried to load the 6x6 elk rack on him. Chief wouldn't have anything to do with the rack. I was worried that he was going to get all worked up and buck all the meat off, so we backed off. Rusty agreed to carry the elk rack back to camp. On the way back to camp

Roundy laughed and said, “Are you guys sick of eating hotdogs yet?” Rusty started to gag and said, “OH GOD, don’t even mention that word right now. I never thought I could eat my body weight in hot-dogs.”

New stove and pipe

We arrived back at camp. Roundy had some elk hunters from Kansas in camp who he was going to take hunting. The Kansas hunters were drooling at the size of Rusty’s elk rack. They had never seen anything like this before. They shook Rusty’s hand and congratulated him several times. I told Roundy that we never did get his new stove and pipe hot enough to burn all the paint off of it. Roundy smiled and said, “Well, let’s just pull that stove out in the meadow and have us a hot fire and I’ll make you guys a cup of coffee while you finish packing up your belongings.” We stayed for a bit and drank a cup of coffee with the Kansas hunters. Rusty would walk out leading Chief with the elk, and I would ride Champ and lead Spook who was packed with all our hunting gear. We would have to leave the elk rack in camp with Roundy. This about killed Rusty to have to leave his rack from his first bull elk. Roundy said he would bring it on his next trip out. As we were leaving the camp the Kansas hunters were sitting on a log by the campfire. Rusty looked back and said, "Don't any of you even think about stealing my elk rack." I thought he was kidding, but he was plumb serious. I was proud of my twelve-year-old son.

Roundy warming his buns

We were about one mile from the trailhead. I could see our truck parked in the parking lot. I looked back and the saddle on Rusty's pack horse had started to roll. I figured we better fix it even though we were almost home. Rusty was tired, he had just hiked about eight miles leading his horse. I parked my horse under a tall limber pine tree with low-hanging branches. My pack horse knew we were almost home, so she tried to go around the back of Champ's ass and head home. While doing so she jerked the lead rope up Champ's ass and under his tail. Champ did not like this. He went to bucking trying to get me off. We had been standing under the low-hanging branches of the tree. He couldn't even buck me off because my head kept hitting the branches above me. I finally lay down on his neck and grabbed his neck with both arms. Once out from under the tree, I slid off his left side and landed on the horse trail. I had a hold of his reins as he dragged me down the trail for a short distance before stopping. The dust was flying in the air, I was lying face down in the trail and Rusty was walking towards me with his pack saddle turned sideways on Chief. I looked up at Rusty with the dust still lingering in the trail and said, "What did you think of that, Rusty?" Rusty never even broke an expression and replied, "Oh Dad, we are on a pack trip, you'll have that."

I got up and repacked Chief as Rusty held onto Champ and Spook. We made it to the trailhead safe and sound with Rusty's first bull elk. This is what memories are made of. However, I don't think Rusty has been on a wilderness pack trip since that day. I may have ruined it for him with the family pack of hotdogs, I don't know. As for the elk ivories, Rusty forgot all about them. I would later have a guy make him a really cool ring with a bull elk on it and give it to him for his college graduation. They were beautiful brown ivories, some of the prettiest that I have ever seen.

Chapter 16

No Time to Rest

The winter of 2003-2004 was another bad one. We would end up running out of hay on Jewett and Bench Corral feed grounds. We also nearly ran out of hay at Scab Creek and Fall Creek feed grounds. Roads into both feed grounds were plowed and opened up with heavy equipment so that hay could be hauled.

Long time hay hauler Lane Walton hauling hay into Bench Corral feed ground during late winter

Approximately 700 elk on Jewett had left the feed ground when the heavy equipment showed up to open the road. They headed south to a neighboring ranchers place who didn't tolerate elk on the ranch. I received a call from this man to come get my damn elk out of his haystack. I told him they were as much his elk as they were mine. He did not like that comment and began screaming at me on the phone. I immediately jumped on my snow machine and headed up to Jewett feed ground to look for the elk. He was right, there was not a single elk in site on the feed ground. I followed the swath of elk tracks to the south to see where the elk had gone. To my amazement approximately 700 elk had walked right through a stack yard with hay in it and never took a single bite. A gate was left open at each end of the stack yard, and all the elk walked straight through without ever touching the fresh green hay. I absolutely could not believe that could ever happen. I could just see myself trying to explain to the landowner that he had over 700 elk walk through his stack yard, and they never damaged or ate his hay. But, if he didn't believe me, he could go look for himself. I ended up finding the elk a short distance away from the feed ground and successfully moved them all back to the feed ground by myself. If you have never moved over 700 elk on a snow machine, this is quite an experience, especially when you actually get them where you want them to go. I learned over the years that elk move really well, especially if you take them the direction that they want to go!

Wolves were still a problem. They had moved all the North Piney elk to Bench Corral. This is why we ran out of hay at Bench Corral. Wolves also moved all the elk from Black Butte feed ground to Soda Lake feed ground. Game and fish personnel spent most of the winter moving elk out of private property and through an elk fence near Soda Lake. One Beer was feeding nearly 1500 elk at Soda Lake that winter. He had to cut their daily rations nearly in half to make it through the harsh winter. I took a horseback ride south of Pinedale on the mesa one day and counted 45 dead deer.

Brucellosis was a big concern to cattle ranchers in the area. It seemed like we were moving elk off private property to prevent cattle and elk from co-mingling somewhere nearly every day. The worst-case scenario finally happened. A local cattle producer east of Boulder had found brucellosis in several of his cattle while testing. The State Vet and officials from the Federal Government with APHIS showed up on the ranch to test the entire herd for brucellosis. The rancher was told that he would have to quarantine his herd and have three negative tests over the next year or so. He was also told that he may never test out of the situation. Feeding hay to large herds of cattle under quarantine can get expensive in a hurry. The final decision was that the Federal Government or APHIS would pay the rancher fair market value to depopulate his entire cattle herd. They showed up on his ranch wearing white suits and blue gloves and helped load cattle onto trucks to be shipped to slaughter. This did not go over well at all in the small community of Pinedale. The game and fish department would now be frowned upon from local ranchers. These were our elk and our fault for allowing this to happen. We would then have a series of very heated meetings with the state veterinarian, cattle ranchers, and game and fish personnel. All these meetings stemmed around how the game and fish department was going to keep their elk out of nearby cattle operations. This situation became very political and rose to the top quickly. The next thing I knew our Director Terry Cleveland was having frequent meetings with Governor Dave Freudenthal.

I walked into the "GRB" (Green River Bar) one Friday evening. This bar was one of the most unique Wyoming bars that I had ever seen in my life. You never knew what you were going to see happen in this bar on any given night. The bar was only about a mile from my home in Daniel. The bar also had a library in it. I would simply tell my wife Lana that I was headed to the library to read for a few hours. She knew that I was full of shit, but generally supported the idea. The bartender at the time was very cute, had a nice figure and knew how to make a good whiskey. I don't think she ever poured a weak drink that I'm aware of. She knew just how I liked my Crown and Coke.

Ninety percent Crown Royal and ten percent Coke. South Pinedale game warden Dennis Almquist once told me that Coke was bad for me, so I eventually eliminated that from my drink.

On this particular evening, I took a good friend of mine into the bar. This would be game warden Bob Trebelcock from Lander Wyoming. Bob was over in the area patrolling the mule deer winter range for poachers. We actually set him up to patrol the winter range in an undercover vehicle. The vehicle was a two-tone brown beat-up and rusted out 1990 Ford Bronco that we had confiscated from a poacher the previous year. I told Bob that he really needed to see this bar, as you never knew what was going to happen on any given night. I had really talked up this bar to Bob. When we arrived, there was only one other guy sitting at the bar. He was a heavy-set guy wearing sweatpants, sorrel snow boots, heavy coat, and a cap with ear flaps. The cute blonde bartender looked at me, smiled and said, "The Usual" I smiled back and said, "Yes ma'am, and a Bud Light for my buddy Bob." She smiled and said, "Of Course." She grabbed the bottle of Crown Royal and filled the glass full of ice clear to the top. Bob looked at me and said, "Damn Hollywood, now that's a drink!" Bob still called me Hollywood because of all the cheap sunglasses that I had worn over the years working with him. Bob said, "Well, Hollywood, it doesn't look like there is much happening in this bar tonight. Do you want to shoot a game of pool?" I agreed and we went in the back room to shoot some pool.

I was a little disappointed that Bob was not going to get to witness a typical night at the GRB. As we were playing pool, I looked into the bar area. The heavy-set man was now lying on top of the bar with his coat and shirt off getting a deep rub massage from the cute bartender. I elbowed Bob as he was shooting pool and said, "Look at that, buddy, you don't see that every day." Bob looked up and said, "Boy I'll say," as he laughed and chewed on his toothpick. We played a couple games of pool. The bar was now filling up with local cowboys and some of the area's most colorful characters. Before long, the entire bar was packed with mostly cowboys. You couldn't even find a spot at the bar to order a drink. It was very loud with people laughing and telling stories. It was also very smoky with nearly everyone smoking a cigarette.

As I was standing in line to get a drink, there was a man sitting at the bar in front of me. I watched him snort two shots of tequila up his nose. This guy was getting way screwed up. He then started saying bad things to the guy next to him about the game and fish department. He was cussing grizzly bears and wolves. He was also cussing the department for wasteful spending. I asked a cowboy standing next to me who that guy was. He replied, "I don't know his name, but I think he's a legislator for this area. He absolutely didn't have a clue what he was talking about and was spreading horrible rumors about the department. I couldn't take it anymore, and I had had a few whiskeys myself. I put my hand on the guy's shoulder and pinched his collarbone a bit. I said, "Excuse me, sir, I was just overhearing your conversation and I would like to set you straight on a few things." The man turned around and looked at me and said with a slur, "Who in the hell are you?" I replied, "My name is Scott Werbelow and I work for the Wyoming game and fish department." He replied with a slur, "I didn't think that you had to be very smart to work for the fish and guts department." This triggered me, I replied, "Probably about as smart as you have to be to become a legislator, I reckon." He quickly stood up and shook my hand very tight and looked me square in the eyes face to face. Before he could say anything, I said, "Why don't you and I go in the backroom and discuss some of these issues where we can hear one another speak."

I took the man in the backroom to the library and sat down at a round table where it was much quieter. I listened to his complaints and rants about this and that for quite some time. I then very professionally explained everything to him and why we did things the way we did. He yelled at me several times about certain game and fish issues. At one point, two cowboys came back to the table and offered to remove him from the bar if I would like. I replied, "Thanks for your concern, we are doing good right now, just hashing some things out." The one cowboy winked and said, "All right, but you just give us the nod if you need help, and we will kindly take him out of the bar." I really appreciated their support. I didn't know either one of them. Maybe someone told them that I was a game warden, and this guy was giving me some shit.

We hashed things out for nearly two hours. He had quit taking tequila shots up his nose and even bought me a few drinks. When our conversation ended, we shook hands. He thanked me numerous times for meeting with him and explaining certain things to him about the agency. I had lost track of Bob, hopefully he wasn't getting a massage on the bar. Nope, he was bellied up to the bar arguing with some cowboy about wolves in Wyoming. The next thing I knew, they had cleared all the drinks off a table and wanted me to arm wrestle the biggest cowboy in the bar. *Here we go again, this is going to be a long night.* I thought to myself.

I paired up with the largest and probably the drunkest cowboy in the bar. Other cowboys were making side bets on who was going to win the arm wrestling match. I sized this large man up and decided that there was a good chance that I may get beat in front of a large crowd of my home town buddies. I decided to try something different. I asked the drunk cowboy if he had ever arm wrestled British style before? He replied, "BRITISH SYLE, WHAT THE HELL IS THAT?" I responded, "This is where you make a fist with your hand and I try to pull it towards me. If I can touch your hand on my chest, you lose. If you touch my fist on your chest, you win." The large man yelled, "ALRIGHT, LET'S DO IT GAME WARDEN!!" We paired up and another cowboy started the match. I pulled the man's fist towards me as hard as I could for a few seconds until the man was pulling back as hard as he could. Suddenly, I let go of the cowboy's fist and it smacked himself right-square in the nose. It his him so hard that he fell over backwards off his bar stool. Everyone in the bar broke out in laughter and the large man was not getting back up. I looked at Bob and said, "I think it's time we make a mile Bob!" Out the door we went and I never seen that man again. Thank God!!

The department had started its first Leadership Development Program, also known as LD-1. I had read about it in an earlier email. If an employee wanted to attend the year-long training class he/she would need to complete an application, submit a resume, and write a summary of why he/she should be selected for the leadership program. I had heard through the grapevine that you had to be a top hand and have inspirations to become a supervisor to ever get selected for this class. Wildlife Administration would carefully select their top twenty candidates from all divisions in the state to attend the training. The training was top notch and a very expensive undertaking for the department to put on for their employees. I read the email and decided that I was probably not very worthy or likely to get selected into the program. Besides, I'm not sure that I could write a full page or two of what a good sumbitch I was. I would really have to make some stuff up. I decided to pass on it, the deadline was approaching fast, and I didn't have time to complete all the necessary paperwork.

It was Friday at 4:38 PM. I was sitting in my office just getting ready to turn off my computer for the week. Office manager Des Brunette called my phone. I picked up the phone and she said, "Hey.

Swerb, Jay Lawson on line one." My heart sank, what could the Chief Game Warden want from me on a Friday just before closing time? The chief game warden had never called me for anything before. I nervously pushed the button for line one. Jay was very upbeat and cracked a couple jokes. He asked me if I had put in for the Leadership Development Program. I told him that I had considered it but decided not to.

Jay replied, "Well the application is due today at 5:00 PM and I would like you to apply for the training." This was very exciting news for me, but shit I only had less than fifteen minutes to meet the deadline and submit my application. Heck, I didn't even have a resume anymore. Nonetheless, I hurried through the paperwork and made the 5:00 PM deadline.

I received a letter from the Directors office the next week in the mail. It was a congratulations letter from the Director himself congratulating me for being selected into the department's first leadership development program. I couldn't believe that I had been selected. It certainly wasn't because of the good job that I did with my resume or the application. My wheels started to spin, *why did the Chief Game Warden want me to attend this high-level leadership training?* This would take up a great deal of my time as the group would meet a couple times a month for about one year. This would require a great deal of travel all over the state of Wyoming. I was excited about it and looked forward to the professional training.

The next big surprise that I received came in a letter from the Governor's office. Governor Freudenthal had appointed me to the Wyoming Governor's Brucellosis Coordination Team. I couldn't believe what I was reading. Why me? I guess this all stemmed from the cattle producer getting brucellosis in his cattle herd and having to depopulate his herd. I was also the feed ground manager for the department, so maybe that was why? I read down the list of other people selected. There were over twenty members on the team and most of their names started with Dr. I had never seen so many names that started with DR. in all my life! The director of every federal and state agency was on the list. There were ranchers, outfitters, senators, and congressmen. Every important person that I had ever heard of or knew of were on the team. The team would meet a couple times a month for at least one year. We would travel all over Wyoming. I also learned that we would be flying in the Governors jet to all of our meetings. I later learned that the legislator who was snorting tequila up his nose in the GRB was responsible for getting me on the team. He evidently had told the Governor that I was straight up and honest and told things the way they needed to be. He stated that I was very knowledgeable about the department and would serve well on the team. I guess you never know who you might meet in a bar. I always believed that everyone that crosses your path in life is for a reason.

I attended our first brucellosis meeting in Pinedale. My first assignment would be to give a power-point presentation on the effects of wolves on elk feed grounds to the team and the Governor himself. This intimidated the hell out of me. All I ever wanted to do was become a Wyoming game warden. Now I'm evidently an expert about wolves and elk feed grounds. I didn't feel like an expert at all, but I probably got to see more interactions with wolves and elk than anyone else. I hadn't really thought about it that way before. I never dreamed I would be standing up in front of a group of people way smarter than me giving a damn power-point presentation. The meeting got contentious. There were environmental groups and news reporters in attendance. I made a statement that if game and fish decided to shut down elk feed grounds, we would have to eliminate approximately seventy percent of the elk herd in the Jackson/Pinedale area. Environmental groups yelled at me for this statement. They yelled, "That is simply not true. That figure is not based on sound science and biology." Well, actually it was an estimate from all the wardens and biologists in the region after careful consideration and was probably a pretty accurate number.

The group meetings started out very contentious. Everyone had their own professional opinion regarding elk feed grounds. I was in favor of the feed grounds because I knew exactly what would happen to the elk if we quit feeding. They would be in every cattle feedline in the county, way before any of them starved to death. Feed grounds were the answer to keep cattle and elk separated, period. The more that the group met the closer we became. I now had new friends and could agree to disagree on things instead of arguing. Everyone came to respect one another's thoughts, opinions, and ideas. We ate dinner together, we even played outside games together after the meetings such as corn hole and horseshoes. Over time I became really close with most team members, and we are still good friends today.

We would fly in the Governors jet from Pinedale to Riverton or Lander. The flight only took eleven minutes. I remember leaving Riverton airport at 4:30 PM one day. We flew to Pinedale, and I drove ten minutes to my office. I was logged into my computer at the office at 4:50 PM. This transportation saved us all an incredible amount of time traveling. I'll never forget the day that I showed up to the Pinedale airport with my golf clubs. I was going to meet my brother in Riverton and have a round of golf after the meeting. I looked at the pilot, he smiled and said, "We will fit them on the plane somewhere," as he took my clubs from me.

During this time the game and fish department was getting a great deal of pressure from APHIS over elk feed grounds. APHIS was trying to get control of wildlife as it pertained to disease in domestic livestock. They simply wanted control of the elk, meaning they could kill as many as they deemed necessary to prevent the spread of brucellosis or any other diseases. This had Wildlife Administration very nervous. At the end of the year the Coordination Team came up with about eighteen different recommendations to the Governor. The top recommendation was to initiate a test and slaughter program on three feed grounds for five years. The feed grounds would be Muddy Creek, Fall Creek, and Scab Creek. The game and fish department would trap and test elk for brucellosis on these feed grounds for five years with an effort to reduce the prevalence or eradicate brucellosis. All test positive elk would be shipped to a USDA approved slaughterhouse in Idaho and killed. The meat from the elk would be donated to needy people statewide. In my opinion we would never eradicate brucellosis on elk feed grounds no matter how much testing and removal we did. There was too much interchange with elk and feed grounds to ever trap them all. Besides, how would we ever construct an elk trap large enough to catch several hundred elk at one time? How would we work this many elk without killing them? How would we open the roads in the winter to get personnel in and test positive elk hauled out in a horse trailer? This would be very costly and near impossible. But we had to show that we were going to do something very serious to solve this problem. I think they call this POLITICS!

Several weeks later my boss Ron Dean (Feed Ground Supervisor) and myself were requested by our Director Terry Cleveland to travel to Cheyenne and meet with him regarding the "Test and Slaughter" of elk on feed grounds. I hated driving to Cheyenne; I called it the "Big City". I hated going to headquarters, too many people, too big of a city for me. We stepped into Mr. Cleveland's office. He greeted both of us with a firm handshake and closed the door. His office was very nice and roomy. I was nervous to be meeting with the Director. *What would this meeting be all about?* Director Cleveland cut to the chase and looked me directly in the eye and said, "Scott, can you guys develop a trap large enough to catch an entire herd of elk at once?" I didn't know how to respond. This would be a huge undertaking and very expensive. I replied, "I suppose if we have enough funding and the right people, we can probably figure something out." Cleveland looked at us and said, "I want this to be your priority over the coming months, we need to pull this off and we need to do it well. My goal is to catch as many elk as possible on those three feed grounds over the next five years. I will be making assignments to who will be serving on your team very soon." We were given our marching orders very clearly and out the door we went. This gave Ron and myself something to talk about on the six-hour drive back home.

Meanwhile, I had been attending Leadership Development classes all over the state. The classes were awesome. I felt very blessed to receive this level of leadership training and not have to pay for it myself. If you were in the private sector and attended this training, it would cost you thousands of dollars. This training really helped me understand other people's personalities. When you combine this training with the Reid Interview and Interrogation training that I had attended earlier, it really helped me understand people and how they click. Basically, the message was to choose good people on your team first and then decide the "what" that you want the team to accomplish. The key is hiring good people first and utilizing every one's strength to accomplish the job. It also really helped me understand my strengths and weaknesses and why I think and do things the way that I do. We were assigned to a team of people and given an assignment to increase communications from the top level to the bottom and across all divisions in the department. This would later prove to be a very difficult assignment.

Between the Leadership Development classes and the Governors Brucellosis Coordination Team my plate became very full. I was having a difficult time keeping up with my day job. Now, I would need to figure out how to design an elk trap large enough to trap and handle hundreds of elk at one time. I would need to meet with other professional agency personnel who had trapped many elk before. I would need to research if anyone had ever built a trap this large before to catch elk or even possibly buffalo.

Regional wildlife supervisor Bernie Holz invited me to ride to Dubois with him to meet with the Bighorn Sheep Foundation and Chief Game Warden Jay Lawson. I'm not sure why Bernie wanted me to attend this meeting, but I was happy to make the trip with him. After our meeting with the Sheep Foundation, Bernie and I met with Jay Lawson. I felt important meetings with the Chief Game Warden. It didn't even matter what the meeting would be about. During this meeting, I learned- that game warden supervisor Scott Edberg had been selected as the regional wildlife supervisor of the Casper region. I didn't even know that Scott had put in for this position. Jay asked Bernie if he had any ideas of a good candidate to replace Edberg in Pinedale. They discussed several different names. I just sat back and listened. At the end of the conversation, I looked at Jay and said, "Heck, I might be interested in applying for that position myself, sounds like an awesome job." Jay looked at me with his eyes wide open and nodded his head up and down. I felt like Jay had never even thought of me as a potential candidate for the position. Now his wheels were turning. He replied, "Well, if you are interested, I would recommend that you apply for the position." I was just kind of kidding to see what kind of a response that I may get from Jay. He didn't laugh uncontrollably and even supported the idea of me applying. Bernie had a surprised look on his face as well. It was a pretty quiet trip on the way back to Pinedale. Bernie hadn't mentioned anything about our conversation with Jay about a replacement for Scott Edberg. This kind of concerned me. Maybe Bernie didn't support me in that position as his right-hand man?

My wheels were now spinning fast. I couldn't believe that I was actually going to put in for this supervisor's position. Different thoughts went through my head. *Could I handle the job, was I qualified for the position? Heck, all I ever wanted to do was become a game warden, not a game warden supervisor.* Things were moving too fast for me. I was now enrolled in the department's Leadership Development program, assigned to the Governor's Brucellosis Task Force, and applying for the game warden supervisor position all in one year. I spent a great deal of time writing my letter of interest for the position and updating my resume. I wanted this to be perfect. I had never been a good writer and my grammar and writing absolutely sucked. I remembered my college English professor who gave me an F- in writing and marked my paper up with red ink everywhere. He told me in large red ink across the front of my paper to consider taking a remedial English class sooner than later. So, if you are reading this book today, I apologize for my grammar and screwed up sentences. I'm going to need one heck of an editor to ever be a successful writer.

The letter and resume were now complete. I nervously hit the send button on my work computer. I thought to myself, *what in the hell did I just do?* I hadn't even told my wife Lana about it yet. I probably didn't have a chance in hell of getting the position. Heck, I didn't have a wildlife degree, nor had I been a game warden with my own district yet. I had no experience as a game warden supervisor. I always believed that you should attempt to walk through every open door in life. If you aren't meant to travel through the open door, it will slam in your face and maybe even catch your fingers and break your nose while doing so. I was embarrassed to apply for the position knowing that there were many, way more qualified candidates than I for the position. I later told only my wife and a few close friends that I had applied for the job. I didn't want to get embarrassed or laughed at from others.

It was late April 2004. I received a phone call from Chief Game Warden Jay Lawson. He asked me if I could drive to Cheyenne to interview for the game warden supervisor position in Pinedale. I about dropped the phone. I couldn't believe that I actually got an interview. I replied, "HELL YES, I have time to drive to Cheyenne for an interview, I'll see you in a few days."

I was extremely nervous about the interview. *Should I wear my red shirt, or should I wear a suit and tie?* I felt out of place in a suit and tie. Hell, I didn't even own one. Nor did I own a red shirt that had all of its buttons and didn't have a stain on it somewhere. I ended up going to a second-hand store and the cute gal fixed me right up. She even showed me how to tie a tie. The knot was complicated so I just left the knot in the tie and would slip it over my head when the time came. I was never good with knots. Other game wardens always accused me of tying a "Swerbe Knot". This was a knot that never came undone, nor could you ever get it undone without a sharp knife. The suit pants were way too tight. I would have to be careful not to split the ass end out of them when sitting down. But heck, I walked out of the second-hand store looking like a rock star for about twenty-five dollars. I returned home and dressed up for Lana. She just laughed her ass off and said, "Hope you don't have to bend over to pick anything up because you are going to split your ass wide open!" I replied, "Thanks honey, are you saying I have a fat ass? I will just not eat next week, and they will fit just fine."

There I was headed for the "Big City" wearing my suit and tie. I was afraid to even fart because I might rip out my new five-dollar dress pants. I was stressed out and tried to think of every question that they might ask me. I hadn't been through very many interviews before and was pretty sure that I was not going to do very well. I was just lucky to find the headquarters office on my own. I had never even lived in a town with over three hundred people before. Heck, none of the towns that I had lived in even had a stoplight. So, to say the least, heavy traffic scared the hell out of me. This was before GPS units, but I safely arrived at headquarters. I slowly and carefully exited my truck, being careful not to split out my pants. I walked to the front door of headquarters. I'm sure I looked like I had a Ruffles potato chip stuck up my butt that I was trying not to break. I met a cute receptionist at the front desk. I told her my name and that I was there to interview for the game warden supervisor's position in Pinedale. She smiled and said, "Oh, I have heard of you before, Swerbe, right?" I smiled and tilted my new cowboy hat and said, "Yes, Ma'am", I hated new cowboy hats, they never fit just right. It was hard not to look like a dork in a new cowboy hat, especially when your pants were too tight. Every hat needed time to develop character. This meant rainstorms, mud, horse wrecks, and sweat from hard work.

The receptionist showed me where the meeting room was located. I slowly sat down in a guest chair waiting for my time to interview. While sitting there, I noticed a woman walk out of the interview room. I knew her as a previous game warden. She was dressed up in her red shirt, I started to doubt my suit and tie get-up. I guess it was my turn to interview. I walked up and knocked on the door. Chief Game Warden Jay Lawson opened the door and said with a laugh, "Oh Swerb, we aren't ready for you yet." He was laughing almost uncontrollably. I'm not sure what this was all about but it made me feel uncomfortable. A short time later he opened the door, still laughing and said, "Come on in, we are ready." I entered the room to see eight redshirts starring me down. Maybe it was my tight dress pants, I don't know? Everyone in the room introduced themselves. I knew most of them, they were all Administrators. Jay told me that each person was going to ask me two questions and go around the table. I wasn't very good at math, but this told me that I would have to answer sixteen questions in total. I started to feel even more nervous.

Jay said, "I will begin, Scott, have you ever worn women's panties before?" That question blew me away. I responded with a laugh, "Only once, and they were on my head." Everyone in the room exploded with laughter. This took all my stress away and lightened the tension. Jay laughed and said, "Alright, the questions will get more difficult from here on out." I ended up answering some very difficult questions during the interview. At the end, I felt like I had done alright but may have blown a few questions. At least I didn't blow my dress pants out in the process. I shook everyone's hand again and thanked them for their time. Jay told me that they would be making their final decision by next Friday and would be in touch either way. I was so relieved to leave that room. A huge weight had been lifted off my shoulders. I didn't care if I got the job or not. That interview was a stressful experience for me to go through. I just wanted to get back on the interstate and get back home to my home and bed. I walked out to my truck, threw my leg up to get in the truck and heard a terrible noise. I had ripped my ass crack out! I smiled, took off my drugstore cowboy hat and threw it in the backseat. I tore off the suit coat and tie and threw them in the back seat as well. I grabbed my ol' crusty cap and put it on my head. I felt relieved. The tie felt like it had been choking me and my pants were way too tight. I undid my dress belt and unbuttoned my torn pants. If I had a beer, I would have drunk it. I grabbed a stale bag of Cheetos and headed north. As I was driving home, I was curious how many people had been interviewed and if I would even be considered for the job. But I did it, and it had been a good experience to go through. I was proud of myself, even if I was not selected.

I returned home and could hardly sleep at night wondering if I would get the phone call from Jay telling me that I had been selected for the position. I was nervous that I might actually get the position. *Could I handle it, was I making a mistake and getting into something that I couldn't handle*? Time would tell. I always believed that if something was meant to be, it would happen. God would guide me and take care of me just like he has always done.

Shed elk antlers collected on state feed grounds

It was Friday May 7th, 2004. I hauled over 1000 lbs. of shed elk antlers to the National Elk Refuge in Jackson Hole, Wyoming. These were shed antlers that the elk feeders had gathered on the 22 state-operated feed grounds. These antlers would be sold at the annual antler auction held in Jackson Hole every May. The proceeds from the antlers would be credited to the Game and Fish Department's annual feed bill. I hadn't heard anything all week from Chief Game Warden Jay Lawson.

It was 4:45 PM. I had left Jackson Hole and was headed back to my home in Daniel. I turned left at Hoback Junction and my cell phone rang. There was very poor cell service in this mountainous area. I'm surprised that my phone even rang. I looked at my flip phone and it read Cheyenne, Wyoming. My heart stopped, could this be the call that I had been waiting for all week from Chief Game Warden Jay Lawson? Was he going to offer me a job as the Jackson/Pinedale game warden supervisor? I opened the phone and answered it with very poor cell service. I said, "Hello." I could barely hear anything. I pulled my patrol truck off the highway, jumped out of the truck, and ran up the side of a steep mountain. The whole time saying "HELLO, HELLO." I jumped up on a large rock on the side of the mountain and held my flip phone up in the air while on speaker phone and said, "HELLO, IS THIS JAY?" I heard a crackling voice respond, "Yes this is Jay, I want to talk to you about the......The call dropped, my heart sank! What was Jay going to tell me? Dammit!! It would be well after 5:00 PM before I had cell service again and Jay would be out of the office until Monday morning.

Scott C. Werbelow

Stay tuned for my next book, Son of a Poacher IV-Game Warden Supervisor??? To see how this story and many others end! Thank you all for your support and friendship along the way over the past three years. I hope you have enjoyed reading my last three books of my incredible journey through this crazy thing they call life. Keep your powder dry, you may need it someday!

If you enjoyed this book, please consider leaving a review on Amazon.

Enjoy other books by Scott C. Werbelow
Son of a Poacher: Wyoming Warden in the Making
Son of a Poacher II: Blast From My Past

Made in the USA
Columbia, SC
16 September 2024

41666882R00172